Our Man
in
WARSZAWA

Our Man in WARSZAWA

How the West Misread Poland

Jo Harper

Central European University Press
Budapest–New York

Published in 2021 by
Central European University Press
Nádor utca 9, H-1051 Budapest, Hungary
Tel: +36-1-327-3138 or 327-3000
E-mail: *ceupress@press.ceu.edu*
Website: *www.ceupress.com*

ISBN 978-963-386-395-4 paperback
ISBN 978-963-386-396-1 ebook

LIBRARY OF CONGRESS CATALOGING-IN-PUBLICATION DATA

Names: Harper, Jo, 1968- author.
Title: Our man in Warszawa : how the West misread Poland / Jo Harper.
Other titles: Our man in Warsaw
Description: Budapest ; New York : Central European University Press, 2021.
  | Includes bibliographical references and index.
Identifiers: LCCN 2020052462 (print) | LCCN 2020052463 (ebook) | ISBN
  9789633863954 (paperback) | ISBN 9789633863961 (pdf)
Subjects: LCSH: Poland--Politics and government--1989- | Political
  culture--Poland | Prawo i Sprawiedliwość (Political party) |
  Rhetoric--Political aspects--Poland. | Discourse analysis--Political
  aspects--Poland.
Classification: LCC DK4449 .H37 2021 (print) | LCC DK4449 (ebook) | DDC
  943.805/7--dc23
LC record available at https://lccn.loc.gov/2020052462
LC ebook record available at https://lccn.loc.gov/2020052463

Table of Contents

Foreword by Urszula Chowaniec vii

Acknowledgments xi

How to Read the Book xv

Part I: A Personal Voice 1

Chapter 1: Mr. Kaczyński, *The Guardian* and Me 3

Chapter 2: At Her Majesty's Service! 21

Part II: An Academic Voice 27

Chapter 3: Modern Poland's Political Blocs 29

Chapter 4: Post-Post-Colonial? 51

Chapter 5: The Confused Hopes of "Civil Society" 65

Chapter 6: Class Struggles 73

Chapter 7: An Imported Middle Class 81

Part III: A Reporter's Voice 89

Chapter 8: Election-Year Issues 91

Playing the Race Card 91

When a Man Loves a Woman 94

Don't Shoot the Messenger! 97

Still the Economy, Stupid! 100

History: War and PiS 101

Brussels or Death 103

Culture: Reaching for the Revolver 105

Between Iraq and a Hard Place 105

Part IV: A Lay Voice 113

Chapter 9: Diary of British Media Coverage of the October 2019
Parliamentary Election 115
Part 1: Floating Frames 116
Part 2: "Some Losers" 132
Part 3: Post-Mortem 140
Chapter 10: Hiatus—The Election that Wasn't, May 2020 147
Chapter 11: Diary of British Media Coverage of Poland's July 2020
Presidential Elections 163
Part 1: Britain's Media Picks its Polish Horse 163
Part 2: Round Two in the Presidential Election 172
Part 3: Unfinished Business 180
Chapter 12: Synthesis: Finding a Voice Between the Sublime
and the Ridiculous 187

Index 197

Foreword

Our Man in Warszawa: How the West Misread Poland was prepared for publication in the most extreme of circumstances—as the world was stunned by an unprecedented pandemic and an unrivalled inability to find the best method of combatting the Covid-19 virus and dealing with its devastating consequences. The world seemed divided between two blocs: skeptics and people in denial, on one hand, and of those who took the situation extremely serious and were increasingly scared. Who was right? I have no idea. But one thing is for certain: the pandemic did not stop the growing tempo of populist politics. In this year of elections, we saw in both the Polish presidential election (June/July 2020), and in the US election (November) the spectacle of ruthless demagogy at its very best. Moreover, the UK was experiencing the ostensibly never-ending turmoil of the Brexit referendum and its effects—yet, this was the year of the official exit from the EU.

It is in the middle of this spectacle that Jo offers us his very personal and insightful, but equally very informative, overview of post-transitional Poland. It is, in its postulation, a book by a British person living in Poland, who wished both to give us a valuable account of Polish contemporary politics, as well as a comparative outline as to how Polish politics differs from the UK's and how the use of stereotypes and patronizing tones when commenting on each other's politics can mislead the target audience.

As a Pole who has lived abroad for the majority of my life, and who has devoted most of my research to "Polish studies abroad," I found the perspective to be a much needed, fresh look into our contemporaneity. Jo dismantles the complicated web of strategies needed to essentialize contemporary politics (as seen clearly from a distance), he shows from the outsider's perspective the discourse of "the best Pole" (or, conversely, "the best Brit"). Jo scrutinizes the methods of stereotyping, foreignization and patronization. All these strategies are always present in the discourse between national politics, but it is not always so easy to see their workings as clearly as in this book.

I can easily anticipate some of the criticism that will be directed towards a book such as this about Polish politics from a foreigner's perspective. Jo is a foreigner in Poland (although, one would scarcely believe it judging by his knowledge and accumulated bibliography), and I am a Pole abroad and even though we occupy supposedly opposite positions, I feel like this is the very same location occupied by someone who will never be completely credited as being unbiased, who can always be accused of not being fully empathetic towards the country, although abroad the foreigner's perspective often gives their opinion somehow the best of credibility! Because nowadays whenever we talk about a nation, any nation, it is always seen as a confrontation, somehow there is no source, no magazine that can be fully trusted, and Jo shows this in an ingenious way. Furthermore, this is very important when we talk about who is entitled to speak and to whom we should listen, because it is also part of contemporary political discourses: in the populist era, we all are part of populist politics, and sometimes we all neglect to listen to those around us. Jo knows all this: this is why he presents us with a broad background, always taking into consideration various opinions and—he is contextualizing his own position—the book starts with an explanation about how he came to Poland and why he decided to write this book; as well as, how his attitude to the British press has changed.

This book is an extremely detailed, very informative, fresh portrayal of post-transitional Poland with many references to the national myth and literary debates. Jo does not aim at academic objectivity (if such a thing should truly exist), but his journalistic approach is to gather many voices and standpoints, juxtapose them and then expose the practice of both how often they are misrepresented and silenced and also how frequently one of them is sometimes particularly successful. This strategy of presenting an issue from many angles makes the book very valuable and recommended to all students and researchers of history, politics, society and culture, both in the region and in general. It is also a good read for any reader who simply wants to know what the situation is today in Polish politics.

To reiterate, this book is a very striking account of the Polish post-1989 transition and of contemporary politics. As I already stressed, it combines personal views and experiences with very careful systematic research and a description of events and processes. It also has a journalistic style, which is very attractive for the readers language with a trustworthy research-based examination. It is principally the result of threading together previously written essays that work really well together.

Stockholm, July 2020

Urszula Chowaniec
cultural and literary scholar, professor at AFM Kraków University
and researcher at SSEES University College London

Acknowledgments

I thank all those who have tried to teach me over the years that journalism is not a poor man's anthropology[1] or some esoteric epistemological exercise, lessons I still haven't fully mastered. Knowing things and verifying them—"sourcing," in the trade—has posed problems, touching notions of truth and how journalism plays its part in creating news. Facts in this "post-truth" era still exist, need context and someone must choose what constitutes a fact, which of them to use and how to use them. In the Covid-19 era this also became especially salient. We can know things inductively, after all, I would say to myself and sometimes (unhelpfully, as it turned out) also to other journalists. Not everything we know—and indeed report—is a priori unknown without empirical confirmation, i.e. the principle that informs Anglo-American journalism and indeed English common law. Journalists are inherently a part of the process of news making, shaping events and personalities and framing ideas. In other words, we are participants as well as observers and our participation informs our observations. But double source we do, as if those doing the confirming are beyond fallibility, given that we select them ourselves. Some semblance of a humanist spirit survives—journalists as hermeneutical beings, therapists or doctors, listeners and healers, rather than accountants.

First off was Martin Jacques,[2] then, then editor of *Marxism Today*, where my internship as a 21-year-old entailed traveling the Circle Line of London's Underground, stopping off at the mainline railway stations to check that copies of *Marxism Today* were as visible as those of *The Economist* and *The Spectator* on the (obviously "hostile" and "reactionary") newsstands of W.H. Smith.

---

1   Elizabeth Bird, *The Audience in Everyday Life: Living in a Media World* (New York: Routledge, 2003).
2   See Jo Harper, "China: Creaking tiger, hidden dragon?" October 18, 2019, *Deutsche Welle*.

I also made tea during the monthly's last few months in existence, my sojourn and the start of its demise coinciding with Poland's semi-free elections of June 1989. *Marxism Today* valiantly tried to explain the rapid subsequent collapse of communism in Eastern Europe from a, well, "Marxist" (or its strange cousin, "Marxian") analytical perspective, but by September, and the start of my Master's degree in International Relations at Bristol University, there was really no going back, for me or for it. While, I hope, retaining some of the best elements of an analytical, critical, humanistic approach to understanding the world, the idea of overthrowing anything was decidedly eschewed.

The Berlin Wall came down in my first two months in Bristol, with the teaching staff both excited and worried, rewriting curricula on the hoof less than ideal. But it was perhaps for the best. "Being" a "Marxist" would be a tiring business, every day confronting a reality you despise. I was too lazy, too skeptical and perhaps ultimately too shallow. In fact, I sometimes quietly hoped there actually was a "Deep State," the one that the conspiracy theorists talked about, given how badly the shallow one seemed to be doing. Perhaps, after all, someone should know what they were doing. As the Greek economist Yanis Varoufakis wrote, he had waited all his adult life as an outsider assuming that his leftist rantings were actually against something, an establishment—adults—whom he hoped to meet when he became Greece's finance minister during the 2008/9 financial crisis. On his first trip to Brussels he realized, he wrote, there were no adults, at least not in that room.[3]

The curious thing was that the more Marxism itself became politically irrelevant, the more the Right attacked what it liked to call "cultural Marxism."[4] For the attackers, liberals—in the U.S. sense (including centrists, in a Western European sense, and those on the Left)—were as "culturally Marxist" as, well, actual Marxists. But, in my experience, many of these said Marxists were, counterintuitively, often even less "culturally Marxist" than many liberals (in the UK sense, i.e., often centrists and conservatives). The Right, on

3   Yanis Varoufakis, *Adults in The Room: My Battle with Europe's Deep Establishment* (London: Random House UK, 2018). I am also reminded of a chat with a senior banker in 2008 working with the UK government on a rescue plan for the UK economy, who told me that then Prime Minister Gordon Brown and his Chancellor of the Exchequer (finance minister), Alistair Darling, were "completely untrained in economics and out of their depth."

4   The term "cultural Marxism" refers to a far-right antisemitic conspiracy theory which claims that the post-war Frankfurt School is part of an effort to weaken Western culture by undermining traditional conservatism and Christianity using multiculturalism, progressive politics and political correctness. David Jenemann, *Adorno in America* (Minneapolis: University of Minnesota Press, 2007).

the other hand, was often a hotbed of "cultural Marxism." A brief glimpse into the private lives of Boris Johnson and Donald Trump, for example, reveals serial disregard for traditional family values. The UK politician Michael Goves's choice of Italian Marxist Antonio Gramsci as an intellectual precedent for his views on education in Britain was also a fascinating glimpse into how terms once heavily tribalized had seemingly shifted. UK prime minister, Boris Johnson's one-time advisor, Dominic Cummings, also used a language more akin to Gramscian notions of institutional wars of attrition in his battles to reform the UK civil service in 2020.

A year in Kraków under the supervision of a professor it took three months to find at the Jagielonian University political science department left me with an ambivalence towards Polish student life, but a love for all (well, most) things Polish. Back in the UK, there were then two years as a clerk at the government propaganda unit, the Central Office of Information (COI) in Lambeth, one of the first to have this new thing called "the internet," while writing a PhD on Polish politics at the London School of Economics (LSE) under the supervision of the later-to-be (right-wing Hungarian) Fidesz MEP György Schöpflin (known to me then as George Schöpflin). The eternally helpful LSE historian Anita Prazmowska told me she thought I was married to my PhD, a notion I never quite understood. A night-shift taxi driving gig in South Kensington paid the fees, assisted by living in a squat-like council flat near the Elephant and Castle. An actual marriage to one of my squat-comrades-in-arms, a "Gdynianka" (she hailing from the great northern Polish port city of Gdynia) called Joanna, and a brief unhappy teaching stint at the British Council in Gdańsk followed, living at Joanna's parents' flat overlooking a huge crane that still read in big letters "Stocznia im. Komuny Paryskiej," (The Paris Commune Shipyard) in Gdynia, before David McQuaid gave me my first real journalistic job at Dow Jones Newswires in Warsaw in 1999, where for 12 months I observed at close hand the odd love affair that is Polish-American relations. As a meta case study of postcommunist know-how transmission along the information supply chain it took some beating. The American teacher and the Polish student, roles that were often reversed when the American sought a dose of "European culture" and the Polish student would willingly oblige. Markets reigned supreme, of course. This was followed by a half-decade in Gdynia, working for some time as Reuters' "Northern Poland" reporter, an intriguing if not very regular supply of work. The Polish journalist Marek Ostrowski befriended me after an article I wrote for his weekly, *Polityka*,[5] on the London riots in 2010, while Bartosz Węglarczyk, then foreign news editor at *Gazeta Wyborcza*, accepted and published some often oddly personal articles for his newspaper written from London[6] following (my) divorce and 12 months of loneliness in Finsbury Park, exacerbated by three months at *Debtwire*, then owned by *The Financial Times Group*, in the Strand.

I thank Maria Bnińska, until late 2020 at the *Financial Observer* in Warsaw, Hardy Graupner at *Deutsche Welle* in Berlin, William Smale at the *BBC* in London and Jan Cieński at *Politico* in Brussels in particular. I also thank Jurek Mączyński, the *Mergermarket* chief in Warsaw, who put up with my ignorance and indifference for several years covering the M&A market in Poland. I thank Craig Smith for his services to Warsaw's expat publishing community. He provided me with work and also a great insight into and respect for American entrepreneurialism. I am also grateful to *CEE Marketwatch* and some wonderful "team-building" breaks in Bulgaria and Greece with Georgi Kadiev, Ventsislav Penchev, Scott Salembier and David Kennedy between 2005 and 2010.

I apologize to Patrick Graham, a *Reuters* reporter, with whom I once enjoyed playing football for Warsaw Wanderers, for using him as a peg on which to hang my various irritations with the often-petty world of Warsaw expat journalism. I also apologize to journalist Christian Davies for not attributing a line of his about Poland's "accursed soldiers" in my earlier work of collected essays on PiS (*Poland's Memory Wars: Essays in Illiberalism*[7]).

I thank my wife, Ola, and our three boys, Henry, Max and Oliver, for their love and support. I am grateful to Peggy and Mike Lunan for their research help. I also thank Brian Porter-Szűcs, a professor of history at the University of Michigan, for his advice and guidance, Patricia Ladly for her often brutal criticisms, Jan Darasz and John Harper for their insights and anecdotes, and Lawrence Fahrenholz and John Stavrellis for proofreading.

5   Jo Harper and Marek Ostrowski, "Afera pedofilska w BBC," May 7, 2013, *Polityka*.
6   Jo Harper, "Anglik za granicą," August 3, 2009, *Gazeta Wyborcza*.
7   Jo Harper, ed., *Poland's Memory Wars: Essays on Illiberalism* (Budapest: CEU Press, 2018), 32.

How to Read the Book

The first part of the book is an overview of my personal reasons for coming to Poland and studying about the place, and why that might matter in the context of writing this book. The second part provides a kind of extended literature review, noting the main strands of social science thought on post-communist Poland and is written in a largely academic style. The third part deals with the key issues during the election years of 2019 and 2020. This section is written in a journalistic style, based mainly on notes and articles I had written in the press during that period. The style is deliberately less academic and often based on personal interviews. The fourth part adopts a combination of my own private reading voice and use of the academic method to interpret both it and the text it is engaging with. Critical Discourse Analysis (CDA)[1] is useful here. CDA tries to discover which strategies, patterns and communicative "events" are characteristic of certain types of texts.[2] Teun Van Dijk meanwhile offers an overview of the parts that constitute the organization of journalistic articles.[3] Norman Fairclough's three-dimensional framework for studying discourse, where the aim is to map three separate forms of analysis onto one each other, is also a guide.[4] The first is textual analysis (description), the second, analysis of discourse practice (processes of text production, distribution and consumption) and the third, analysis of discursive events as

---

1   Ruth Wodak, "What CDA is About—A Summary of its History, Important Concepts and Its Development," in *Methods of Critical Discourse Analysis*, ed. Ruth Wodak and Michael Meyer (London: Sage, 2001).
2   Paul Baker et al., "A Useful Methodological Synergy? Combining Critical Discourse Analysis and Corpus Linguistics to Examine Discourses of Refugees and Asylum Seekers in the UK Press," *Discourse and Society* 19, no. 3 (May 2008).
3   Teun A. van Dijk, *Communicating Racism: Ethnic Prejudice in Thought and Talk* (London: Sage, 1987).
4   Norman Fairclough, *Critical Discourse Analysis: The Critical Study of Language* (Abingdon: Routledge, 2013).

instances of sociocultural practice (explanation). This "triple voice" is used as a way of introducing the reader to the multi-layered process of reading and assimilating information and knowledge. It is intended to engage the reader in multiple ways and hopefully in the process pick out sometimes hidden meanings. It is also the way I—and I suspect others—actually read and understand complex issues, whether in academic papers, newspapers or conversations in the pub. I was driven to adopt this methodology also by a realization that quite often I couldn't find my own voice in a journalistic or academic setting, but that I had something I wanted to say, and thought was valuable. The process of writing the book was therefore a dialectical one, with layers of understanding built up often on top of each other, via competing and sometimes complementary modes of expression, each at times in conflict with the others. Exploring these contradictions is a part of the process, for both the writer and the reader.

Part I
A Personal Voice

Chapter 1

Mr. Kaczyński, *The Guardian* and Me

As the historian Norman Davies nicely put it in an interview with Poland's biggest daily newspaper, *Gazeta Wyborcza*, "gdybologia" (loosely translated as "'what-if'ology") is a very Polish hobby.[1] One such alternative history with resonance in 2019 and 2020 was *what if* communism had collapsed in Eastern Europe in 1968—as it appeared close to doing—and not 1989? It would certainly have been a very different transition, or perhaps a lack of one. Instead of Oxford historian Timothy Garton Ash and his "Liberal Internationalism,"[2] it might have been Daniel Cohn-Bendit and his anarcho-syndicalism landing at Okęcie airport in Warsaw, or Zygmunt Bauman's humanistic Marxism staying at home rather than being kicked out of communist Poland.[3] Depending on your point of view, the region either dodged a bullet or took one in the chest, then, when it embarked upon its post-communist journey at the peak of neoliberal optimism in 1989.

Not My Monkeys: So Garton Ash it was. A primetime news interview on Polish commercial television channel, *TVN*, with the historian sometime in the 2000s fascinated me. I had always liked his work but had never heard Garton Ash speak. His attempt was noble and impressive. He crunched his way through Polish grammar and pronunciation, never easy.[4] But something nagged. It felt

---

1 "Norman Davies: Jestem za 'underdogs.'" *Gazeta Lublin*, September 11, 2008.
2 Commonly cited examples include NATO's intervention in Bosnia and Herzegovina; the 1999 NATO bombing of Yugoslavia; British military intervention in the Sierra Leone Civil War; and the 2011 military intervention in Libya. Some defined it as liberal idealism backed by muscle.
3 Zygmunt Bauman was a Polish-British sociologist and philosopher driven out of Poland during the 1968 anti-Semitic purges.
4 A later TVN interview with Garton Ash in 2018 showed a decided improvement: https://tvn24.pl/polska/fakty-po-faktach-prof-timothy-garton-ash-o-polsce-i-kaczynskim-ra830600-2357771.

a little as if, having learned ancient Greek, Garton Ash had finally been given an opportunity to try it out on some actual ancient Greeks. And boy did he want to try it out! A slightly effete, extremely self-confident Anglicized Polish. Wow, I thought, the guy has some chutzpa! But it was also, as *The Financial Times* journalist Gideon Rachman perhaps wouldn't say, "problematic,"[5] at least for me, living in Gdynia at the time, in a Poland I didn't much recognize in Garton Ash's words about solidarity and, again, "Liberal Internationalism." Hidden depths of meaning in the Polish expression *"Nie mój cyrk, nie moje małpy"* (*"Not my circus, not my monkeys,"* loosely meaning "not my problem") were revealed to me that day. As a fellow Brit trying to make sense of Poland, I would wonder about that circus and who was making monkeys of whom. A February 28, 2019 article in *The Economist*[6] was an early reminder of such monkey-business at the outset of preparing to write this book. The article "explains" the Law and Justice (PiS) government's social spending policies.

> A 1,100 zloty bonus for state pensioners and cuts in taxes, especially for young people, are part of the package, which is worth up to 40bn zlotys ($10.5bn), almost 2% of this year's projected GDP. That is pretty blatant stuff, especially when you take into account the fact that the new child payments will go into effect in July, just three months before the expected date of the next general election. (...) Some worry that the new promises are unaffordable. (...) Ruling-party strategists scoff that the opposition said the same thing when the 500+ scheme was first introduced in 2016; but last year the budget was close to balance. Debt is 50% of GDP, and falling. (...) The universal benefit, which will disproportionately help those on lower incomes, is good for consumption. A bit more stimulus might be just what is needed if business is dragged down by weakness in Germany.

The notion that *"populists"* will always promise *"money to splash around"* was by then a common one. The language asks the reader to take on board a worldview and understanding of proceedings premised on sharing certain

---

5   Gideon Rachman, Twitter post, Mar 3, 2019, 3:07 pm. https://www.twitter.com/gideonrachman/status/1102344890153922560. "One of the most threatening word's in the left's vocabulary is 'problematic,'" he tweeted.

6   "The $10 Billion Bung: Ahead of Elections, Poland's Ruling Party Offers Huge Handouts," *The Economist*, February 28, 2019.

assumptions, principally that markets as self-evidently not only the best but the only righteous method of divvying up the economic pie. When governments start promising "handouts" and "bribes" to the people, is it because "they"—i.e., "the people"—won't understand how economies work, while "we" do? Leave it to the professionals? When we are told that "some worry that the new promises are unaffordable," it is not clear who these "some" are. In turn, the "ruling-party strategists scoff" at the claim made by the "some." The final shake in the tail also tells us a lot. "But maybe it's good for consumption" is quite clearly a nod in the direction that sometimes fiscal priming is needed to steer the ship back on course. Even if the money has to go into the pockets of the proles and not the banks, this—we are asked to assume—is an unavoidable price to pay when the economy needs a boost. Redistribution—if this is what it was—is not just a bad idea, but morally circumspect. There is a weary and lofty tone of righteous indignation when the laws of free market economics are seen to have been tampered with. In the situationist manifesto, Guy Debord noted that official culture was what he called a "rigged game," where subversive ideas are sidelined, then trivialized and sterilized, and safely incorporated back into mainstream society, "where they can be exploited to add new flavors to old dominant ideas."[7] The thought made me feel better when rereading *The Economist* article, for a while anyway.

Covid-19 Empties the Circus: The need to rethink things, collective and personal, during the first phase of the Covid-19 pandemic in spring 2020 drew me back to the basics of my trade as a journalist and my original academic discipline of sociology. How to explain this strange new world? New books on the subject published in 2020 also whetted the appetite.[8] But as much as I'd like to say I had deliberately spent the previous 20 years diligently and single-mindedly conducting research using my "cover" as a (British) foreign correspondent working in Poland, I couldn't. Much of the analysis and insights contained here are based on often painful professional experience. I am not an "ideal writer"[9] for many media folk in Warsaw. Having said that,

---

7   See, McKenzie Wark, *50 Years of Recuperation of the Situationist International* (New York: Princeton Architectural Press, 2008).

8   Agata Kondzińska and Iwona Szpala, *Prezes i Spółki. Imperium Jarosława Kaczyńskiego* (Warsaw: Agora, 2020); Karolina Wigura and Jaroslaw Kuisz, *The End of the Liberal Mind: Poland's New Politics* (Warsaw: Kultura Liberalna, 2020).

9   The "ideal reader" is discussed in Stuart Hall, "Encoding/Decoding," in *Culture, Media, Language: Working Papers in Cultural Studies, 1972–79*, ed. Stuart Hall et al. (London: Routledge, 1980) 136–138.

my proclivity for posing "problematic" questions in editorial offices meant I was often "moved along" (sacked) the supply chain, working at or freelancing for some of the main news agencies, several newspapers and trade publications during my time in Poland after 1997 and that journalistic promiscuity proved to be a mine of anecdotal and more "scientific" material, invaluable in conducting this "research."

Inspired by Ryszard Kapuściński, Marek Edelman, Jack Kuroń, and Claude Lanzmann,[10] I set off to Poland in July 1993, aged 25, copies of Norman Davies' The Heart of Europe and Garton Ash's The Polish Revolution[11] in my bag. I had been accepted to write a PhD dissertation on the Polish transition at the LSE; the one condition of entry being the ability to read Polish. A month in the coastal spa town of Sopot, at Poland's then only language school for foreigners, was a crash course in the art of surviving in Poland. I had come in many ways to escape a Britain I found a mess, or perhaps I found myself a mess in it. It was not long after the Maastricht Treaty, the "Up Yours Delors!"[12] headline in The Sun, "Black Wednesday" and the emergence of the ambiguous concept that became "George Soros."[13] It was also just before the post-communists won the September 1993 parliamentary election in Poland, only four years after communism had fallen, and the world was asking how this was possible. But Britain followed me, or perhaps it was there waiting for me (or maybe I just took it with me in the shape of Garton Ash in my bag).

"So, are you Australian?" one bastion of the emergent Anglo-Polish elite boomed on a visit to his office next to the Sejm (parliament) in Warsaw. I assumed he couldn't quite place me in the British social hierarchy, so I assumed he had assumed (we did a lot of assuming) I was somehow outside of it, a

---

10 Artur Domosławski, Ryszard Kapuściński: A Life (London: Verso, 2012); Shoah, directed by Claude Lanzmann, (1985; Paris: Les Films Aleph, 2003), DVD; Marek Edelman, The Ghetto Fights (London: Bookmarks Publications, 2014).

11 Timothy Garton Ash, The Polish Revolution: Solidarity (London: Coronet Books, 1985); Norman Davies, Heart of Europe: The Past of Poland's Present (Oxford: Oxford University Press, 2001).

12 "Up Yours Delors!" The Sun, November 1, 1990.

13 George Soros, a Hungarian-born American billionaire investor and philanthropist, is known as "The Man Who Broke the Bank of England" because of his short sale of $10 billion worth of pounds sterling, which made him a profit of $1 billion during the 1992 Black Wednesday UK currency crisis. Soros is a supporter of progressive and liberal political causes, something that has made him a figure of hate for European nationalists. As the New York Times reported in October 2018, "conspiracy theories about him have gone mainstream, to nearly every corner of the Republican Party." Scott Shane, Kenneth P. Vogel, Patrick Kingsley, "How Vilification of George Soros Moved from the Fringes to the Mainstream," The New York Times, October 31, 2018,

"colonial type" perhaps. The fact he couldn't tell Sussex from Sydney was also probably designed to show me he was so far above this social class thing that it didn't matter. Everywhere was somewhere below Oxford, after all. But it was not a great performance, merely another line in trying to project the self-regulating social hierarchies that those hanging on to the lower end of the British upper middle classes have finely tuned over the years, from a Jane Austen hero to a Harry Potter villain. The doxa was unambiguous, a body language that screamed assumed superiority through the medium of feigned curiosity. Pierre Bourdieu's concept of habitus,[14] in particular at the level of what he called "bodily logic," seemed to jump from the page into this man's every move. If I had been Australian, I'd have probably given him a hard time, but we exchanged pleasantries, quietly located each other in the British class hierarchy and went our separate ways. The hierarchy is normal, natural, and anyone who questions it is a humbug, to quote another Old Etonian at the time in Downing Street. Before I finished my PhD, I started work at the British Council in Gdańsk, with Poles teaching English using books about a Britain of bowler-hatted men marching across London Bridge, a world in which old Etonians still ran the country. How absurd! These voices do, granted, have—even if unintentionally—a touch of self-parody about them, appealing to a feudal deference sold as British and which many of the Polish-British cohort squeezed into their travelling luggage after 1989. An ex-*Financial Times* Warsaw reporter, for example, fired off a typically searing analysis over the phone to me in late 2019. "PiS are a bunch of shits," he snorted, "And I want them out."

Twenty-odd years later, having become a doctor of philosophy and a freelance writer in Warsaw, I decided to write some notes, mainly for my own consumption, about *The Guardian's* coverage of Poland, a kind of personal stress test—or perhaps a loyalty test—and the more I read, the more irritable I became. The paper's voice felt a little too righteous, its attacks on what became known as illiberalism ever more shrill and pious. Cut to July 12, the day of voting in the second round of the presidential election and a wonderfully odd piece in *The Observer* by Nick Cohen on the journalist Anne Applebaum.[15]

---

14 Pierre Bourdieu, *Outline of a Theory of Practice*, trans. Richard Nice (Cambridge: Cambridge University Press, 1990).

15 Nick Cohen, "Anne Applebaum: How My Old Friends Paved the Way for Trump and Brexit," *The Observer*, July 12, 2020. See also: Gavin Rae, "Poland in the Mirror," *The New Left Review*, July–August 2020.

Anne Applebaum can look at the wreck of democratic politics and understand it with a completeness few contemporary writers can match. When she asks who sent Britain into the unending Brexit crisis, or inflicted the Trump administration on America, or turned Poland and Hungary into one-party states, she does not need to search press cuttings. Her friends did it, she replies. Or, rather, her former friends.

We, the readers, are then taken on a journey. Buckle up. The piece is worth reproducing here in almost its full form. Cohen oozes sycophancy of a genuine Cold War Warrior—and post-Cold War Warrior to boot—from the pages of an ostensibly left-of-center British newspaper. The notion that Applebaum had helped bring down communism and supported all the "right" causes was somewhat hard to understand. The Left, meanwhile, Cohen stresses, was cowardly in its appeasement of the Soviet Union, a view taken by Applebaum and others, but one that requires unpicking, something Cohen is firmly disinclined to do here. Others at *The Guardian* might well also have disagreed with this version.

Millennium Eve, a housewarming for a manor house in western Poland they had helped rebuild from ruins. Unlike the bulk of the left of the age, they had stood up against the Soviet empire and played a part in the fall of a cruel and suffocating tyranny. They had supported free markets, free elections, the rule of law and democracies sticking together in the EU and NATO, because these causes—surely—were the best ways for nations to help their people lead better lives as they faced Russian and Chinese power, Islamism and climate change. They were young and happy. History's winners. (...) Even when she was young, you could see the signs of the inquiring spirit that has made her a great historian. She went to work as a freelance journalist in eastern Europe while it was still under Soviet occupation and too drab and secretive a posting for most young reporters. She then made a standard career move and joined The Economist. But it was too dull for her liking and she moved to the Spectator in the early 1990s. The dilettante style of English conservatism charmed her. She came to know the conservative philosopher Roger Scruton and Margaret Thatcher's speechwriter John O'Sullivan. They had helped east European dissidents struggling against Soviet power in the 1980s and appeared to believe in democracy. Why would she doubt it? How could she foresee that Scruton and

O'Sullivan would one day accept honours from Viktor Orban. (...) What was life in the English right like then. 'It was fun,' she said. Her husband knew Boris Johnson. They were both members of the Bullingdon Club at Oxford. She assumed that he was as much a liberal internationalist as Sikorski was. (...) When the couple met Johnson for dinner in 2014, she noted his laziness and 'all-consuming narcissism', as well as the undoubted charisma that was to seduce and then ruin his country. They asked about Europe. 'No one serious wants to leave the EU,' he replied. (...) Heretics make the best writers. They understand a movement better than outsiders, and can relate its faults because they have seen them close up. Religions can tolerate pagans. They are mere unbelievers who have never known the way, the truth and the light. Although Applebaum has left the right, and stopped voting Conservative in Britain in 2015 and Republican in the US in 2008, she can make a convincing case that the right betrayed her. (...) You can read thousands of discussions of the 'root causes' of what we insipidly call 'populism.' The academic studies aren't all wrong, although too many are suspiciously partial. The left says austerity and inequality caused Brexit and Trump, proving they had always been right to oppose austerity and inequality. The right blames woke politics and excessive immigration, and again you can hear the self-satisfaction in the explanation. (...) Applebaum offers an overdue corrective. She knows the personal behind the political. She understands that the nationalist counter-revolution did not just happen. Politicians hungry for office, plutocrats wanting the world to obey their commands, second-rate journalists sniffing a chance of recognition after years of obscurity, and Twitter mob-raisers and fake news fraudsters, who find a sadist's pleasure in humiliating their opponents, propelled causes that would satisfy them. (...) Rather than grab at standard explanations, Applebaum understands that a society based on merit may sound fine if you want to live in a country run by talented people. But what if you are not yourself talented? (...) Among her friends who became the servants of authoritarian movements, Applebaum sees the consequences of the lust for status among resentful men and women, who believe the old world never gave them their due. (...) Readers should be glad she bided her time. Applebaum can bring a candle into the darkness of the populist right precisely because she stayed on the right for so long. (...) She does not know whether it can be beaten. She's a journalist not a soothsayer. But I know that if you want to fight it, her writing is an arsenal that stores the sharpest weapons to hand.

Among many, a favorite line is, "a society based on merit may sound fine if you want to live in a country run by talented people. But what if you are not yourself talented?" Well, indeed. It is a question that has bedeviled thinkers from, you know, Socrates to the Talented Mr. Scruton: the untalented, what to do with them? They ought to know their place, like those second-rate journalists sniffing a chance of recognition. The thought occurred that what—if nothing else—had the rise of Trump and Johnson and the mainstreaming of notions such as structural racism during the Black Lives Matter protests taught us about meritocracy and talent? Even for those not in agreement with the view that something was askew in the societal allocation of rewards, surely the existence of people saying things were askew deserved at least a reference in this article?[16] We go on. The Left blames the rise of populism—a term pedaled without much critical analysis in *The Guardian, The Observer*'s sister paper—on austerity, the Right on immigration, Applebaum pontificates. It was unclear if Cohen was simply unaware of Applebaum's continued rightwing positions on key issues. Furthermore, it seemed odd to think that only insiders (and "heretics") could understand the likes of Johnson, Scruton and O'Sullivan, given that Applebaum seemed incapable of doing precisely that when they were sat across the dinner party table. What was so confusing about these people that she couldn't see and many others not at the table could? They were amusing, we are told, and "we were young, History's winners." Naked ambition, perhaps, blinds one to one's friends' ("ex-friends'") vices? Sadly, Applebaum typified a culture of intellectual bullying and ruthless snobbery that afflicted many aspiring opinion formers in the 1990s in Poland. A new class was emerging and demanded to be heard. This

---

16 Mark Blyth, a professor of economics at Brown University in the US, told me in an interview for Forbes in 2019: "So the critics have a rather obvious point. If most people are working longer hours for less money, which they are, then why should they be happy about it." "It takes a monumental effort to look around at a world with Trump, the AfD, Brexit, and all the rest and declare that everyone is really quite happy with everything after all," Blyth says. Elizabeth Anderson in *Private Government: How Employers Rule Our Lives (and Why We Don't Talk about It)* (Princeton: Princeton University Press, 2017) calls it "Private Government," arguing that neoliberal freedom for capital has necessitated a despotism for workers where employers control all the levels of power, not just wages but off hours behavior, access to health care, bathroom breaks, etc. "Maybe the workers at *The Economist* suffer no such indignities, but millions of other workers do," Blyth goes on.

new salariat was a creature created by almost three decades of raw capitalism in Poland, an irony not lost on those whose analysis of the rise of PiS adopted a dialectical understanding of history. So, perhaps it was no surprise that Applebaum took refuge in a country manor house and wandered around in tweed jackets. These things only go so far, however, when your project is meritocracy and modernization. But perhaps the real tragedy for Applebaum was that her husband, ex-foreign minister, Radosław (Radek) Sikorski, had picked the wrong Rightwing grouping within the emerging sub-elites to join when the post-communist Left imploded in the early 2000s. Sikorski had in fact been a member of PiS for a while, and then jumped ship to PO, a fact conveniently omitted from the article. A new elite without a political foothold is a fragile flower. But—to grossly paraphrase Oscar Wilde—one that can't pick the right Rightwing faction of the new elite to join looks a bit careless.

A "Symmetrist"? Such a view would, I suppose, cast me into the category of "Symmetrist," or as Cohen and Applebaum—at least on the basis of reading this article—might call it, appeaser.

I met a couple of *The Guardian*'s reporters in Warsaw in 2018 and my itch refused to be scratched. I was surprised to hear one of them had not heard of Władysław Gomułka, one of the key figures in postwar Polish communism. Her next foreign assignment was in Africa, so who really cared anyway? But PiS was "terribly exciting" and "jolly good fun," she said. I was immediately transported in my imagination to a Belsize Park dinner party, full of others from this world of the "talented." The focus and style for the most part seemed to be what an idealized *Guardian* reader might want to read. I wasn't sure if they were aware of this and my questions elicited little by way of self-awareness. Another journalist in Warsaw, bureau chief of a major international news agency, wondered wistfully on Facebook if there had been any "research" undertaken into the rise of "all this modern-day hatred." I still am not entirely disabused of the idea that she wasn't joking. The talented's cup did indeed overfloweth.

A Reality Check: That was until one day in September 2019, when a picture of the increasingly bigoted singer Morrissey wearing a shirt that read "Fuck *The Guardian*"[17] appeared in, well, *The Guardian*. Heaven knows I was miserable. It was as if I had betrayed my own side. But it also felt like a watershed

---

17   Josh Halliday, "Morrissey Performs in LA Wearing Explicit Anti-Guardian Vest," *The Guardian*, October 27, 2019.

moment. *The Guardian*, if anything, had been, after all, the one newspaper in Britain that had consistently challenged the status quo on most fronts, supported progressive and democratic causes, driven the climate change agenda and so on. And who, after all, could begrudge a paper with the likes of John Crace, Simon Hattenstone, Marina Hyde and John Harris on its books?

The period between round one and two of the 2020 presidential election in early July also added to this sense of a misjudged project. President Andrzej Duda attacked July 3's *Fakt*, Poland's most popular tabloid, which had reported on his pardoning of a convicted child abuser. "Mr. President, how could you pardon someone like this?" the paper asked.[18] PiS attacked *Fakt* and especially against its owners—Switzerland's Ringier Holding and Germany's Axel Springer. "Does the Axel Springer company, with German roots, which is the owner of the Fakt newspaper, want to influence the Polish presidential election?" Duda asked. "Do the Germans want to elect Poland's president?"[19] Duda also unleashed an attack against Philipp Fritz, the Warsaw correspondent of *Die Welt*, a German paper owned by Axel Springer, accusing him of promoting the campaign of Duda's opponent in the election Rafał Trzaskowski. "Today, ladies and gentlemen, we have yet another German attack during these elections," Duda said. Justice Minister Zbigniew Ziobro hinted that the government would have to "look closely" at foreign media ownership. Foreign correspondents covering Poland for international publications—including *The Financial Times, Le Monde, De Volkskrant, Le Soir* and *The Guardian*—published a joint statement on July 14 condemning the criticism of Fritz. In the statement they said Fritz had received thousands of threatening messages. In response, Poland's state broadcaster, TVP ran a news segment entitled "German interference in the Polish elections," accusing "German media of standing on one side of the barricades" in Poland, using "manipulations" to attack Duda. It named and showed an image of Fritz, alongside a commentator saying that German foreign correspondents have a "long tradition" of performing a "double role" of reporting news while also representing their country's "national interest."[20]

---

18   "Andrzej Duda ułaskawił pedofila? Prezydent zabiera głos," July 3, *Fakt*.
19   Jan Cieński, "Poland's Duda goes to war against foreign media," July 7, 2020, *Politico*.
20   "Foreign correspondents in Poland condemn president's attack on German journalist," July 20, *Notes from Poland*.

So, the initial premise for the book was threatened from the start of writing and my own motives for writing thrown into doubt or even exposed as trivial and personal. Was I not in danger of adding fuel to the far-right's accusations of "fake news," of undermining "'liberal" media, of myself normalizing performative references to "mainstream media" and undermining the very traditions of reporting that papers like *The Guardian* had fought for?[21] What would Cohen make of it all? Was I one of his leftist apologists for rightwing authoritarianism? Wasn't I, after all, just doing what I accused others of, namely "essentializing" and "Orientalizing" Poles, and Poland, othering them, but also myself as a foreigner living in Poland? I was haunted by the possibility that I was just following the narrative established by PiS and a set of discussion points (gender, history, etc.), myself just another performative signpost along a well-trodden path? Was I an enabler, another Useful Idiot or just a common or garden "Symmetrist"?[22] Another problem was falling into the trap of endowing journalism and journalists with an agency they didn't (don't) have. And what of my own telos? Where did I want to go and what kind of society would I prefer to live in? Above all, was I not in danger of placing my own my own insights, methods and style of presentation above others', the claim I make throughout the book about "Mainstream media"? Was I not just another one of those second-rate journalist sniffing around for recognition after years of obscurity, another of the untalented?

I am no fan of PiS, after all, and probably closer to the Fabian traditions of the Labour movement in Britain, if not the Labour Party. My mum's Quaker family background probably had it about right—a line I never thought I would write. My aim, I told a friend, was to help "us" define what it is "we" wanted, before "we" could decide how to go about achieving it. He smiled. "Us?" he sighed. "You're dreaming." He told me I would alienate any remaining friends I had in the Warsaw foreign press and not be befriended or rewarded by "the other side." It was "professional suicide" another told me. The path between exploring why people voted for PiS and somehow appearing to be condoning or normalizing its politics turned out to be a rather narrow one. Journalistic friends unfriended me on Facebook, invitations to events

---

21 Nick Cohen, "The Far-left Origins of No 10's Desperate Attack on all Things 'Woke,'" *The Guardian*, June 20, 2020.
22 See https://kulturaliberalna.pl/2019/04/02/co-dzieli-opozycje-10-lat-kultury-liberalnej/#more-75146.

dried up and the people at *The Guardian* with whom I had had some, albeit minimal, contact stopped answering emails.

But I couldn't claim to have had a remarkable Warsaw career as a journalist. The best I could say was that I had survived and written a handful of decent articles. Most of the rest was long days spent wading through relentlessly dreary business news for British or American news agencies, papers or magazines. At times it became hard to remember what I'd written that someone else hadn't already copied and pasted into an earlier article that had then been reborrowed. Then there were those endless industry conferences by "groundbreaking" Polish start-ups and conventions for paper bag producers and the like. All the while watching, noting the often-pompous behavior of fellow reporters, and of course reading their Warsaw pieces, some from the top drawer, but most not so much. Bourdieu's notion of "habitus" helped me relieve the boredom and do something I considered vaguely journalistic, casually exploring what he calls the "semi-autonomous logic" of journalism—"the interplay between individual journalist, social process in the news room and the commercial ideology of the media company." That thought keep me awake during many a plastic cutlery producers trade conference at Warsaw's Sheraton hotel.[23] This incestuous, inherently plagiaristic (and not in the Bauman sense[24]) mini-world of Warsaw foreign journalism seemed ripe for some kind of overhaul.

Then, on finishing the first draft of the book a week later, I watched on YouTube—by chance obviously—a chat between the Rightwing British hack, Rod Liddle, and British nationalist politician, Nigel Farage.[25] I disliked how easy it was to agree with their comments in the symptoms of the crises unfolding across the Western world. How did Farage understand this so well and we, the good liberal-left, didn't? The Situationists seemed the only ones able to grasp this apparent contradiction. "In the autocratic reign of the market economy (...) which had acceded to an irresponsible sovereignty, and the totality of new techniques of government which accompanied this reign, the mass media are its most glaring superficial manifestation," as Debord had

23 Bourdieu, *Outline of a Theory of Practice*.
24 See, Alberto Bellan, "Zygmunt Bauman—liquid copyright or solid plagiarism?" *The IPKat*, April 11, 2014.
25 "Nigel Farage Meets Rod Liddle, Stepping Up with Nigel Farage #1," YouTube video, 39:17, posted by Nigel Farage, October 6, 2019, www.youtube.com/watch?v=weAruOCjMRc.

it.[26] The spectacle—that notion that once commodities rule us as both workers and consumers, instead of being ruled by us, we become passive subjects that simply contemplate the reified spectacle—also lent a helping hand when shaking sweaty palms over cake and coffee in the carpeted London Lounge of the Sheraton in Warsaw. Thank God for György Lukács, I would mutter.

I was reminded while watching Liddle and Farage of how, as a 17-year old I had gone to our local pub in Lewes, East Sussex, with visiting South Wales miners towards the end their year-long strike in early 1985. The local Labour Party, full of "intellectuals" from nearby Sussex University, had collected several hundred pounds for their families. My friend Gwyn and I went with the miners, while our parents stayed at home. "Keep your hands in your pockets, boys," we were told as round after round of warm Harveys bitter appeared and disappeared. The collected money was duly spent in the pub and the next morning they left in clapped-out Ford Cortinas, beer cans on board, back home. We wanted to support them but couldn't find a language with which to talk and were probably privately relieved when they returned home and peace was restored to the sedate little town. Hope may lie in the proles, to paraphrase Orwell, but let's hope they keep their distance from us.

There seemed to me to be many similarities with how the idea of "Poland" had been constructed since 1989 by the British middle class: plucky underdog, proud and on the right side, but only a few lucky ones can join our club.

Whose Side Are You On? The idea that the term "liberal elites" is a cliché used by populists or lazy journalists had already itself become something of a cliché by the time of writing this book. But the struggle over ownership of the term itself was perhaps indicative of a wider problem, namely how we named things we don't like. Simply writing about "elites" and "the people" thus became fraught with danger.[27] The worse things got (democracy unwinding, dents to the rule of law), the more this seemed to be so. But populists, it seemed to me, could simply be anyone you don't like or agree with. Most of us, after all, might ourselves share in some aspects of some conspiracy theories, and some elements of other peoples' versions of populism. After Donald Trump entered the White House, anyone found using

---

26   McKenzie Wark, *50 Years of Recuperation*, 185.

27   Godwin's Law state's that any online discussion, if it continues long enough, will always devolve into an accusation that someone is a Nazi. See Mike Godwin, "Meme, Counter-Meme," *Wired* (October 1994).

the term "Mainstream media," however banal or blunt their criticism, however sane and balanced their sense of self and evidenced-based and rational their method, the temptation was to cast that person into the same pot as David Icke and Tommy Robinson in the UK and in Poland, Max Kolonko or Wojciech Cejrowski.[28] *The Guardian* started a campaign of trying to explain, define, and measure populism in 2019.[29] It struck me as a particularly interesting exercise, but one that also highlights this problem. One thus needs to tread very carefully. This is a particularly difficult problem when talking about hegemonic rhetorical frameworks, because without great care, those frameworks appear to take on a power of agency that they do not possess, as a wise professor told me.

The majority of analyses of populism refer to Cas Mudde's definition,[30] namely that it is "an ideology that considers society to be ultimately separated into two homogeneous and antagonistic groups, 'the pure people' versus the 'corrupt elite,'" and which argues that politics should be an expression of the general will of the people."[31] Mudde argues that populism is a "thin ideology," which on its own is too insubstantial to provide a blueprint for social change. It differs from "thick-centered" ideologies such as fascism, liberalism and socialism. Populism in this definition is a rejection of key elements of modernity, based on assumptions of a unity of "the people," a promotion of "solidarism," "the people" being the only "legitimate sovereign" distinguished from, and counterposed to, the power elite, from whom power is to be retrieved. So, what unites populist movements on both left and right is their rejection of elite culture and values. On the Right were Trump, Marine Le Pen in France, Geert Wilders in the Netherlands, and Hungarian Prime Minister Viktor Orbán, and, on the Left, Syriza in Greece, Podemos in Spain, the Five Star Movement in Italy, Bernie Sanders in the US, and Jeremy Corbyn in the UK. Populism is by this definition against the status quo and not much else.

28 Max Kolonko was an iconic figure, reporting from Washington in the 1990s. He then went a little David Icke: YouTube video info, https://www.youtube.com/channel/UCN4mm7HcfpjgVYQUeqRkCuQ.

29 See, for example, Peter C. Baker, "We the People: The Battle to Define Populism," *The Guardian*, January 10, 2019.

30 Cas Mudde, "In the Name of the Peasantry, the Proletariat, and the People: Populisms in Eastern Europe," in *Democracies and the Populist Challenge*, ed. Yves Mény and Yves Surel (New York: Palgrava, 2002); Olga Wysocka, "Populism in Poland," (paper presented at ECPR General Conference, Florence, European University Institute, 2007).

31 Cas Mudde, "The Populist Zeitgeist," *Government and Opposition* 39, no. 4 (2004): 543.

"I don't think 'the Western model' has any real meaning, outside of specific ideological (and often ethnocentric) meanings it is being given in the contemporary debates," Mudde told me for an interview with *Deutsche Welle* in 2018. He argued:

> Liberal democracy is currently the legal system of western democracies and the moral norm for the vast majority of people. Populism, as defined by a majority of scholars is in direct breach with fundamental aspects of liberal democracy. It is 'emancipatory' in the sense that it will break from the liberal constraints on majority rule. It's a (populist) cliché to argue that the political establishment has not been listening--just look at the shift in the debates on austerity, European integration, or immigration. At the same time, the liberal democratic system has not failed. Mainstream politicians have depoliticized politics. They should again publicly defend their political position, argue why they are good/better, and put them at the center of election campaigns.

Mudde's defiant defense of liberal democratic tolerance struck me as a bit rigid, and in fact rather intolerant. The tone of his communication also suggested exasperation with (yet another) wannabe populist harboring most likely quasi-ethnic driven antipathies. But he didn't bother to find out if this was the case, regurgitating a defense of a model whose unchallenged continuation was to be put to the test within the subsequent 12 months by the Black Lives Matter protests and the social crisis caused by Covid-19. His argument that "the political establishment" had been listening seemed to be weakening by the day.

The Essex School of Discourse Analysis provides some way out of the Mudde impasse.[32] The question is not how to fight populism, but rather which type of populist you want to be, Ernesto Laclau argues. Conflict is an inescapable and defining feature of political life and there is always a "we" and a "they." He maintains that populism is just another word for real politics:

---

32 Ernesto Laclau and Chantal Mouffe reinterpreted Antoni Gramsci's theory of hegemony to highlight the processes of interpellation and identification in the creation of political identities. Chantal Mouffe, "Centrist politics will not defeat Boris Johnson's rightwing populism," October 1, 2020, *The Guardian*. Nick Cohen wrote a damning criticism of the ideas in: Nick Cohen, "The spectre of censorship and intolerance stalks today's left," July 11, 2020, *The Guardian*.

for people ("us") creating a sense of how our dissatisfactions relate, who is to blame ("them"), and how to force change.

Towards a Definition: An interesting political-linguistic research proposal that allows a broadening of the view of populism is a cognitive methodology using the category of the "linguistic picture of the world." In proposing cognitivism in the study of populism, Małgorzata Kołodziejczak and Marta Wrześniewska-Pietrzak[33] point out that among the characteristic elements supporting the definition of a text as populist, a specific vision of the world is created within this discourse. Among the rhetorical mechanisms of narrative creation, those typical of populist narratives include the following:

(1) *Topos of power. The authorities exploit people. The roles "good" and "bad" are rigidly assigned in this narrative. The populist, always "good," often does not declare his hostility towards democracy as such, but against its representative component while affirming the will of the people.*

(2) *Topos of oppression: Certain groups (elites) pose a threat to the people. In this role, the populist arouses fear of a political opponent, mobilizes the people against the oppressor. Performative speech acts in this narrative flatter "the people."*

(3) *Topos of complaint: The populist laments the fate of the people exploited by evil power, exposing its unjustifiable wrongs, traumas and feelings of being underestimated. The populist is the voice of the people here, he complains on their behalf.*

(4) *Topos of change: Populism is a reaction to crisis. In this narrative, in which the people are a victim, the ruler is an oppressor, the populist is a savior, and the proposed change is that the savior will tame the oppressor. This opens up space for speech acts, such as promises, to manage collective hopes and dreams. They may refer to an ideal from the past or future.*

(5) *Topos of integration: Populists refer only to collectives, because it guarantees the collective emotions that give a sense of cultural community of experience and values, and this is possible thanks to rituals and shared narratives.*

---

33 "Kognitywizm jako sposób interdyscyplinarnego (politolingwistycznego) badania populizmu na tle polskich analiz dyskursu populistycznego," (Cognitivism as an interdisciplinary (politolinguistic) method for research on populism against the background of Polish analyzes of populist discourse), Małgorzata Kołodziejczak i Marta Wrześniewska-Pietrzak (*Badania nad dyskursem populistycznym: wybrane podejścia*, by Agnieszka Stępińska and Artur Lipiński, Uniwersytet im. Adama Mickiewicza w Poznaniu Wydawnictwo Naukowe Wydziału Nauk Politycznych i Dziennikarstwa Poznań 2020.

(6) ***Topos of compensation:*** *By articulating claims, the populist will help compensate the people for what they lack and settle the bill with bad authority.*

The analytical process might as easily thus also focus on how these "populist" tendencies define what are ostensibly non-populist politics and political discourse. Does this taxonomy also apply to Liberalism, Marxism and so on?

Chapter 2

At Her Majesty's Service!

In the 1990s it was quite cool to be British in Poland.[1] We had helped "win" the Cold War, been on the "right side of history," weren't Germans and were almost Americans. We were, to borrow the Applebaum line, "History's winners." Then there was the Beatles, Monty Python, good manners, language, schools, that "soft power" we carry around as informal "Britishness," however overused, tired and dreary it may be.[2] The dominant (neo)-liberal narrative of that decade was also tinged with elements Brits could legitimately claim to have played a part in establishing and maintaining: modern democratic institutions, the rule of law and separation of powers, an open mixed economy, open(ish) borders, small state, strong civil society, secular, and individualistic. Margaret Thatcher was something of a hero in Poland at the time, as was Adam Smith. Britain was also, under Prime Minister Tony Blair after 1997, a key player in the EU and supportive of Poland's accession to the bloc, even if New Labour's quasi-social democratic ("Third Way") language was a misleading precursor of its later "Neo-Con" subservience before and during the 2003 Iraq War. Meanwhile, the government of Donald Tusk, 2007-2015, had a not-insignificant British contingent.[3]

---

1   Notwithstanding the small matters of Neville Chamberlain, Yalta and, of course, Britain's post-war silence over Katyń.
2   Ben Sixsmith, "Poles Apart," *The Spectator*, July 18, 2019; Ben Sixsmith, *Kings & Comedians: A Brief History of British-Polish Relations* (London: CreateSpace, 2018).
3   Jacek Rostowski from 1989 to 1991 was advisor to Finance Minister Leszek Balcerowicz and and was finance minister until 2013 under Tusk. Stanisław Gomułka was a Polish born economist, from 1970 to 2005, a reader in economics at the LSE, and between 1989–2002 advisor to the Ministry of Finance. Radosław "Radek" Sikorski was a journalist and later Minister of Foreign Affairs in Tusk's cabinet. A graduate of Pembroke College, Oxford, between 1986–1989 he worked as a journalist for *The Observer* and *The Spectator*. At the Oxford Union he was elected to the Bullingdon Club, with David Cameron and Boris Johnson.

By 2019, if not before, much of this legacy had slipped, in large part be-cause of Brexit and the anti-immigrant rhetoric that underpinned it, as had the generally rather benign image in some of the tabloid press of Brits' new, post-2004 neighbors from "the East." A notorious Panorama report on the BBC from Poland and Ukraine before the 2012 European soccer champion-ships was illustrative.[4]

This was also reflected in the Right's attacks on immigration and immi-grants. As Ariel Spigelman observed,[5] some politicians, parts of the media and of the public in Britain started to weaponize quasi-colonial tropes of Eastern Europe, "Orientalizing" Poland and Poles as lower down on a civi-lizational hierarchy. "Mention concerns about the rule of law in certain EU countries, and people, even EU officials, automatically assume you are re-ferring to Hungary and Poland," as Agata Gostyńska-Jakubowska writes.[6] This perspective is based on a division of the East and West of Europe, which makes the experiences of Eastern European nations invisible from a postco-lonial perspective.[7] The election victories of PiS in 2015 and again in 2019 seemed to reinforce these tropes, at least as far as domestic Poland figured at all in British popular awareness. Poland went from being the golden child of western capitalism to "problematic": from the Radical-Right thesis (Mudde), to the mild authoritarianism thesis (Daniel Ziblatt and Steven Levitsky), and the illiberal democracy thesis (Yascha Mounk[8]).

Projected Fantasies: This book looks at how the British press covered Po-land and PiS, in particular after 2015, asking if it exemplified and perhaps ac-centuated pre-existing (even if dormant) notions of Eastern Europe[9] within British society? It is very much, then, a British perspective on Poland, partly

---

4   "Stadiums of Hate': Legitimate and Fair," *BBC*, June 8, 2012.
5   Ariel Spigelman, "The Depiction of Polish Migrants in the United Kingdom by the British Press after Poland's Accession to the European Union," *International Journal of Sociology and Social Policy* 33, no. 1–2 (2013): 98–113.
6   Agata Gostyńska-Jakubowska, "Make No Mistake: Poland and Hungary Aren't the Only EU States Abusing the Law," *The Guardian*, January 22, 2020.
7   Claire Cavanagh, "Postcolonial Poland: An Empty Space on the Map of Current Theory," *Common Knowledge* 10, no. 1 (2004): 82–92. See "Occidentalization," the labelling of outdated, post-imperial Western fantasies as Asia takes over global hegemony.
8   Cas Mudde, "Poland's Rightwing Populist Win Should be a Wake-up call for Democrats Worldwide," *The Guardian*, October 21, 2019; Steven Levitsky and Daniel Ziblatt, *How Democracies Die* (New York: Crown, 2018); Yascha Mounk, "Democracy in Poland is in Mortal Danger," *The Atlantic*, Octo-ber 19, 2019.
9   Adam Burgess, "Writing off Slovakia to 'The East'? Examining Charges of Bias in British Press Report-ing of Slovakia, 1993–1994," *Nationalities Papers* 25, no. 4 (1997): 659–682.

because it is an area I felt best equipped to describe and explain and partly because of the heuristic insights it afforded. The sense of writing about something so apparently new and historically unprecedented—the transition from socialism to capitalism—and a Poland that had been submerged for a long time, was also appealing.

But, curiously, at the same time, it felt a little as if one was writing allegorical tales about Britain, as Kapuściński had done about Edward Gierek's regime in early 1970s Poland via Haile Selassie's rule in Ethiopia.[10] These were the Britains and Polands as they would like to see themselves against how they were actually seen by others, the virtual against the real. The migration of hundreds of thousands of Poles to the UK after 2004 also added to a process of cultural mirroring. Writing about Poland's overly deferential attitude towards the Catholic Church was another semiotic minefield, but perhaps also an allegorical look at how Brits idolize their Royal Family, idealize the past, the importance of social hierarchy, tradition and notions of purity and good breeding. Both countries, meanwhile, harbored their own colonial hankerings of sorts, Poland's for its 18th-century Commonwealth, as much a political and a mental space as a real one, stretching 'From Sea to Sea' (Baltic to Black) and the UK for its imperial prowess on the High Seas. Neither had yet to fully come to terms with its actual size and status. Then there was writing about Poland's anti-Semitism. Perhaps this was easier than writing about England's anti-black and anti-Irish (if not also its own anti-Semitic) history. The two countries also seemed to share a legacy of class cleavage drenched in ancient—and ethnicized—difference: in Poland the Sarmatian[11] myth and in Britain the Norman one, both invading noble, warrior castes imposing their will, language and religion on a peasantry defined as "Other" and lesser. As George Orwell once remarked, England is a family with the wrong members in charge. The same could perhaps be said of Poland.

Admonishing plucky little Poland for its naughty anti-democratic ways worked quite well as long as Westminster remained somehow a functioning model of how politics should work. But as Brexit ripped through the institutions and institutional culture of the Westminster Model in 2019, the tone towards Poland and others changed. Indeed, some of the key issues that

---

10 Ryszard Kapuściński, *The Emperor: Downfall of an Autocrat* (New York: Vintage Books, 1984).
11 See Tadeusz Sulimirski, *The Sarmatians* (New York: Praeger Publishers, 1970). See also footnote 39 on p. 58 in this book.

had been brought up in the first four years of PiS's rule in Poland were also center stage in UK debates over Brexit: the independence of the judiciary in a democratic system of government, the role and power of the legislature versus an overbearing executive, and media independence. Then there was a rise in ethno-nationalism, in the UK case perhaps most clearly English nationalism, and Euroskepticism. There was also a strong majoritarian theme running through elements of both PiS and the Conservative party discourse and political behavior in particular after the Brexit referendum in June 2016. The rise of what became called "Culture Wars" was another area of overlap, with a narrative of "traditional values" counterposed against a narrative of change. This also took place in an atmosphere of increasingly vitriolic social media commentary and growing political polarization. UK press coverage of Poland and its election on October 13, 2019 was therefore, to some extent a product of an internal struggle within the UK as much as a simple reflection of events as they actually happened in Poland. PiS's Poland and the other populists in the EU could either be held up as examples of why a stronger EU needed Britain's continued input or why it should leave the Europeans to their own devices.

Poland was then at once a blank page for many Westerners, a place of projected fantasies, of new starts and mistakes to be corrected, but also historical guilt, shame and betrayal. Both of Poland's leading parties' stories share roots in a mythological sense of betrayal: Civic Platform's (PO's) in the betrayal of democratic norms and PiS's narrative in the alleged selling out of Polish society and identity to "foreign interests."[12]

The Veil Slips: When I started writing about Poland's descent into illiberalism, we were still in a pre-Brexit and pre-Trump era. In early 2016 a paradigmatic shift in what was acceptable in UK and US public discourse was not widely expected. During the course of writing my first book on the subject, Trump and Brexit seemed to creep up behind Washington and Westminster, respectively, and by 2017 a new set of rules had apparently claimed large chunks of the public discursive space. We saw a slipping of the UK's veneer, revealing a picture of Britain that few outside had seen so obviously as two sides of the same coin, the beauty and the beast, the gent and the hooligan,

---

12 Barbara Törnquist-Plewa, *The Wheel of Polish Fortune: Myths in Polish Collective Consciousness during the First Years of Solidarity* (Lund: Lund University Press, 1992), 115–74.

the sublime and the ridiculous.[13] This was a process of national self-revelation. Britain as a "normal" mid-sized European country, precisely the thing most Poles when asked in 1989 said they wanted.[14]

Meanwhile, for the first time in a generation some of the apparently fixed (post-1979/80) ideological tectonic plates appeared to be shifting. While the values that underpinned the liberal/neoliberal paradigm—individualism, self-reliance, low tax/small state, etc.—were embedded, the operational end of the discourse seemed to move towards a more nuanced and mixed version of capitalism and liberal democracy. What of *"Life after Neoliberalism?" The Economist* asked in November 2019.

Earlier phases of neoliberalization in the 1990s had been executed by centrist parties, with the center-right committing to socially progressive politics in exchange for center-left support for economic neoliberalization. But after 2016, a new alliance emerged between center and Far-Right, which saw the latter mainstream as center-right parties such as the US Republicans and UK Conservatives steadily radicalized themselves, relinquishing any commitments to what Tariq Ali calls "the extreme center."[15] Reijer Hendrikse calls this process political illiberalization, which seeks to undo the institutional setup of liberal-democratic checks and balances, seeing legislative and judicial branches of government subjected to a power-hungry executive. "The rejection of 'two major emancipation movements—socialism and liberalism'—is what the Western far right wants," he writes.[16] The new synthesis is perhaps best described as neo-illiberalism, a mix of neoliberalism and identitarian nationalism. Hendrikse argues the rise of neo-illiberalism also suggested the center of capitalist gravity had shifted, with parts of the traditional periphery assuming characteristics of traditional core countries. The West in this light was witnessing a reverse process of what Immanuel Wallerstein called semi-peripheralization.[17] According to Wolfgang Streeck, beginning in the 1970s governments had tried various methods to redress the politically

---

13 Jacek Tebinka and Iwona Sakowicz-Tebinka, "Brytyjczycy i Polacy: Jak kształtował się obraz Polski w Wielkiej Brytanii od Churchilla do Camerona," *Kultura Współczesna* 1 (2015): 100–106.

14 Timothy Garton Ash, "Poland: a country getting to grips with being normal at last," April 4, 2011, *The Guardian.*

15 Tariq Ali, *The Extreme Centre: A Second Warning* (London: Verso Books, 2015)

16 Reijer Hendrikse, "Neoliberalism is Over," May 7, 2020, *OpenDemocracy.*

17 Immanuel Wallerstein, *The Modern World System I: Capitalist Agriculture and the Origins of the European World-Economy in the Sixteenth Century* (Berkeley: University of California Press, 2011), 151.

unacceptable outcomes of market allocation: first the toleration of inflation, then public debt, and finally the deregulation of private credit that led to the crash of 2008, at which point democratic capitalism appeared to have run out of options, and some countries abandoned all pretense of democracy in favor of technocracy. But following the global financial crisis, it was the authoritarian Right, not the Left, that managed to gain a foothold.[18]

---

18 Wolfgang Streeck, "How Will Capitalism End," *New Left Review* 87 (May–June 2014): 50. See also: Laura Amico, "Do Democracy and Capitalism Really Need Each Other?" *Harvard Business Review*, March 11, 2020.

Part II

An Academic Voice

Chapter 3

Modern Poland's Shifting Political Blocs

Scene Setting: *"PiS, PO, jedno zło"* (*"PiS/PO: as bad as each other"*). That was a common refrain on the far right and "Symmetrist" left from 2015 onward, if not before. Some called this emergent party system a duopoly. But for many others, the divisions between the two parties were real and mattered. Retracing a brief history of how Poland arrived at this two-party model may be instructive.

PO and PiS were children of the period when the Solidarity movement emerged in the 1980s and broke apart in the 1990s. Since then has been a long and drawn out struggle over symbolic succession: who will inherit the mantle of the Solidarity movement of the 1980s? One child appeared to have veered towards the European mainstream and the other stayed much closer to home. Or that is how it has been largely written, in particular from afar, in the Western press and elsewhere.

The focus here is mainly on the post-2001 period, following the electoral failure of an influential post-Solidarity centrist party, Freedom Union (UW), a precursor of PO. UW's electoral collapse in 2001 and subsequent political marginalization opened up a new phase, one marked by a shift of the center-right to the Right and the emergence of a clearer gap between a "harder" (PiS) and "softer" (PO) right-of-center discourse in Poland.

In many ways, the UW "buckle" that held the post-Round Table political consensus[1] together ended in the early 2000s and permitted the unleashing of a more clearly defined national oriented discourse that sought, openly and dogmatically, to break up what it saw as the tainted (post-1989) Third

---

1   Krzysztof Dubiński, *Magdalenka, Transakcja Epoki* (Warsaw: BGW 1990); Konstanty Gebert, *Mebel* (London: Aneks, 1990).

Republic, which grew out of the compromises of the—"flawed"—Round Table agreement of 1989.

After the split within the Solidarity movement in the early 1990s (the so-called "War at the Top"), some fetal elements of the ideological and discursive divisions on the center-right that were to emerge after 2001 started to become more visible. For a while they were largely subsumed under the banner of the Solidarity Election Campaign (AWS) umbrella party that won the 1997 election and was ousted four years later by a resurgent post-communist Democratic Left Alliance (SLD). It was not until the 2005 election, four years after they were both established, that PO and PiS emerged as more or less clearly identifiable representatives of competing narrative interpretations of a shared ideological patch and discursive space in Polish public life. The "liberal," secular and internationalist PO up against the conservative, Church-supported and nationalist PiS. This was a fashionable dichotomy and easily slotted into the media news cycles and narrative assumptions underpinning them.[2]

Sociologically, much has been made in this apparently post-ideological (Left versus Right) age of PO and PiS seeking to articulate the voices and latch on to the votes of a changing society, with the former articulating many of the demands of an emerging, mainly urban, middle class that is perhaps more materialistic than previous generations, more open to Europe (in a wider and narrower sense), better educated, more affluent, and more aspirational, and the latter representing those of an older constituency, often more rural, less affluent, more closely linked to the land and to tradition.

But PiS often deployed a language that was closer to social democracy, or perhaps a cruder statism: the protection of the elderly, pensioners, traditional industries, a strong state-funded health and pension system. It wrapped up what is, therefore, in many ways a call for post-communism to be reversed, for the state to remain an important allocator of collective resources, in a language of patriotism and populism rooted in a well-understood, often rather covertly articulated discourse of "us" versus "them." The "us" was clean,

---

2   As Brian Porter-Szűcs argues, the actual shifts in public opinion over the decade preceding 2015 or so were small. If we group all the parties of "illiberal democracy" together, and set them against the proponents of liberal democracy, the two sides have been locked in a nearly stable 50-50 split for quite some time. Because of the d'Hondt method used to allocate Sejm delegates, small shifts can have enormous consequences.

decent, honest, hard-working Poles, invariably Catholic, who are manipulated, lied to, and betrayed by a combination of mythically constructed "Others" ("them"), both inner and outer: "liberals," "communists," Jews, Muslims, "urban elites," foreign investors, and others.

Original Sins—the Round Table: Wiktor Soral and Mirosław Kofta at the University of Warsaw[3] in research conducted in 2018 found that attitudes towards the 1989 Round Table were an important marker of the fundamental political cleavage in Poland. Those who supported the rule of PiS (and who held a nationalistic-authoritarian orientation) tended to agree with PiS-driven conspiracy theories about the Round Table, whereas those who supported PO tended to reject it.

PiS first came to power in 2005 under the banner of a "moral revolution." It claimed it was necessary to bring about a "Fourth Republic" to replace the existing (post-1989) Third Republic and which, according to the PiS narrative, had failed and was tainted by "układy."[4] This Polish term does not lend itself to easy translation into English, but it refers to a nebulous series of networks, as PiS constructs them, of semi-covert groups operating in a half-world comprised of (mainly ex-communist) politicians, secret service officials, and apparatchiks (civil servants), and which grew up as a direct consequence of the Round Table deal between the communists and intellectual-liberal wing of Solidarity.

PiS's narrative was held together by the defining myth—the original sin—of the Round Table, endowing it with a mythical significance and setting it up as the origin of all the post-communist period's ills. This was a discourse that spoke to a particular national tradition, evoking a certain strand of that tradition, one that divided the world into "good" and "bad." It was a mode of political thought and action that also placed the Catholic Church at the heart of the concept of the nation, and Catholic Poles, by extension, at the center of the national identity and PiS as the party of the Catholic faithful. The discourse played on an old set of grievances: a nation that saw itself as governed by foreigners or their local proxies; a society divided against itself, stripped of the power to define itself.

---

3   "Belief in the Round Table Conspiracy and Political Division in Poland," *Social Psychological Bulletin* 14, no. 4 (March 2020): 1–19.

4   Jo Harper, "Negating Negation," *Problems of Post-Communism* 57, no. 4 (2010).

The PiS attack on the Round Table agreement and what it refers to as the "pathological networks" that stemmed directly from it, finds a direct discursive link to later battles via the process of lustration: cleansing. Since the first days of the post-communist era, voices on the nationalist Right called for a national accounting of what it called the "crimes of the communist period," to open the official files and allow the legal process to take its course. "Cleansing" is, of course, a heavily loaded political metaphor, implying there is dirt to clean up and implicitly equating dirt with "the other," i.e. not "us."[5] It found a rather ugly expression in the PiS leader Jarosław Kaczyński's equation of refugees from the Middle East with disease in mid-2015. The discourse stamps a restrictive framework on a complex and multi-layered reality. But it was a central feature of PiS tactics of dividing the world into those who supported lustration, and therefore the PiS "project," and those who did not.

Are We There Yet? The split that was subsequently to lead to the birth of PO and PiS in 2001 appeared to be a marginal feature of post-communist politics in the 1990s. Infighting in the post-Solidarity movement was an intermittently vexing sideshow to the re-emergence of the post-communists, the SLD, and the slow emergence of a more clearly defined and organized extreme nationalist and populist Right.

But after 2005, this powerful dichotomy of PO versus PiS emerged, grounded in a series of shifts in Polish socio-politics: one, the success of the far-right and populist parties at the 2005 election and their subsequent collapse at the 2007 election; two, the collapse of the post-communist Left; and three, the marginalization of UW. The elections of 2001, 2005, 2007, 2011, and 2015 thus see a shift away from the two extremes of Left and Right (however troublesome that ideological distinction had become) and the emergence of a new political center, although shifted decidedly to the Right and devoid of many of the ideological and personnel cleavages that had marked the earlier phase of the post-communist transition.

The Brief Rise and Fall of Extremism, 2005-7: At the 2007 election, the League of Polish Families (LPR) and Self Defense (SO) failed to re-enter

---

5   Łukasz Orylski, *Evolution of Polish Political Discourse after September 2005* (Gdańsk: Uniwersytet Gdański, 2006). The works of Norman Fairclough, e.g., *Language and Power*, 2nd ed. (London: Longman, 2001), and Teun A. van Dijk, *Communicating Racism: Ethnic Prejudice in Thought and Talk* (London: Sage, 1987); Elżbieta Halas, "Symbolic Politics of Public Time and Collective Memory: The Polish Case," *European Review* 10, no. 1 (2002).

parliament after two years in coalition with PiS. While LPR and SO constituencies differed, as did their discursive formulations and political strategies, a combination of the nationalist messianism of LPR discourses and the bottom-up populism of SO is perhaps what an unreconstructed PiS discourse might look like: on the one hand, a hardline call for a moral purge of the ills, as it saw them, stemming from both communism and post-communist liberalism, and on the other, a strong state. These SO and LPR discourses briefly appeared to herald the dawning of a rightward shift after their electoral successes in 2005.

Left Loses its Voice: In the early 1990s, the SLD—then based around the Social Democracy of the Polish Republic (SdRP)—was apparently quietly able to shed much of its communist heritage and focus on secular issues where popular disaffections ran high, such as health, education, abortion rights, and the separation of church and state. It portrayed itself as a modernizing force, while still upholding the ideal of social justice and its recognizable identity as part of a secular left tradition. In 1995, the co-founder of the SdRP, Aleksander Kwaśniewski, became president, and by the elections of 2001, the SLD had what appeared to be powerful political appeal. By the time of its election victory in 2001, it seemed to have succeeded in doing two apparently contradictory things: positioning itself simultaneously as a protector of the underdog and as a natural party of government. But once in power after 2001, it appeared to have no coherent worldview, an identity crisis manifested in contradictory impulses and policies, or a lack of them. It lurched to the Left and back to the Right and in the process, it lost any symbolic historical terrain it may have occupied.

The post-communists' fall from (a highly conditional and societally segmented) grace centered on a lack of vision and alternatives, which was seen by some as a continuation of the PZPR and by others as a sop to neoliberalism. On a personnel level, the post-communist Left was also destroying itself, with several high profile figures that had risen in the aftermath of (and, in the case of Leszek Miller and Kwaśniewski, thanks to) the Round Table negotiations caught up in a series of corruption allegations, reinforcing the party's drifting ideological references.

Secular Center Moves Right: Another important stepping-stone towards the rise of the new center-right was the demise of the old center-right. The 2001 electoral eclipse of UW, the successor of the Democratic Union (UD), a party that had grown out of the rump of the Workers' Defense Committee (KOR), undermining one of the key dimensions of the Round Table agreement. Namely, it weakened the stabilizing role played by the mainly Warsaw-based intelligentsia, both secular and Catholic, centered around KOR.

One needs to understand that PiS is also, in some crucial ways, a reaction to the failure of the secular center and Left. PiS offered a platform that harked back to community, jobs, and decidedly not to emigration. It defined the nation in narrow terms, evoking enemies both real and imagined. PiS also seemed to have learned some lessons from 2005–7. Its economic policies regarding banks, foreign investment, wind power, energy security, and Russia and its fight with the European Commission, all played into the narrative of Polish exceptionalism. In this understanding, PiS was a response to the crisis, not a cause of it. It, thus, offered quasi-Leftism with a touch of religion, conspiracy theory and law and order.

"What happened, not only in Poland, was that at [that] very moment you needed a social democratic kind of regime, which said 'we're going to protect: we know this transition is going to create a lot of losers as well as some winners, but our duty is to try and hold society together,'" Neal Ascherson told Jan Darasz.[6] "And so, the parties of the left in Poland committed themselves to neo-liberalism, leaving a political vacuum in a most sensitive place and it is not surprising that eventually somebody has moved into this vacuum: an ultra-nationalist, highly conservative, traditionalist party. That poses as a party of the losers, a protectionist party to some extent," Ascherson said.

Likewise, the victory of PiS in September 2015 was also, to a large extent, a function of the rudderlessness of PO after its leader Donald Tusk's departure to Brussels in late 2014. The reallocation of pensions in 2014 also indicated a drift away from the party's liberal economic source of legitimacy. There were also arbitrary uses of state power in sweeps of the weekly rightwing magazine *Wprost*, some seemingly deliberate last minute appointments to the Constitutional Tribunal prior to leaving office, and a sense that the party had lost its way and was just as prone to cronyism and corruption as it later accused PiS of being.

---

6   Jan Darasz, "966 and All That," in *Poland's Memory Wars: Essays on Illiberalism*, ed. Jo Harper (Budapest: CEU Press, 2018), 135–152.

The Key Blocs

1: PiS: *"A person whose pockets are empty isn't free,"* Kaczyński said at the 2019 PiS convention.[7] This can be read as a trademark rhetorical device, both quasi-biblical in style but resolutely profane at the same time. And perhaps this is the greatest political trick Kaczyński managed to pull off, namely keeping a wide spectrum of rightwing and traditionally leftwing thought and organization inside the same tent, while persuading enough outsiders in at election time to gain power. PiS itself was in fact a far more variegated entity than many observers chose to admit, with struggles between three main blocs: "ideological praetorians," the most important group as far as political influence and personal aspirations went, including Antoni Macierewicz, Mariusz Błaszczak, Mariusz Kamiński and Witold Waszczykowski. The second main group were the "ideological neophytes" around Ziobro and a counterbalance third force was the "managers," an interesting category including future Prime Minister Mateusz Morawiecki, along with Anna Streżyńska, Henryk Kowalczyk and earlier Paweł Szałamacha. The NSZZ Solidarity trade union was also a supporter, as were large chunks of the clerical aparatus. One should also bear in mind, as Rafał Matyja argues,[8] that at the start of Poland's transformation in 1990, Kaczyński had been very positive about the free market, with the Center Agreement (Porozumienie Centrum, PC) party, which he founded in 1990, a striking advocate of Margaret Thatcher's scorched earth economic policies of the 1980s. Tomasz Sawczuk shows that Kaczyński had in fact mocked the centrist Democratic Union (Unia Demokratyczna, or UD) on this front.[9] Kaczyński, according to Sawczuk, in fact wanted to create a Christian-democratic party that would combine conservatism, liberalism, and social democracy. In his personal history of the Center Agreement, published under the title *Porozumienie przeciw monowładzy* ("Agreement Against Authoritarianism"), Kaczyński recalled John Paul II's 1991 pilgrimage to Poland, observing: "We also tried to translate the Pope's teachings into a political program, but we clung to a particularistic, Christian-democratic

---

7   Jo Harper, "Poland: Where Keynes Meets Jesus," *Deutsche Welle*, May 29, 2019.
8   Rafał Matyja, "Emergency Exit," in *The End of the Liberal Mind, Poland's New Politics*, ed. Karolina Wigura and Jaroslaw Kuisz (Warsaw: Kultura Liberalna, 2020), 37–56.
9   Tomasz Sawczuk, "Reconstruction in Democracy: From Jarosław Kaczyński's Illiberal Shift to Pragmatic Liberalism," in *The End of the Liberal Mind: Poland's New Politics*, ed. Karolina Wigura and Jaroslaw Kuisz (Warsaw: Kultura Liberalna, 2020) 107–133.

format. We failed to grasp what was most significant: the need to bolster our identity as Poles and to universalize the link between Polishness and Catholicism, often expressed in the saying Polak-katolik."[10]

Sawczuk suggests that the irony lies in the fact that Kaczyński in fact managed to build the most ideologically flexible party in the history of the Third Republic. "PiS is not irrational, small-minded, or parochial. It is modern through and through, and that is precisely the source of a paradox that is also the party's biggest problem. PiS is unable to restore tradition or accomplish the 'reconstitution' of Polishness," Sawczuk argues.[11]

Kaczyński's support for liberal market economics remained after the formation of PiS and when in government in 2005–2007 its economic policy was shaped by politicians with liberal leanings, such as Deputy Prime Minister Zyta Gilowska.

But the Kaczyński twins also looked for inspiration to the pre-war Left-leaning Sanacja movement, and its leader Józef Piłsudski, in contrast to the nationalist Endecja led by Piłsudski's political rival, Roman Dmowski.

The party included several nationalist politicians in senior positions, such as former leader of the All-Polish Youth (Młodzież Wszechpolska), and deputy PiS leader, Macierewicz, founder of the National-Catholic Movement (Ruch Katolicko-Narodowy, or RKN).

Matyja notes that a change occurred when PiS was in opposition after 2007. "By gaining the support of SO and LPR, PiS itself adopted some of the stances of these parties, both of which had backed the 'no' vote in the EU accession referendum of 2003 (...) taken hostage by the leader of traditionalist Catholic opinion, Tadeusz Rydzyk and Radio Maryja. Until 2005, Kaczyński had viewed them as a threat and harbored suspicions that they could be potential pro-Russian mouthpieces."[12]

After its 2015 election victory, the government arrived at a political compromise stemming from the establishment of an electoral coalition bloc, the United Right (ZP). Its three components were: PiS, the hegemon, Jarosław Gowin's "Agreement" and "Solidarity Poland" led by Ziobro.

---

10 Sawczuk, "Reconstruction in Democracy."
11 Sawczuk, "Reconstruction in Democracy."
12 "Rafał Matyja: Kto najbardziej przeszkadza PO i PiS? Ten, kto nie chce stanąć po żadnej ze stron," an interview with Grzegorz Sroczyński, June 3, 2017, *Gazeta Wyborcza*.

The party won reelection in the 2019 parliamentary election with 44% of the popular vote, the highest vote share of any party since Poland returned to democracy in 1989, though it lost its majority in the Senate. Unlike its previous tenure from 2005 to 2007, PiS had long since moved away from orthodox neoliberalism, introducing free medication for people over seventy-five, restricting the use of short job contracts, and pushing forward a minimum wage higher than even trade unions were demanding.[13]

But the paradox was clear. While PiS wanted to scrap the Third Republic that was built out of the agreements of the 1989 transition, to settle accounts with the communist past, some believed what was in fact happening was a return to key elements of that past. Porter-Szűcs[14] argues that, on the one hand, PiS presented itself as the most uncompromising opponent of communism and its legacy, but on the other hand, many described the resurrection of the Polish People's Republic (PRL).

Just below the surface of this undeniable anti-communism, PiS has indeed perpetuated a strand of Polish politics that has roots in the PRL, the communist era (...) The PZPR's legitimacy was never recognized by the Catholic Church. First Secretary Władysław Gomułka downplayed many of socialism's goals, but could never fully abandon the anticlericalism and scientism of the Marxist project. For their part, the Church hierarchy had been demonizing socialism for so long that a reversal seemed inconceivable. Given the importance of Catholicism to 20th century Polish nationalism, Gomułka's National Communism was doomed.(...) In this light, it is no coincidence that the SLD collapsed precisely when PiS emerged as a political force. (...) I am not arguing that Kaczyński is a communist. But many in Poland did not want that sort of revolution back in the 1980s. They wanted a state that would preserve the workers party PZPR's commitment to social cohesion, cultural homogeneity, and nationalism, but imbue it with a Catholic rather than a leftist conceptual vocabulary. We best understand PiS as a blend between the post-1956 PZPR

13 Sławomir Sierakowski, "The Five Lessons of Populist Rule," *project-syndicate.org*, January 2, 2017. https://www.project-syndicate.org/commentary/lesson-of-populist-rule-in-poland-by-slawomir-sierakowski-2017-01.
14 Brian Porter-Szűcs, "The Triumph of National Communism," in *Poland's Memory Wars: Essays on Illiberalism*, ed. Jo Harper (Budapest: CEU Press, 2018), 65–70.

(shorn of any ties to the Marxist tradition) with the pre-1939 Endecja. Kaczyński, then, appears as the illegitimate child of Roman Dmowski and Gomułka.[15]

"Like it or not, some of Europe's boldest new social policy initiatives are coming from its most illiberal governments," according to Mitchell A. Orenstein. "The populist right is pressing the rhetoric and policies of social democracy into the service of authoritarian nationalism."[16]

More than Sacred: PiS also recognized that some kind of arrangement with the Church was a precondition of achieving political power, if not yet hegemony. That the Church played a key role in the Solidarity movement in the late 1970s and 1980s and emerged in the post-communist era is well documented. That it assumed an apparently unassailable moral position in Polish society after 1989, equally so. Whether they want to or not, all parties had to factor the Church into any successful political strategy.

The standard unspoken version of the Polish Church is that it is made up of timeless, unchanging values and moral certainties, a closed, self-referential, and confirmed via the power of internal logic and rhetoric, of certainty, good and bad, shame, traditional norms, family, gender and reproduction, and against secular institutions. Artur Lipiński, for example, notes a strong interconnectedness between populist discursive strategies and religious discourse about "Others."[17]

But while PiS may, at times, have sounded like the political wing of the Church in Poland, as if it needed one, it is more complex.[18] Focusing on its pulpit catechisms, which appear to constitute an element of PiS's hybrid form of legitimation, is liable to blind one to the diversity of opinion within the

---

15 This is a common theme in anti-PiS polemics. For just a few examples, see Dariusz Ćwiklak, "Tydzień z wehikułem czasu," *Newsweek Polska*, no. 2 (2016); Jarek Nieten, "Czy wraz z PiS wraca komunizm?" *Wiadomości24.pl*, November 11, 2015; "Rostowski: Rządy PiS gorsze niż komunizm," *Super Express*, May 25, 2016.

16 Mitchell A. Orenstein, "What Europe's Populist Right is Getting Right," *New Europe*, March 18, 2019.

17 Artur Lipiński, "Constructing 'the Others' as a Populist Communication Strategy: The Case of the 'Refugee Crisis' in Discourse in the Polish Press," in *Populist Discourse in the Polish Media*, ed. Agnieszka Stępińska (Faculty of Political Science and Journalism Adam Mickiewicz University, Poznan, 2020), 155–180.

18 Michal Kunicki, then director of the Program on Modern Poland at St. Antony's College, Oxford, told me in 2015: "The fascist mentality, perhaps the fascist personality, will always find a home in a communist system, and the Catholic element, the quasi-religious part of communist ideology, suited this."

Church and within PiS.[19] The Church runs from liberal Catholics in the form of *Tygodnik Powszechny* to hardline Radio Maryja, those that recognize the separation of church and state and those that want the Church's role to be constitutionalized, respectively.

After 2005, PiS's discourse combined a strong "anti-establishment" message with strategic employment of elements of nationalism and Catholicism to out-maneuver its coalition partner, the LPR.[20] It also entailed a change of attitude towards Radio Maryja, which had been criticized for its pro-Russian sympathies and anti-Semitism. But in 2005, Jarosław Kaczyński claimed he had been mistaken in warning against Radio Maryja. "It is not possible to win elections without Radio Maryja," he said.[21] In an interview, Kaczyński said that there should be no space between PiS and those to its right.[22]

This radicalization was even more pronounced after the Smoleńsk catastrophe on April 10, 2010. The event and the allegedly improper reaction to it by the then-governing PO, was used to build emotional links to the electorate by attacking political elites and spreading conspiracy theories. The refugee crisis that broke out during the election campaign in 2015 offered another opportunity for a radicalization of the PiS agenda.[23]

2. The Far-Right: The elections of 2014 and 2015 increased interest in the sources of rightwing parties' success in Poland. Janusz Korwin-Mikke had launched several political parties since the 1990s, with the Koalicja Odnowy Rzeczpospolitej Wolność i Nadzieja-KORWiN (Coalition of the Republic's Renewal Freedom and Hope) taking part in the 2015 elections.[24] At the 2014

---

19 A 2018 study of religious practices by the Pew Research Center found that there was a 23-percentage point difference between young adults and older people in how important religion was in their lives.

20 Jacek Kucharczyk and Olga Wysocka, "Poland in Populist Politics and Liberal Democracy," in *Central and Eastern Europe*, ed. Grigorij Mesežnikov, Olga Gyárfášová, and Daniel Smilov (Bratislava: Institute for Public Affairs, 2008), 71–100; Rafał Pankowski, *The Populist Radical Right in Poland: The Patriots* (London: Routledge, 2010); Artur Lipiński, *Prawica Na Polskiej Scenie Politycznej w Latach 1989–2011. Historia, organizacja, tożsamość* (Warsaw: Elipsa, 2016).

21 Jarosław Kaczyński, Lech Kaczyński, Michał Karnowski and Piotr Zaremba, *O Dwóch Takich. Alfabet Braci Kaczyńskich* (Warsaw: Wydawnictwo M, 2006), 292.

22 Jarosław Kaczyński, "Na prawo Od Nas Tylko Ściana," *Rzeczpospolita*, November 20, 2008, http://www.rp.pl/artykul/222423-Na-prawo-od-nas-tylko-sciana-.html.

23 Majid Khosravinik, "The Representation of Refugees, Asylum Seekers and Immigrants in British Newspapers during the Balkan Conflict (1999) and the British General Election (2005)," *Discourse & Society* 20, no. 4 (2009): 477–98.

24 Agnieszka Stępińska, *Marketingowe strategie wyborcze. Wybory prezydenckie w Polsce 1990-2000* (Poznań: Wydawnictwo Naukowe INPiD UAM, 2004); Artur Lipiński, *Prawica Na Polskiej Scenie Politycznej. Historia, Organizacja, Tożsamość, Warszawa* (Warsaw: Elipsa, 2016).

European parliamentary elections his party came in fourth with 7.15% and 11 seats. A year later, he received 4.76% of votes in national parliamentary elections.

Paweł Kukiz, meanwhile, arrived on the political scene in 2015 with his political movement Kukiz'15, finishing third in the presidential elections (with 20.8% of the vote) and winning 8.81% in the parliamentary elections in 2015. His main focus was replacement of Poland's list-based electoral system with a UK-style single-member constituency system. Although in the 2005 and 2007 parliamentary elections Kukiz supported PO, in subsequent years he shifted towards more conservative and nationalist milieu.

Both Kukiz and Korwin-Mikke grounded their discourse in the strong division between elites and "ordinary people."[25] In Kukiz's discourse, the elites were referred to as "gangs," "cliques," "party system cynics," "party oligarchy," "partocracy," or "bands" and "party minions,"[26] thus grounded in the patriotic language of conservatism. Korwin-Mikke's discourse promoted a neo-conservative vision with its emphasis on the free market, minimal state, and a radical critique of the bureaucratic apparatus, particularly the tax apparatus."

Formally set up at the start of 2019, the radical right-wing 'Confederation' (Konfederacja) grouping was an eclectic mix of economic libertarians, loosely affiliated with Korwin-Mikke, and radical nationalists from the National Movement (RN). Confederation's first electoral outing was in the 2019 European Parliament elections, when one of its leaders summed up the grouping's policy platform as: "we don't want Jews, homosexuals, abortion, taxes and the EU."[27] Its signature issue was its criticism of the alleged failure of PiS to stand up to the US and Israel over the issue of Jewish reparations. Confederation professionalized its image with the articulate Krzysztof Bosak representing it in pre-election televised debates—keeping more controversial figures such as Korwin-Mikke in the background.

3. PO: PO originally combined ordo-liberal stances on the economy with socially conservative policies, including opposition to abortion, same-sex marriage, and the availability of in vitro fertilization, among other things.

---

25 Radosław Markowski, "The Polish Parliamentary Election of 2015: A Free and Fair Election That Results in Unfair Political Consequences," *West European Politics* 39, no. 6 (2015): 1311–22.

26 From Paweł Kukiz's Facebook page.

27 "What are the prospects for Poland's radical-right Confederation?" December 23, 2019, *Notes from Poland.*

But after 2007 the party shifted its stance and in 2013 the PO government introduced public funding for in vitro fertilization programs and in 2017 supported a citizens' initiative for liberalization of the abortion law. During the 2019 and 2020 election campaigns PO was—if not vociferously—pro-LGBT, supporting the possibility for unmarried couples to register their relationship, and stronger women's rights.

But the curse for PO was perhaps the perception that it was Brussels' local proxy. Tusk, for example, spoke at a University of Warsaw event in 2019 commemorating Poland's 1791 constitution, where he cited Immanuel Kant, Edmund Burke, and George Washington, and warned of a civilizational threat facing the world.[28] As Paweł Kozłowski notes, rather than showing that a different politics is possible, PO chose the path of de-politicization. But by doing this, it also depoliticized the success of the transformation. The term "warm water in the tap" refers to a strategy developed by Tusk when he was prime minister. PO's vision was meant to a kind of "conservative modernization."[29] But the new social group, the "precariat," a group of frustrated middle-income people who might under different conditions have looked favorably on PO's offer, turned away as the party. Part of this frustrated electorate chose the latter of Albert Hirschman's[30] exit strategies (emigrating, withdrawing) and voted against the government.

Tusk depicted PiS as twenty-first century Bolsheviks and pointed out that Piłsudski and Wałęsa had each faced far more difficult circumstances when they defeated "their own eras' Bolsheviks." But many Poles saw a man who had escaped to Brussels and was himself deeply compromised as prime minister. As Stefan Sękowski argues, "the history of dismantling and bending the rule of law didn't start with PiS's rise to power."[31] He notes research by Agnieszka Dudzińska illustrating that during the PO-PSL coalition's second term (2011–2015), the executive and legislative branches "constituted a single

---

28 Speech by President Donald Tusk at the University of Warsaw on the occasion of 3 May, Constitution Day, 2019

29 Paradoxically, a few years earlier the model of modernization implemented by PO was criticized as "conservative." Paweł Kozłowski et al., *Dwudziestolecie polskich przemian: konserwatywna modernizacja* (Warsaw: Instytut Nauk Ekonomicznych PAN, 2011).

30 Albert Hirschman, *Exit, Voice, and Loyalty: Responses to Decline in Firms, Organizations, and States* (Cambridge: Harvard University Press, 1972).

31 Stefan Sękowski, "No Change—How the Government and the Opposition Toe the Same Line on Policies, and How to Make a Difference," in *The End of the Liberal Mind, Poland's New Politics*, ed. Karolina Wigura and Jaroslaw Kuisz (Warsaw: Kultura Liberalna, 2020), 57–79.

system of governance. The partisan discipline was unshakable, and members of parliament became virtual voting machines, with amendments being automatically dismissed if they didn't have the support of the prime minister's cabinet." Sękowski goes on to argue that parliamentary debate became an empty ritual, "while PO-PSL politicians suggested more than once that the opposition's participation in the legislative process is of no particular meaning, because it's the voting math that counts. So when it comes to stripping the Constitutional Tribunal of its powers, the current opposition is not guilt-free."[32] In 2015, the PO-PSL coalition, with support from the SLD, picked new members of the Constitutional Tribunal who would replace judges retiring from their posts. That same body (before PiS made its own replacements after 2015) ruled that the process was partly unlawful. The strategy was meant to secure a Constitutional Tribunal that shared a worldview with the soon-to-be opposition. Sękowski, does, however, note that "while PO and PSL bent the democratic rule of law with white gloves on, PiS is doing it openly—bragging that the will of the 'nation,' and not of the 'elites,' can finally be carried out."[33]

PO joined forces with two small liberal groupings to compete in the 2019 national vote. Grzegorz Schetyna pulled out of the race for prime minister in favor of Małgorzata Kidawa-Błonska, deputy speaker of the Sejm. The party outlined six key policy areas, dubbed the Schetyna Six: restoring democratic freedom, increasing wages, improving healthcare, pensions, education reform, and environmental improvements. What was lacking from the proposals was not only passion and detail, but also telos (or what PiS leaders might call "destiny")—how to move Poland into a next level of development. The proposals that did appear were limited to deregulation and cutting taxes. This lack of narrative clarity was perhaps also in part a product of PiS's success, which has set the agenda. As Alex Szczerbiak put it: "copy them and seem redundant or criticize them and risk unpopularity? Outbid them and look unrealistic or irresponsible or ignore them and appear irrelevant?"[34]

4. The Left: As an aside, this sub-section is of particular curiosity to me. My sense of unease at writing about fellow journalists found its manifestation in an exchange with *Politico* in Brussels in August 2020, a month after

32 Sękowski, "No Change."
33 Sękowski, "No Change."
34 *The Polish Politics Blog*, Alex Szczerbiak: https://polishpoliticsblog.wordpress.com/about/

the manuscript of this book was sent for publication. It was also a turning point in my own emerging personal views as to the modus operandi and perhaps ideological predilections of media insiders. A brief description of the exchange is insightful, followed by the article I pitched, which was accepted and then, on completion, "spiked," that is rejected.

My article went through a dozen or more self-edits before it was sent to the editor in Brussels. I wanted it to outline a genuine alternative to PiS and a path for halting the shifts towards authoritarianism. It was about a specific and very interesting and vital part of the emerging post-election political culture. But I felt myself seeking the "Ideal Reader" as I wrote and rewrote the piece. How much did they know, could they be expected to understand? And why, after all should anyone care? After the rejection, given it is difficult to resell a piece that has been written for a single buyer, the piece was effectively culled. It was too specialized and offered no wider resonance, I was told. But it held and holds water and its reproduction here serves the twofold function of explaining the state of the Left in 2020, but also the ideological-discursive problems of framing a discussion that did not posit PO as the sole legitimate opponent of PiS.

The article:

Polish Left Gets its Act Together

Given its confusing ideological heritage, it is hardly surprising the Left in post-communist Poland has had something of an identity problem. But after almost two decades of drifting into electoral oblivion, a new-look left seems to have stopped the rot. The Left electoral coalition won 12.6% of the vote in the 2019 parliamentary election, giving it 49 seats—49 more than it won in 2015—leading some to talk tentatively of a genuinely progressive opposition to Jarosław Kaczyński, leader of the nationalist ruling Law and Justice (PiS).

"The early Polish left was of course anti-capitalist, but capitalism was an abstraction in Poland for most of the 20th century. So their main enemy became the nationalists, the Endeks, and the Church," political scientist David Ost says.

Lest we forget, illiberalism remains in the ascendency in Poland. After 25 years of post-communism just over half of Polish voters rejected liberal internationalism and elected protectionist-nationalist PiS in 2015.

After four years of the party rolling back judicial independence and media freedoms, Poles voted PiS back in at the 2019 parliamentary election and in July re-elected PiS-puppet Andrzej Duda president after he ran an unashamedly anti-LGBTQ campaign.

PiS-opponents rallied around Rafał Trzaskowski, the candidate of the largest opposition electoral coalition, Civic Coalition (KO)—led by the liberal opposition's largest party, Civic Platform (PO). Trzaskowski ran Duda close in the second round, but as the dust settled many looked beyond the young Warsaw mayor and envisaged a different shape of opposition to PiS. One perhaps where the Left played a part.

The "Three Tenors": Three streams of the Polish left put their differences aside and stood under a single banner in the 2019 parliamentary election. With three male figures—Włodzimierz Czarzasty, Robert Biedroń and Adrian Zandberg—representing the coalition, it was nicknamed the 'Three Tenors' pact.

The biggest player—the Luciano Pavarotti if you will—Czarzasty's post-communist Democratic Left Alliance (SLD), held power from 1993 to 1997 and 2001 to 2005 and is largely made up of folks from the united workers (communist) party. As the only party in the Left bloc electorally big enough to get state funding, its role in the Triumvirate is crucial. Wiosna (Spring) is a political project led by the openly gay Biedroń, who is perhaps its main distinctive feature. Its formal integration into the SLD is slated for this later year. The third entity, Razem (Together), was founded in 2015 as an avowedly leftwing party and is a far more interesting proposition.

"The SLD is a key bloc of voters, and its nostalgia and welfarism are important attractions for a group of the electorate," says Adam Ostolski, ex-leader of the Green party and a sociologist at Warsaw University. "But this group, with the other parts of the 'new left,' will probably hit a ceiling of 15–20% of votes in the short-term," he goes on. "The 'reluctant voters' are the key. They may not trust PO, but they don't understand the Left," he says.

"But the SLD has a spectacular capacity to put institutional survival on top of the agenda, and left-wing values squarely at the bottom," says journalist Konstanty Gebert. "And Razem is doing exactly the opposite: values on top, survival irrelevant," Gebert says.

"The SLD followed the [Tony] Blair-[Gerhard] Schröder Third Way path and lost its claim to being a leftwing party," says Julia Zimmermann, a member of the Razem executive board. "But it has changed," she promises, with a wry smile.

Saddling the cow: To challenge PiS in 2023, the Left needs to face its demons—and cross its fingers. Saddling a cow might be easier.

Firstly, face up to communist-era associations. Though far from easy in such a toxic atmosphere, it is where the Left must start, says Gavin Rae, a sociologist at the Koźmiński University in Warsaw.

There is a popular equation of communism and fascism among many Poles, with the Left in its broadest sense seen as guilty either directly in the crimes of the Stalinist era or at least complicit in them.

"This ideology is accepted by both the conservative right and the liberal center and effectively tries to exclude any alternative being formed," he says. "The Left must include stating that the period of the PRL partly involved a civilizational jump for the country, through mass literacy, provision of free health care, etc," Rae says.

Zimmermann says one of the Left's main tasks is reclaiming a stake in Polish history. "There is a history of workers protests in Poland that we aren't taught about in schools," she says. "Also, Poland's first post-independence-era president, Gabriel Narutowicz was a socialist," she says.

Secondly, find a new modus vivendi with the Catholic Church. "The Left has a hard time admitting that the core of its message could go hand-in-hand with a coherent and politically mobilized group of voters who are Catholic or post-Catholic," Wojciech Przybylski of the Res Publica think-tank in Warsaw says. But the presidential election showed there could be an appealing non-rightwing program that has the Church onside, he argues, noting. the electoral success of Szymon Hołownia, an independent presidential candidate who came third in the first round with 13.87%.

Others agree. "Hołownia could be a great asset for the Left. A PSL (the agrarian Polish People's Party)-Hołownia-Lewica coalition could work," Ostolski says.

Michał Kobosko, who works for Polska2050, Hołownia's newly created political association, said his group is open to talks with Lewica, PSL and PO. "We are pragmatic and open-minded, on all fronts," he says.

"There is a strong anti-clerical tradition among the rural community, where the Church has always been a big landowner and employer. That is something we can work on. But we have to make it clear that we are not anti-Church per se, but pro-secularization of the state," says Zimmermann. Thirdly, challenge PiS on social issues. PiS cannot be considered left, says Przybylski. "They are showing candies of the Left in the shop window, but are carrying out a full frontal right-wing economic policy where party officers are using public resources to capitalize private and party gains. That's not the Left."

"The Left has to offer a vision that goes beyond the marginal social handouts, tied to extreme social conservatism, provided by PiS. This should include urgent investments in public services such as health and education," Rae says.

"The Polish left has so often not really trusted 'the people,' but in 1980 it believed the people were on its side. This might well have continued if it hadn't then abandoned the workers after 1989. The Left must remember that the people who supposedly wholeheartedly support PiS and its values are the same people who supported the Left-leaning Solidarity of the 1980s, and who gave the SLD huge votes and parliamentary victories in 1993 and 2001," Ost says.

The strange death of liberal Poland: Some see PO's main concern as maintaining the hegemony of the two main parties, a set up some deride as 'symmetrism.' "It uses some left and green language as a decoy from time to time, but its biggest enemy is any challenger from the Left, whether it be the Left or Hołownia," says Ostolski.

But PO may itself also need to change, and that could help the Left. Liberals need to adopt a more pragmatic approach to the economy, Tomasz Sawczuk writes in an essay in the recent book 'The End of The Liberal Mind.' "Liberalism should not be associated with slavish devotion to the free market," he writes.

The question is if PO wants or sees the need to change course. Some believe not. "In a hypothetical alternative in which the opposition to PiS would be organized around a progressive agenda, the powerful forces of Poland's business community would be pushed into the arms of the government," Porter-Szűcs says.

"The dilemma for the Polish left, ever since early in the last century, is that it has not so much been anti-capitalist as anti-nationalist. And to be anti-nationalist it is sufficient to be a liberal, not a leftist. Thus there's always been this overlap between liberalism and leftism, because both are wary of nationalism," David Ost says. "In this sense, PO has some leftists in its ranks, as liberals, while the official left parties have been anti-nationalist above all."

Jam tomorrow?: "The new generation is promising, with a mix of cultural progressivism and personal dignity messages, but without heavy handed budget spending," Przybylski says. "Within decades they stand a chance of winning over new generations who will be deprived of the social benefits and privileges enjoyed today by pensioners and full time employees."

Some don't want to wait that long. Podemos in Spain changed the conversation on the Left, Agnieszka Wiśniewska, editor-in-chief of Krytyka Polityczna, a leftwing media organization in Warsaw, says, adding that the "Black Protests" (against changes in the abortion law) and the KOD mass movement showed the potential in Poland for similar movements.

"A strong independent left in Polish politics is like the gravitron in physics. Theory postulates that it has to exist and that, indeed, it plays a fundamental role. It simply has not yet been observed in practice," Gebert says. "Until somebody discovers the gravitron, this is where things will remain," he concludes.

-end-

The spiking occurred three days after a front cover *Gazeta Wyborcza* article about Applebaum.[35] It was of course a coincidence, but I really did start to feel like one of her second rate journalists.

Applebaum's work had made it even harder to publish anything remotely curious about the Left in what one might call mainstream media, it being associated forever with the crimes of Stalin or an intellectual dead-end for history's losers—and let's not forget the untalented. This despite much

---

35   Anne Applebaum, "Jeśli Trump wygra, ludzie zaakceptują jeszcze gorsze rzeczy," *Gazeta Wyborcza*, August 8, 2020.

scholarship challenging the teleological version of communism's demise in the region. Dariusz Jarosz argues,[36] for example, that the relations between the Polish authorities and society from 1944 to 1989 in post-1989 historiography led to a one-sided view of the Polish People's Republic (PRL) as a structure that was only repressive, implementing aims imposed by the PZPR and behind it, the Soviet Union. Anyway, back to the smiling, if slightly disturbing, picture of Applebaum which had splashed itself across the newspaper's front page on August 8. It seemed odd, a "story" about a journalist on the front page of a newspaper. Then, as the final edits of this book were almost done, *Matka Polka*[37] appeared. Entering a book store off Plac Zbawiciela in Warsaw in early October, the same forced smile was waiting by the entrance, watching from eye level on the corner of the shelf facing the door. A sense of dread and loathing, fear, and shame, guilt and doubt, a touch of envy, I guess too. Admonishment from a rather severe head mistress. The eyes followed you around the room. We see pictures of Anne's wedding, her family, her cakes. Most of us lower down in the Warsaw media hierarchy probably didn't need that much policing, given our habitus was situated in unerring sympathy for LGBTQ people and our newfound antipathies towards structural racism. Our awareness of other, wider, structures we also benefited from was largely absent. But taking no chances, it seemed the spectacle of Liberalism, if not the real thing, would thus be defined by its moral superiority, its support for minorities and its universalist and legalistic essence and not by grubby compromises with the Left, which was seen to be prone to extremism and populism itself.

The LGBT+ issue had been in the news over the summer of 2020 after attacks on protestors in Warsaw. The liberal media came out in full discursive riot gear. Unable to defend its own actual interests, or even give them a name, it relied on symbolic troops in the form of gay and lesbian people, a new avant guard. The nationalism of PiS was the enemy in public, the Leftism of PiS the enemy in private. There would be nothing about PO's intolerance, its own illiberalism or lack of a plan.

As a US academic expert on Polish history told me:

---

36 Dariusz Jarosz, "Post-1989 Historiography's Distorted Image of the Relation Between Authorities and Society in Poland During the Period from 1944 to 1989," *Revue d'études comparatives Est-Ouest* 2, no. 45 (2014): 307–20.

37 Anne Applebaum, *Matka Polka* (Warsaw: Agora, 2020).

I share your frustration that a cluster of people with weak or non-existent scholarly bona fides get accepted as public intellectuals while more serious and insightful work is ignored. Their books are so deeply flawed that they aren't really worth engaging with; to critique them would be like catching fish from a barrel. They are famous because they have utilized the services of highly skilled and very expensive agents, of the sort most of us will never gain access to. In addition, they write simple stories that fit within a widely shared collective wisdom, and can be comfortably digested without upsetting the worldview of their target audiences. The problem is that pointing this out virtually always backfires, precisely because their fame makes any critique appear like jealous sniping. It's a no-win contest. But whether or not they are arrogant assholes is irrelevant. An emphasis on effect rather than affect is both more accurate, and more likely to resonate among the many people who unwittingly participate in the discourse you are describing.

The problem for the Left was then it seemed similar to that facing the liberals. It seemed common sensical to think about a common front, a radical, progressive set of ideas about work, about the relationship between work and pay, about ownership, about consumption, beyond left and right. An honest and open debate was needed to formulate a new democratic charter. But instead we got sharp-elbowed new middle classes hawking their often second-rate wares.[38]

---

38 I was reminded of an old school friend who later made it big in British banking asking me via Instant Messenger in 2006 on a fleeting visit to Warsaw why the taxi driver was telling—with apparent pride, or dark humor—about the Warsaw Ghetto, through which they happened to be passing. "In our culture, a ghetto is kind negative, right?" he wrote. I later met the banker with Polish journalist Marek Ostrowski at his home in London to talk about the financial crisis, for *Polityka*. He managed to be both patronizing and uninterested at the same time. At a Krynica-Zdrój forum in southern Poland in 2018 I watched a panel moderated by James Shotter of the *Financial Times*, and including then deputy British prime minister, David Lidington. New Labour's defines minister, Geoff Hoon, was also there, working for a defense industry firm. Sharp elbows and plummy voices, not sure about the actual talent on display.

Chapter 4
Post-Post-Colonial?[1]

"We reject the postcolonial concept of Poland as a country of cheap labor, a concept that has already hurt us a lot and should no longer harm us," Kaczyński said during the 2019 election campaign.[2]

It is a common thread in contestations of Polishness. Sikorski, then foreign minister in the PO government, was secretly recorded telling the then finance minister Jacek Rostowski towards the end of the party's 8-year tenure in 2014 that Poles "think like negroes." His use of the word *"Murzyńskość"* (Négritude) evoked a common theme in Polish debates about post-colonial discourse.[3]

Soul to Soul: It is something of a cliché that there are two "Polands" fighting for the country's soul. The conflicts, the contradictions and the confusions are embedded in the country's personality, it is said: liberal, critical, secular versus conservative, patriotic, catholic.[4] This is a common enough representation of Poland and one that despite 30 years of capitalism is still at the forefront of many minds.

Sękowski's notion of "recycled anti-Communism,"[5] a symptom of being mentally stuck in the past, and Jarosław Kuisz's notion of "occupation

---

1   The notion of "intra-European colonization" was first used to describe Ireland's subordination to the British Empire. See Seamus Deane, *Irish Literature: Nationalism, Colonialism, and Literature* (Minneapolis: University of Minnesota Press, 1990).

2   Matthew Day, "Poland's Ruling Party Pledges to Double Minimum Wage and End Country's 'Post-Colonial' Reputation as a Source of 'Cheap Labour,'" *The Telegraph*, September 18, 2019.

3   Łukasz Lipiński, "Polish FM Said to have Called US Ties 'Worthless,'" *EU Observer*, June 23, 2014. See Susan Bayly, *Asian Voices in a Post-Colonial Age: Vietnam, India and Beyond* (Cambridge: Cambridge University Press, 2007).

4   George Burnett, *View of the Present State of Poland* (London: Longman, Hurst, Rees, and Orne, 1807).

5   Stefan Sękowski, "No Change."

mentality," shaped over decades of subordination, are both apt here.[6] Kuisz's argument is psychoanalytical, as co-author Karolina Wigura rightly posits: "like it or not, history has caught up with Poles, and until they understand this, they will remain trapped in the closed loop of habit."[7]

"At first glance, it seems that the country's reclaiming of sovereignty after years of foreign occupation would come as an incredible relief. But when a collective identity is predicated upon a desire for sovereignty, its reclamation might, paradoxically, produce an insolvable political problem. There is nothing more to reclaim, yet old habits persist. Subjugation is like phantom limb: it might not be there, but the pain lingers. A bevy of examples clearly demonstrates this," Kuisz writes.[8]

For Czaja, two coffins govern Polish collective mythology those of Henryk Sienkiewicz and Witold Gombrowicz.[9] These two names are legible emblems of two antagonistic attitudes. "Either we find eternal trauma and dotage, or sobriety and intellectual maturity. These coffins carry very different sets of values," Czaja writes.[10]

These divides are, of course, arbitrary, contingent, and cross party lines. One should remember that PiS's rise to power was certainly not predestined, nor was it an unequivocal expression of all Poles' needs and wishes.[11] It was also not irreversible. It had explicable and contingent causes woven into the fabric of post-communist life and history since 1989.

Perhaps the key question was whether Poland has actually changed or if PiS reflects a set of societal values that have remained largely unchanged but publicly latent—a sphere not apparently occupied only by nationalist football hooligans, as much of the media rhetoric might have it, but one in which habitus is occupied—peopled—by neighbors, friends, work colleagues, family

6 Jarosław Kuisz, "The Central European Mind: The Trauma of the State Collapse," in *The End of the Liberal Mind, Poland's New Politics*, eds. Karolina Wigura and Jaroslaw Kuisz (Warsaw: Kultura Liberalna, 2020), 20–36.
7 Kuisz, "The Central European Mind."
8 Kuisz, "The Central European Mind."
9 An enduring dichotomy in Poland is between *Idealists* and *Realists*. See Adam Bromke, "The Revival of Political Idealism in Poland," in *Poland: The Protracted Crisis* (Oakville: Mosaic Press, 1983).
10 Dariusz Czaja, "Poland's Theater of Death," in *Poland's Memory Wars*, ed. Jo Harper (Budapest: CEU Press, 2018), 171. See also Elżbieta Halas, "Symbolic Politics of Public Time and Collective Memory: The Polish Case," *European Review* 10, no. 1 (2002): 115–29.
11 Luke Coppen "Sorry, Bono, but 'Hyper-nationalists' aren't Running Poland," *The Spectator*, May 21, 2016; Jan-Werner Müller, "The Problem with Poland," *The New York Review of Books*, February 11, 2016.

and even spouses who, when pushed, might also betray a quiet predilection for Polish exceptionalism, even if only at a micro level, when disparaging the over-liberalism of English attitudes to child rearing, Germans' tolerance of the so-called Multi-Kulti society, or American commercialism, for example. These values tend to be less informed by secular and multi-cultural influences and while not overtly fueled by a sense of inward-looking patriotism there is a clear and strong a sense that "what we do is the best way of doing things." Laced with Catholic values in relation to the family, women's rights, homosexuality and in other areas it is a formidable agent of social control.

Sawczuk refers to a 2004 interview with Kaczyński by Andrzej Nowak, entitled "How Do We Go Home?"[12] He suggests this is the question that best sums up the nature of PiS. He suggests it defines attitudes towards "adversaries" who have impeded "our" return. "PiS's fundamental goal as the ruling party is to fulfill a national Identitarian mission, an indivisible unit joining symbolism (the politics of memory, for example) with economics. Whether or not a task is carried out successfully doesn't matter as long as it's framed as part of a larger endeavor." The sentiment, he suggests, is the longing for what Poles call *swojskość*, the sense of familiarity associated with one's home or homeland. "We must juxtapose virtual Poland with real Poland," Nowak writes.

Another interesting position is Poland as a gendered entity. In the Eastern European variant of postcolonial theory, as George Mosse shows, a central position is taken by a vision of an enslaved nation as a woman.[13] The colonial discourse assumed that the male West must conquer the female East. The female embodiment of the fatherland was usually a suffering body: tormented, unhappy, chained. Cultural gender identity research, after all, shows links between sexuality and the nationalist ideal. Nationalism is a movement that overtly dissociates itself from any contamination or deviation. Mosse argues that the nationalistic male ideal has been strengthened in its search for perfection by isolating itself from a despised femininity, seeking out "countertypes": a Jew, a homosexual, a pansy, a hysteric. As Maria Janion and others had hoped, this part of the national psyche did not fade away after 1989.[14]

---

12 Sawczuk, "Reconstruction in Democracy."

13 George L. Mosse, *The Image of Man: The Creation of Modern Masculinity* (Oxford: Oxford University Press, 1996).

14 Maria Janion, *Niesamowita Słowiańszczyzna. Fantazmaty literatury* (Kraków: Wydawnictwo Literackie, 2006); Maria Janion, "Polska między Wschodem i Zachodem," *Teksty Drugie* 3 (2006); Robert Blobaum, *Antisemitism and its Critics in Poland* (West Virginia University Press, 2006).

A brief aside here adds color to this assertion. "It seems that the soul of a small Eastern European nation, the soul that suffers from the father complex and is immersed in sadomasochistic perversion, is unable to exist without a great oppressor, whom it could blame for its historic failures, nor without a national minority, this scapegoat, on which it could vent, releasing the surplus of hatred and resentment, which accumulated in the course of daily defeats." Imre Kertész's[15] comments, originally referring to Hungary, also seem applicable to Poland.

"Transitional Society": Critical anthropology describes "transitional" societies moving from socialism to capitalism and dictatorship to democracy as "postcolonial" due to the neoliberal tendency that enjoyed a hegemonic status in the region when the transitions took place. CEE societies, the argument goes, underwent similar processes to those of Europe's maritime colonies. This "neocolonial" view notes the presence and influence of advisors from international organizations, such as the International Monetary Fund, advocating liberalization, democratization and marketization in the region, and on the other hand, the internationalization of domestic policies caused by accession to the EU.[16]

Triple Relation: The process in the CEE region, however, can perhaps be better traced to three colonizing forces: the West (European/global modernity), the East (Russia/the Soviet Union) and the countries in the region that have historically had imperial ambitions (Poland and Hungary). Notions of Polishness[17] then might well be understood in terms of a triple relation: Poland as a former colony, as a former colonizer, and in relation to the western hegemons as a hybrid-colonee perhaps. What seems clear is that Poland's position within this discursive framing is not simply "inbetweeness" (between East and West). This triple perspective resonates with Merje Kuus's[18] analysis of discourse on EU and NATO enlargement. Kuus suggests that the Cold War era binary division of Europe into communist and capitalist changed as

15 Imre Kertész, *Valaki más: A változás krónikája* [Someone else: a chronicle of the change], (Budapest, Magvető, 1997), 44.
16 Michał Buchowski, "The Specter of Orientalism in Europe: From Exotic Other to Stigmatized Brother," *Anthropological Quarterly* 79, no. 3 (2006): 463–82. See also Samuel Huntington, "The Clash of Civilizations?" *Foreign Affairs* 72, no. 3 (1993): 27–49.
17 Geneviève Zubrzycki, "Nationalism, 'Philosemitism,' and Symbolic Boundary-Making in Contemporary Poland," *Comparative Studies in Society and History* 58, no. 1 (2016): 69.
18 Merje Kuus, "Europe's Eastern Expansion and the Reinscription of Otherness in East-Central Europe," *Progress in Human Geography* 28, no. 4 (2004): 472–489.

powerful European actors began to divide the continent into three different regions: the European/Western core, the Central European applicants and eastern peripheral states not yet European enough to join the EU (e.g., post-Soviet republics), or at all (i.e., Russia, Turkey). As Attila Ágh argues, there has always been a fight between two main narratives within the EU: the modernization narrative and the traditionalization narrative:

> In some progressive periods the modernization narrative was the dominant, but in the decline periods the traditionalization narrative came back with a vengeance. (...) The dream of quick Europeanization in the semi-periphery relied on the conceptual framework of the Western fallacy, according to which the rapid Western developments after WWII could be repeated. Public discourse has been split more and more between the two dominant narratives of the EU-centered Modernization and the Nation State-centered Traditionalization (...) the major change due to the global crisis is that the Nation-State/Traditionalization narrative has defeated the Europeanization/Modernization narrative.[19]

In the Cold War period, from a Western perspective, the Iron Curtain set a clear-geographical division into "us" and "them."[20] The two systems' border was inscribed in the mental map, places inhabited by two tribes: the civilized "us" and the exotic, often uncivilized "them." Elaborated by Edward Said and Maria Todorova, the notion of Orientalism[21] and the perception of the process of creation of the Other, were contiguous with this world: the Other was, to use Arjun Appadurai's term, "spatially incarcerated." As Anna Azarova suggests,[22] historians of Eastern Europe agree that the idea of "Eastern Europe" originated in Western Europe in the eighteenth century, created by Western geographers, philosophers and travel writers.

---

19   Attila Ágh, "Cultural War and Reinventing the Past in Poland and Hungary: The Politics of Historical Memory in East-Central Europe," *Polish Political Science Yearbook* 45 (2016), 32–44.

20   Bogusław Bakuła, "Kolonialne i postkolonialne aspekty polskiego dyskursu kresoznawczego (zarys problematyki)," *Teksty Drugie*, no. 6 (2006): 11–33.

21   Edward W. Said, *Orientalism* (New York: Pantheon Books, 1978); Barbara Harlow and Mia Carter, *Imperialism and Orientalism: A Documentary Sourcebook* (Malden: Blackwell Publishers, 1999); Maria Todorova, *Imagining the Balkans*, (New York: Oxford University Press, 1997).

22   Anna Azarova, "Eastern Europe According to British Media: More Likely to go to Italy for Cappuccinos than Join the Ethnic Fighting in Kosovo," *Krytyka Polityczna*, August 17, 2017.

Symbolic Borders: Since the early 1980s, many Western intellectuals who had ignored "Central Europe" as a distinct geographic, political and cultural entity, started to look more closely, Kristina Andelova argues.[23] She notes that the decline of Marxism as a political theory in Western Europe from the 1970s and the increasing attention towards Central Europe were closely interrelated processes. Once revolutionary ideas were discredited within Western intellectual debates, legitimacy for the existence of a giant and seemingly united "Eastern Bloc" dissolved, she writes.

As Maria Todorova's study of the symbolic geography of Eastern Europe shows, during the 1980s a new concept of Central Europe appeared, which saw the region as an independent cultural entity, differentiating itself from Soviet Russia and the rest of the Eastern Bloc.[24] The "new order" that emerged in the 1990s thus allowed Orientalism to escape the confines of space and time, with the border now mostly within societies.[25] During 2020, for example, a new symbolic division was floated by some, namely the so-called "pink line."[26] Added to this, Poles may tend to make sense of their encounters with ethnic diversity by relating it to non-linear representations of the past, present and future, via a collective imaginary that is relational and fluid.[27] Attitudes towards other nationalities thus are not merely a result of the "East–West split."[28]

Anti-Russian: Todorova argues that both Orientalization and subsequent counter-Orientalization after 1989 produced a form of racism towards the "East," specifically Russia. She argues that the emancipatory idea of Central Europe became a "politically expedient tool" enabling Central European countries to gain acceptance from Western European institutions. Janion likewise notes practices in Polish identity discourse that describe Russia as strange to Europe, and thus reduce it in the Polish national imagery to "defamiliarized monstrosity."[29]

---

23 Kristina Andelova, "Reinventing Central Europe and the Decline of Marxism: Czech 'Orientalism' through the Lens of Intellectual History," *IWM Junior Visiting Fellows' Conferences* 35 (2016).

24 Maria Todorova's presentation "Spacing Europe: What is a Historical Region?" at "Europe's Symbolic Geographies," a conference held at the Central European University on May 29, 2004.

25 Richard Rorty, *Objectivity, Relativism, and Truth: Philosophical Papers* 1 (Cambridge: Cambridge University Press, 1991).

26 Mark Gevisser, "Duda's Victory in Poland Helps Draw a 'Pink Line' through Europe," *The Guardian*, July 17, 2020.

27 Buchowski, "The Specter of Orientalism in Europe."

28 Marysia Galbraith, "Between East and West: Geographic Metaphors of Identity in Poland," *Ethos* 32, no. 11 (2004): 51–81.

29 Maria Janion, "Farewell to Poland? The Uprising of a Nation," *Baltic Worlds* 4 (2011): 4-13.

Relatedly, Kristina Andelova argues that a key contribution was played by a critique that didn't blame the tragedy of Central Europe on Hitler and Nazism, "without which we cannot explain Stalin's presence in the region," she suggests. "The tragedy of Central Europe started without Russian participation; Jews, who were crucial for the 'Central European spirit,' according to Kundera, were not liquidated by communists, but by Nazis."[30]

The West as Surrogate Hegemon: Ewa Thompson describes the relationship between Poland and the "West" as a "surrogate hegemon," which she traces back to the period of the partitions (1795–1918)[31] and argues that similar processes were at work in the communist period. In both periods large numbers of Polish intelligentsia emigrated and with them a key narrative on Polish socio-cultural life was relocated outside Poland. Habermas once described Eastern Europe's intellectual and political development as merely reiterative, but rarely interactive during the second half of the 20th century.

Some scholars argue that the aspirations of being included as part of Western Europe and accepted as not a "barbarian Slavonic"[32] people, led to the creation of a para-colonial relationship with western countries,[33] while Bolesław Domański suggests the ideology of "catching up" actually reinforced the acceptance of external influences and added another layer to a pre-existing sense of exclusion from European integration after the Second World War. This in turn added to the acceptance of the recipient role and to the reproduction of the East–West mental division.[34]

Thompson describes Poles' attitudes towards western countries as a mix of desire and resentment, a negotiation, an ambivalent hybrid. Over the decades Poles adopted the discourse of the conquerors, blaming themselves for the

---

30   Kristina Andelova, "Reinventing Central Europe and the Decline of Marxism."

31   Ewa Thompson, "Whose Discourse? Telling the Story in Post-Communist Poland," *Slavic and East Europe and Cultures Abroad, Past and Present* 1, no. 1 (2010), 1–15.

32   Tony Judt, "The Rediscovery of Central Europe," *Deadalus* 119 (1990); Milan Kundera, "The Stolen West, or The Tragedy of Central Europe," *The New York Review of Books,* April 26, 1984. See also: Isabelle Davion, "The Concept of Central Europe in French Historiography in the 20th Century," *Historyka, Studia Metodologiczne,* 153, 2013.

33   Larry Wolff, *Inventing Eastern Europe* (Stanford: Stanford University Press, 1994). See also Magdalena J. Zaborowska, Sibelan Forrester, and Elena Gapova, "Introduction: Mapping Post-Socialist Cultural Studies," in *Over the Wall/After the Fall: Post-communist Cultures Through an East-Wast Gaze,* eds. Forrester, Zaborowska and Gapova (Bloomington: Indiana University Press), 1–41.

34   Bolesław Domański, "West and East in 'New Europe': The Pitfalls of Paternalism and a Claimant Attitude," *European Urban and Regional Studies* 11, no. 4 (2004): 377–381.

failure of the Polish state, at the same time as the belief in Western suprem-acy grew stronger.[35]

The narratives developed by Polish intellectuals in Western Europe—who were seeking explanations for the partitions or commenting on internal af-fairs in communist Poland—confirmed the inferiority of Polish society, and according to Thompson (for a critique see Claudia Snochowska-Gonzales[36]), Poles started "internalizing the Orientalizing gaze of the West," but at the same time "they tended to transfer the notion of inferiority onto the lower social strata in Poland, or onto those strata that did not subscribe to the En-lightenment slogans about progress and secular development of humanity."[37] This would posit Poland as a country colonizing its own citizens, who are defined by the elites not in terms of their nationality or race but in terms of class differences. In Polish scholarly discourse, an "internal colonization ap-proach" based on the assumption that cultural elites colonize other social strata, is posited by Tomasz Zarycki.[38]

Ossowska, meanwhile, compares the aristocratic ethos of England and Po-land. The hereditary szlachta were referred to as "nobilitas" and could be com-pared in legal status to British peers of the realm, she suggests. Only szlachta members, irrespective of their ethnicity or culture of origin, were considered as "Poles." Two English journalists, Richard Holt Hutton and Walter Bage-hot, writing in 1864 saw this clearly:

> The population consisted of two different peoples, between whom there
> was an impassable barrier. There is the Sliachta,[39] or caste of nobles (the

---

35 Joanna Średnicka, "The New Romantics," in *Poland's Memory Wars*, ed. Jo Harper (Budapest: CEU Press, 2018), 128.

36 Claudia Snochowska-Gonzales, "Post-Colonial Poland: On an Unavoidable Misuse," *East European Politics & Societies* 26, no. 4 (2012): 708–723.

37 Ewa Thompson, *Imperial Knowledge: Russian Literature and Colonialism* (Westport: Greenwood Press, 2000).

38 Tomasz Zarycki, *Ideologies of Eastness in Central and Eastern Europe* (London: Routledge, 2014). Alex-ander Etkind, *Internal Colonization: Russia's Imperial Experience* (Malden: Polity Press, 2011); Emilia Kledzik, "Inventing Postcolonial Poland: Strategies of Domestication," in *Postcolonial Europe? Essays on Post-Communist Literatures and Cultures*, eds. Dobrotva Pucherova and Robert Gafrik (Leiden: Brill Rodopi, 2015), 85–103.

39 One theory of its origins involved a descent from the ancient Iranian tribe known as Sarmatians, who in the second century AD occupied lands in Eastern Europe. Adam Zamoyski asserts that the szlachta were not a social class, but a caste. See Adam Zamoyski, *The Polish Way* (New York: Hippocrene Books, 1987).

descendants of Lekh), on the one hand, and the serfs or peasantry, who constitute the bulk of the population, on the other...Nowhere in history—nowhere in the world—do we ever see a homogeneous nation organise itself in a form like that which has prevailed from the earliest times in Poland. But where there has been an intrusion of a dominant people, or settlers, who have not fused into the original population, there we find an exact counterpart of Polish society: the dominant settlers establishing themselves as an upper caste, all politically equal among themselves, and holding the lands of the country.[40]

At the same time, Poles acknowledge that they are not always seen as desirable citizens in the West, and the complex of the unwanted child is often cited as a symptom.[41] Being "unwanted" results in a sense of uneasiness about one's own position among other European countries, being not European enough, which is overcome by attempts to prove Polish superiority over the West in other dimensions. Poland is therefore sometimes depicted in political and media debates as morally superior to Western countries and as a society that has not been "spoiled" by changes brought about by "civilizational" processes.[42] This internal Orientalization justifies a para-colonial relationship with western societies, casting them as more modern and representing a future which Poles aspire to.[43] Some societies are "behind" western ones, existing in their past rather than in a global present.[44]

Polish Truth? Add in to this mix, questions of what one might call, at a stretch, Polish truth. Is there a truth only Poles by virtue of their experience can know or a way of knowing that is specific to Poles? One thing seems sure, as Przemysław Rotenbruber argues, many Poles prefer national mythology

---

40 Richard Holt Hutton and Walter Bagehot, "The Races of the Old World," *National Review* 18 (January 1864): 482.

41 Lucy Mayblin, Aneta Piekut, and Gil Valentine, "'Other' Posts in 'Other' Places: Poland through a Postcolonial Lens," *Sociology* 50, no. 1 (2016). See also: Rafal Smoczynski, Ian Fitzgerald and Tomasz Zarycki, "The Intelligentsia Informed Habitus in Social Distance Strategies of Polish Migrants in the UK," *Ethnic and Racial Studies* 40, no. 6 (August 2016).

42 Anna Horolets and Kozłowska, "Provincializing Europe, Orientalizing Occident or Reproducing Power Imbalance? Representations of the UK in Post-2004 Polish Migrants' Narratives," *Word and Text: A Journal of Literary Studies and Linguistics* 11, no. 1 (June 2012).

43 Magdalena Kania, "'Here Comes the Rest.' A Sociological Perspective on Postcolonial Rethinking of the 'Second World,'" *Postcolonial Europe*, May 15, 2009.

44 Lucy Mayblin, *Asylum after Empire: Colonial Legacies in the Politics of Asylum Seeking* (London: Rowman & Littlefield, 2017).

to facts.[45] This is highlighted in the publication in 2010 of a biography of Kapuściński in which the reporter was exposed to have been somewhat cavalier with the truth.[46] The author, journalist Artur Domosławski, believes this can be seen as a form of allegorical journalism. "There is a kind of New Journalism, if you like, that sometimes alters facts to create atmosphere, create links and make sense of complexity where often there is no link," the *Polityka* journalist told me in an interview in 2013. "There is a confusion at times between facts and the truth and I think Kapuściński believed in telling a truthful story, sometimes at the expense of facts."

Domosławski argues that Kapuściński belonged to an "East European" tradition with a logic that most Anglo-American journalists could not or choose not to understand. Kapuściński was simply a product of his time and place, he suggests. Domosławski acknowledges that the Anglo-journalism tradition has it that fiction dressed up as fact is always wrong. "The Central European tradition assumes that what readers want is entertainment and enchantment as much as information," he argues. "Writing in totalitarian environments clearly makes both fact and fiction problematic," he says. "But then this is not unique to this time and place, look at Truman Capote's *In Cold Blood*, for example." Kapuściński himself called it reportage d'auteur (reportaż autorski)—where the subject matter is filtered through the author's personality. Some believe it can be traced to a tradition of *gawęda szlachecka*, a traditional Polish anecdotal narrative running through parts of the literary history of the seventeenth to the nineteenth centuries, depending on real historical people, facts, and situations as raw material for literary stories.

However, as Anna Duszak notes, after 1989 this strand clashed head in with a new language of politics in Poland which was more dialogic, direct, expressive and open, using colloquial speech, clichés and buzz words.[47] Anna Wierzbicka argues that pragmalinguistic analyses confirm that Poles rarely

---

45 Przemysław Rotengruber, "The Problem of Polish (Self-) Stereotypes: The Perspective of Applied Cultural Studies," *Journal of Applied Cultural Studies* 2 (2016): 29–44.

46 Domosławski, *Ryszard Kapuściński: A Life.* In the biography, Kapuściński's time mainly in Africa and Latin America is tracked down, his conversations, meetings and whereabouts detailed. But oddly perhaps, the Anglo (mainly British) press (for example, *The Guardian*) ran numerous pieces in his defense, including by Neal Ascherson and Timothy Garton Ash. When *The Emperor* was published in New York in 1983, it was to great critical acclaim, and *Shah of Shahs* was equally successful two years later.

47 Anna Duszak, "Why 'New' Newspeak? Axiological Insights into Language Ideologies and Practices in Poland," in *Language Ideologies, Policies and Practices: Language and the Future of Europe*, eds. C. Mar-Molinero and P. Stevenson (New York: Palgrave Macmillan).

apply hedging techniques and this refers to the ways in which opinions are voiced.[48] Cliff Goddard and Wierzbicka argue that in most contexts Polish culture is likely "to actively encourage 'directness' of expression" rather than to advocate means of toning messages down.[49] Paweł Boski claims meanwhile that "Polish scripts of interpersonal communication encourage spontaneity of affective expression, including negative moods and feelings."[50]

This is of course also complicated by the history of fake news, or simply "the news" up until 1989.[51] A largely uncontested public voice floating on a sea of unreported dissent, filtered through conspiracy theories and old family tales. The post-1989 landscape was supposed to change all of that—open, free to discuss, dealing with the past, coming to terms with Poland's own mistakes, traumas and identity. And this appeared to be the case up to 2010. Poland had since 2004 been a keen member of the EU, had avoided the worst of the financial crises from 2008 and had started a process of transforming itself into a "normal" European country. PiS, in fact, appeared to be a busted flush, with declining support. But then came Smoleńsk, Russia's attack on Ukraine, the rise of Euroskepticism and a fragmentation of the PO message in government. The underlying discourses of conspiracy and national survival regained traction in various parts of social media and in the darker parts of the Right-wing press.[52]

Three cases of rhetorical "Othering" stand out in Poland. The first is the historian Jan Gross and his work on massacres of Jews by their Catholic Polish neighbors at Jedwabne during World War Two. The second is the April 2010 plane crash at Smoleńsk. PiS has sought to portray ex-president Lech Kaczyński as a man of historical significance, and many in the party believe his death in the 2010 air crash was no accident. The third is *Bolek*: the figure of Lech Wałęsa has provided a fertile terrain for PiS discourse, allowing

48 Anna Wierzbicka, *Cross-Cultural Pragmatics* (New York: Mouton de Gruyter, 1991). See also Zbigniew Oniszczuk, "Mediatyzacja polityki i polityzacja mediów. Dwa wymiary wzajemnych relacji," *Studia Medioznawcze* 4, no. 47 (2011): 11–22.

49 Cliff Goddard and Anna Wierzbicka, "Discourse and Culture," in *Discourse as Social Interaction*, ed. T. A. van Dijk (London: Sage Publications, 1997), 231–259.

50 Paweł Boski, Fons Van de Vijver, Helena Hurme, and Jolanta Miluska, "Perception and Evaluation of Polish Cultural Femininity in Poland, the United States, Finland, and the Netherlands," *Cross-Cultural Research* 33 (May 1999): 131–161.

51 Ewa Gieroń-Czepczor, "Verbal Warfare in the Polish Media: An Analysis of Conceptual Metaphors in Political Discourse," *Research in Language* 11, no. 2 (2013).

52 *The Financial Times*' editorial from May 30, 2016. Others deserve credit for noting at least some of the contradictions. Adrian Karatnycky in *Politico*, for example, December 15, 2015.

it to (attempt to) requisition the anti-communist struggle, to possess it symbolically, downplaying and attacking Wałęsa's role and contribution. Wałęsa is constructed discursively as having jumped into the fray (and literally over the wall of the shipyards in 1980, another powerful symbolic association) over the heads of the established underground opposition, and quickly acquiring a cult status that made him indispensable to the movement. All three elements, almost by a magical alchemy, bring together and then juggle the notions of foreign intervention (and hence the need for domestic unity and self-protection) and domestic betrayal.

Messianism and Conspiracy Theories: Piotr Urbanowicz argues [53] that we could observe after the 2010 plane disaster an occupation of part of Polish public discourse by figures of rhetoric associated with the country's rich Romantic tradition. He argues in particular that Messianism became an attempt at a negotiation of national identity and reconciliation of political interests and resembled conspiracy theories. As Mickiewicz's Slavic literature lectures in 19th-century Paris were widely seen as an attempt to include marginalized nations in European political discourse, part of the messianic view of the Slavs' role in the renewal of the European order, thus PiS adopted a similar rhetoric after 2010. Andrzej Walicki, meanwhile, calls the phenomenon of Polish messianism in essence a "millenarization" of the modern idea of progress. [54]

The traction gained by such conspiracy theories, Urbanowicz argues, lie in the way they allow interpretation of events by merging narratives originating from different sources: social, philosophical, and religious, with the potential to encompass individual experience, offering an opportunity for affective participation and connect with extra-institutional areas of knowledge, via new media, a cultural countermodel opposing the symbolic schemata established by state institutions. Marek Dybizbański argues, [55] the government's procedural approach was being questioned, as was the credibility of traditional media, by a metaphysical understanding of truth, turning away from traditional forms of representation, perceived in institutional rituals and media

53   Piotr Urbanowicz, "Metaphysical Despair. Messianism and Conspiracy Theories in Polish Media Space," *CzasKultury*, 2016, no. 2.

54   Andrzej Walicki, *Filozofia a mesjanizm. Studia z dziejów filozofii i myśli społeczno-religijnej romantyzmu polskiego* (Warsaw: PIW, 1970), 292.

55   Marek Dybizbański, *Od epiki romantycznej do teatru science fiction. Studia i szkice* (Opole: Wydawnictwo UO, 2016), 199.

narratives, a transcendental division between "deep reality" and media reality. The ontological difference between an event and its representation becomes effaced. "The hyper-real level develops invisibly, resonating in the space of media communication, by means of a mechanism that, while providing the illusion of approximating truth, is actually pushing us away from it."[56]

---

56   Clare Birchall, *Knowledge Goes Pop. From Conspiracy Theory to Gossip* (Oxford–New York: Berg, 2006) 34.

Chapter 5

The Confused Hopes of "Civil Society"

The central discursive strand that runs through this and other works in this field is the contested meaning of "1989." One thing is clear, "1989" brought independence and a chance to re-establish and reassess relationships with both the West and the East and with Poland's own national identity.[1] "The phrase people use to sum up what is happening," Garton Ash noted in 1990, "is 'a return to Europe.'"[2] The "revolutions" of 1989 represented, from this perspective, a return to the traditions of the pre-war era, a return to pre-1939. "1939," from this perspective, represents not only the last period of Polish sovereignty, but also the last period of democracy. Communism from this perspective was seen exclusively as an aberration, a product—in Poland, as elsewhere—of Soviet imperialism and the division of Europe after the Second World War. But "1989" is messy. Who "won" "1989" and what did they win: a return to Europe, a return to the liberal West or to an indigenous Polish model of democracy that many in the West might find far less liberal than they would like? Polish politics during the 1930s must be located within the context of a still semi-colonially penetrated national economy, weakly legitimated democratic—and at times authoritarian—structures of power and a multi-ethnic and diverse society.

Furthermore, varied and complex sets of political, ideological and constitutional relations and matrices have emerged since 1989. The post-communist political map in Poland is not easily amenable to the traditionally

---

1   Piotr Sztompka, "Looking Back: The Year of 1989 as a Cultural and Civilizational Break," *Communist and Post-Communist Studies* 29, no. 2 (1996): 110–123; Dariusz Gawin, *Polska, wieczny romans: O związkach literatury i polityki w XX wieku* (Kraków: Ośrodek Myśli Politycznej, 2005).
2   Timothy Garton Ash, *We the People: The Revolution of '89 Witnessed in Warsaw, Budapest, Berlin & Prague* (London: Granta Books, 1990), 154.

dichotomized notion of political ideology along a left/right continuum. Much of the post-communist left—comprised of the PZPR's successor, the Social Democratic Party of the Polish Republic (SdRP, the largest party in the SLD), and the post-Solidarity left, made up of the Labor Union (UP) and the Socialist Party (PPS)—was committed to more market deregulation of the national economy than one might associate with traditional Western European social-democratic parties, although that was also changing in its heartlands. It also had significant support from the emerging ownership classes, many of whom benefited from communist-era networks and social capital. The Right, on the other hand, made up of post-Solidarity (mainly nationalist and Catholic-sponsored) parties, was often attached to a stronger redistributive, active state. The political landscape of post-communist Poland was therefore marked very early on, then, not simply by a dichotomy of those committed to market and democratic reformism and those against, but also by a dichotomy of those attached to one version of "Poland" and those attached to another.

Civil Society as Double-Edged Sword: David Ost argues that the spread of a notion of civil society in the 1990s became a way to cope with the underlying class dynamics of the transition. He suggested that liberals in Poland could "make progress and still remain patriots."[3] To the extent they said this aloud, he argues, they got run over by the "patriots." To the extent that they hid it, they were unable to challenge the patriots. At least that was the vision of the 1970s New Left, and of much of Solidarity in the 1980s. Ost suggests that many years in power after 2007 enabled liberals (PO) to change the subject and become associated with modernity instead. But with "modernity" having resulted in economic crisis, PiS had success with the contention that modernity had failed, he adds.

Jean Cohen and Andrew Arato argue in turn that the lack of clarity regarding the type of civil society that was to be constructed or reconstructed was paradigmatic for the Polish case and reached back to the transition period.[4] This is a view supported by Aleksander Smolar, who argued in the early 1990s that the conception of civil society that won popularity in

3   David Ost, "Authoritarian Drive in Poland," in *Poland's Memory Wars: Essays on Illiberalism*, ed. Jo Harper (Budapest: CEU Press, 2018), 63.
4   Jean L. Cohen and Andrew Arato, *Civil Society and Political Theory* (Cambridge: MIT Press, 1992).

Central and Eastern Europe had "little in common" with Western European debates, "with the thinking of Locke, Ferguson, Smith, Hegel, Tocque-
ville, Marx and Gramsci."[5] According to Smolar, the concept of civil society
turned up "in the language of the emerging opposition under the influence
of their contacts with Western intellectuals. For various reasons, the idea of
civil society fascinated both Western, post-Marxist left-wing and circles and
neo-conservatives. Both were looking in the East for a major ally in the ideological struggles being fought out in their own world." He suggested that
Solidarność combined the call for "reform of the market with the ethos of
egalitarianism" and "formulated the traditional left-wing idea of social self-
government in the language of national solidarity."[6] Paweł Śpiewak in turn
argues that the subject of political liberty was relatively unexplored among
Polish liberals: "Few in these circles have reflected on the quality of civic
participation in politics or considered whether it's possible to broaden the
sphere of public dialogue."[7] Ireneusz Krzemiński, meanwhile, wrote that the
"experience of Catholic personalism has left a significant mark on Polish liberalism in that the latter has rather unquestioningly adopted the Catholic
ethic as well as the church's social and moral teachings as expressions of universal values."[8] As Sawczuk observes, the Polish liberal tradition was shaped
under the direct experience of totalitarianism and its intellectual roots can
be traced back to the dissident movement. "A common response to the moral hypocrisy that characterized authoritarian regimes was to ground the social order in a firm foundation: first, in the absolute truth of religion and second, in legalism, which kept politics at arm's length," he writes, adding that
the purpose of liberal conservatism was limited to maintaining the rule of
law and preserving tradition.[9] He continues:

---

5   Alexander Smolar, "Przygody społeczeństwa obywatelskiego," in *Idee a urządzanie świata społecznego.*
    Księga jubileuszowa dla Jerzego Szackiego, eds. Ewa Nowicka and Michał Chałubiński (Warsaw:
    Wydawn. Naukowe PQN, 1999), 387.
6   The proceedings of the conference were published by the National Humanities Center, cf.: Bronisław
    Geremek, "Civil Society and the Present Age," in *The Idea of a Civil Society* (Research Triangle Park,
    NC: National Humanities Center, 1992), 11–18. Geremek's paper also appeared in 1992 under the ti-
    tle "Civil Society Then and Now," *Journal of Democracy* 3, no. 2 (1992): 3–12.
7   Paweł Śpiewak, "Edukacja liberalna," in *Liberalizm polski*, ed. Ireneusz Krzemiński (Warsaw: Sedno,
    2015), 172–182.
8   Śpiewak, "Edukacja liberalna."
9   Śpiewak, "Edukacja liberalna."

But its anti-totalitarian sources eventually dried up, and by the time the economic transition was complete, anti-communist emotions had exhausted their potential for modernization, becoming Identitarian fuel for the right. Liberal conservatism has nothing to contribute and has ceded the field to PiS without a fight. The liberal bloc needs to abandon its free-market dogmatism in favor of a completely pragmatic approach to the economy. Liberalism should not be reduced to its economic concerns, much less associated with slavish devotion to the free market. There is no reason for liberals to adopt any particular economic religion, nor to have an immutable set of views regarding the economy.[10]

Beyond ideology? As Dariusz Gawin asked: "if neither right nor left, what else?" The parting with Marxism after 1968 described by Jacek Kuroń (in his case 1964) and driven by Leszek Kołakowski and others required the search for new conceptual frameworks.[11] Gawin argues that between 1968 and 1976 a new intellectual coalition developed in Poland which abandoned the dialectical conflict between reactionary and progressive forces, uniting the "lay left" and "liberal Catholics" in an approach to action, later to be defined as the building of civil society.[12] The intellectual foundation for this was set out in a book by Bohdan Cywiński, a Roman Catholic journalist connected with the Catholic organization *Znak* and Tadeusz Mazowiecki, later to be Poland's first post-communist prime minister.[13]

It was this approach that Adam Michnik also proposed in his text "New Evolutionism"[14] in 1976. Michnik identified two main groups of oppositionists for that period: revisionists and neo-positivists. The revisionist group was made up of the Left-wing and, to a large extent, openly Marxist intellectuals who had supported Gomułka in 1956 in the hope that there could be humanization and democratization of the system. "Neo-positivism" was linked to the *Znak* group. The *Znak* group not only had a network of the clubs of

---

10 Sawczuk, "Reconstruction in Democracy."
11 Leszek Kołakowski, "Tezy o nadziei i beznadziejności" in *Czy diabeł może być zbawiony i 27 innych kazań* (Krakow: Społeczny Instytut Wydawniczy Znak, 2012), 289.
12 Dariusz Gawin, "Civil Society Discourses in Poland in the 1970s and 1980s," WZB Discussion Paper (im Erscheinen).
13 Bohdan Cywiński, *Rodowody niepokornych* (Warsaw: Wydawnictwo Naukowe PWN, 2010).
14 See Robert.Brier, "Adam Michnik's Understanding of Totalitarianism and the West European Left: A Historical and Transnational Approach to Dissident Political Thought," *East European Politics and Societies*, 25, 2 May 2011.

Catholic intellectuals. *Tygodnik Powszechny*, together with the Warsaw community of *Więź* played a role of licensed political opposition in the 1960s. According to Michnik, both the revisionists and neo-positivists were defeated in 1968. The anti-intellectual and anti-Jewish campaigns launched after the March events cut the link between the Leftist intelligentsia and the PZPR.

Agnes Arndt's exploration of the rise of notions of civil society in Poland between 1968 to 1989[15] is fascinating in this context. She touches on misunderstandings in the Western European reception of the notion,[16] suggesting that "Solidarność surprising still uncritically laid claim to be a 'civil society' phenomenon." But, as she argues, Polish civil society discourse was much more likely to have been influenced by Karl Popper's concept of the Open Society.

"In sum, the concept of civil society allowed Polish intellectuals to join in this transnational discourse, to find common terminological ground for Eastern and Western European politicians and intellectuals interested in social reform, and hence to catch up with Western Europe in reform-oriented communication as had been qualitatively impossible prior to 1989," Arndt argued.

This in turn had repercussion for what Jerzy Szacki and Lech Mażewski described as an inadequate understanding of the relationship of the democratic opposition to the economy. Debates addressing the issue were concerned not with eliminating the planned economy but with involving the population in shaping it. Jerzy Szacki described the situation as follows: "In the East... civil society appeared as an ideological creation. What is more, it focused on the creation of a new moral and social order whose economic foundations were highly unclear."[17]

Arndt further suggests there was also a failure in the West to take account of the Polish contribution to the rediscovery of civil society, even while recognizing the importance of the Eastern European opposition movements. She posits what she calls "a triple distortion," where elements of Poland's contribution were either set aside, or constructed one-sidedly from a Western

---

15   Agnes Arndt, "Renaissance or Reconstruction? Intellectual Transfer of Civil Society Discourses Between Eastern and Western Europe," in *From Samizdat to Tamizdat: Transnational Media During and After Socialism*, 2nd ed., eds. Friederike Kind-Kovács and Jessie Labov (New York: Berghahn 2015), 156–171.

16   Jacques Rupnik, "Dissent in Poland, 1968–78: The End of Revisionism and the Rebirth of the Civil Society," in *Opposition in Eastern Europe*, ed. Rudolf L. Tőkés (London: Basingstoke, 1979), 60–112; Chris Hann, "Civil Society at the Grassroots: A Reactionary View," in *Democracy and Civil Society in Eastern Europe*, ed. Paul G. Lewis (London: Palgrave Macmillan, 1992), 152–165.

17   Jerzy Szacki, *Liberalism after Communism* (Budapest: CEU Press, 1995).

European theoretical understanding, interpreting the concept as a continuity of modern, Western European developments. Thirdly, the elements in the Polish discussion that arose in connection with Western European and American developments were dissociated from this context. In a 2005 essay, Jan Kubik also pointed to the fragility of a line of argument that equated the emergence of civil societies with modernization and Westernization,[18] a position shared by Alan Renwick[19]

Polish Liberalism and Conservatism: Despite ambiguity over the types of civil society, there was a re-emergence of vibrant thinking on the Right inside Poland in the late 1980s and early 1990s. From the beginning of the 1990s, many Polish conservatives had been fascinated by Anglo-American capitalism.[20] This was entwined with what Wlodzimierz Mich termed the dominance of a certain form of "integryzm" (integral Catholicism)[21], a conservative stream in Catholic thought hostile to changes concerning the doctrine of the Church and its position in state and society.

Publications during the communist era inside Poland had provided an opportunity for conservatives to publish their points of view. The Catholic paper *Tygodnik Powszechny* had been published in Kraków since 1947. *Znak* was another, while *Res Publica*, was published by Marcin Król from 1979. National conservatism was also visible in *Tygodnik Warszawski* at the end of 1940s, in the underground organization Ruch in the 1960s, in the Movement for the Defense of Human and Citizen Rights (ROPCiO) in the 1970s and in the Movement of Young Poland (RMP) in 1980, and in the Christian-National Union (ZChN) in 1990. All stressed the role of the individual in society and the connections between Catholicism and liberalism.

The issue of defending liberalism became part of a wider evolving understanding of the threat posed to liberal democratic traditions and institutions

---

18 Jan Kubik, "How to Study Civil Society: The State of the Art and What to Do Next," *East European Politics & Societies* 19 (2005): 113.

19 Alan Renwick, "Anti-Political or Just Anti-Communist? Varieties of Dissidence in East-Central Europe and Their Implications for the Development of Political Society," *East European Politics & Societies* 20 (2006).

20 Adam Folvarcny and Lubomir Kopecek, "Which Conservatism? The Identity of the Polish Law and Justice Party," *Politics in Central Europe* 16, no. 1 (March 2020): 159–188.

21 Wlodzimierz Mich, *Myœl polityczna polskiego ruchu konserwatywnego* (Lublin: Uniwersytet Marii Curie-Skłodowskiej 1995); Piotr Korys, "Conservatism as an Answer to Liberalism in Politics: The Case of Contemporary Poland," in *A Decade of Transformation, IWM Junior Visiting Fellows Conferences* 8, no 5 (Vienna, 1999).

after 2015. It highlighted, among many things, the degree to which centrists had yet to see the Left as natural allies against populism and the need to grasp deeper structural problems, the effects of which many had had to face, largely unnoticed, after 1989. The failure to tackle these questions echoed a common refrain that defending liberal democracies requires those of us who believe in them to herald their achievements better and more loudly. This awkward strategic moment was highlighted by an article in *The Journal of Democracy* in April 2020 by Karolina Wigura and Jarosław Kuisz from the Warsaw-based thinktank, Kultura Liberalna.[22] They framed the debate among opponents of PiS within Poland as a discussion between what they called "Symmetrists" and "Alarmists." The former tried to keep a distance from both PiS and PO, arguing that both were worthy of each other. The latter, however, believed one should group together to fight "totalitarianism." A brief summary of their ideas is illustrative.

Not Enough to be Right: "It is not enough to be in the right: We have to understand why (the populists won) and the factors that have enabled triumphs by the political opponents of ruling populists...More empathy is needed, also toward those who are particularly difficult for liberals to understand, such as voters who support populist parties."

It is a common theme and one that was obviously real, but also one that opens a lot more questions. But the assumption appears to be that "we" are right.

The Past and the Future: The article goes on to argue that populists' successes are in part due to their better harnessing of discourses of the past: "In postcommunist Europe, liberals lost the battle for the legacy of 1989. To mount an effective challenge to populism, liberals must offer a more convincing narrative about the democratic breakthroughs that took place thirty years ago and the decades of change that followed. Similarly, the populists have thus far done better than their opponents at promoting their visions of the future. This does not have to remain the case."[23] That still leaves the present.

Understand Loss and Dislocation: "Populism appeals to those experiencing loss because it is reactive: Populists position themselves as the defenders of social mores or forms of community under threat from the pressures of

---

22 Jarosław Kuisz and Karolina Wigura, "The Pushback Against Populism: Reclaiming the Politics of Emotion," *Journal of Democracy* 31, no. 2 (April 2020), 41–53.
23 Kuisz and Wigura, "The Pushback Against Populism."

a changing world...The populists may have been correct in sensing that a feeling of loss is today the dominant collective emotion."

Cool Those Emotions: "Liberal intellectuals urge a cooling of emotions, if not their complete rejection (...) Martha Nussbaum ... called for the liberal education of emotions...employing reason to eliminate emotions." But above all, the authors suggest, the liberal order "needs a passionate defense and not a cold one." Still a bit confusing.

Reclaim Patriotism: "One needs to consider, then, the possibilities for combining patriotism with liberalism, without slipping into nationalism."

Understand the Modern World: "Only if liberals can offer voters a new, attractive vision of the future can they hope to win." The authors note also that accelerating technological advances, the advent of new and transformative forms of communication, soaring standards of living, and rising social mobility created a sense of loss and that liberals "erred seriously by ridiculing this emotion, which is felt across the social spectrum—not only by the so-called losers of the transition, but also by its 'winners.'" Liberals, they argue, must catch up with their populist competitors in learning to convey their narrative "in a manner that is not only engaging and authentic, but also sufficiently entertaining to hold the audience's attention."

Poverty Comes Last: In what appears a kind of afterthought, the article offers some brief recognition of the "humiliation of poverty," the scale of which "became evident only gradually, just as people only gradually came to know the real Western Europe. Relative deprivation is one type of emotion of loss that is widespread in these societies." It perhaps only became evident to the authors when PiS was elected and people asked them how this had happened. A little like the Black Lives Matter movement in the U.S., most white middle class Americans had little real idea of the structural problems black people faced daily, just as the enlightened Polish middle class/intelligentsia, the "winners," perhaps failed to see the reality of the structural socio-economic post-1989 transition.

Chapter 6

Class Struggles

A Bifurcated Middle Class: Stefan Sękowski notes the absence of a stable middle class in Poland.[1] Middle income earners have little wealth in the form of property or investments and occupy a position that is both aspirational and precarious, he suggests. The traditional intelligentsia, meanwhile, possessed more of the social capital needed to survive in the new Poland, with access to languages, EU posts in Brussels and international schools. This group in effect converted some of this[2] into post-communist positions in think-tanks, startups and investment funds and so on. But the positions of both the new (moneyed) middle class and the traditional intelligentsia were both still precarious.[3]

Similar class dynamics in fact, if counter-intuitively, shaped much of the communist era. Iván Szelényi's theory[4] of state socialism as a class society dominated not by the party elite but by the intelligentsia is useful here.[5] It is the stratum he terms the sub-intelligentsia where the contradictions were strongest and the mechanics of dialectical change located, he suggests. These were those working at state planning agencies, technicians and humanist intellectuals who pushed to establish a new kind of society within communism in which intellectuals would be the dominant class and use redistributive

---

1   Stefan Sękowski, "No Change—How the Government and the Opposition Toe the Same Line on Policies, and How to Make a Difference," in Wigura and Kiusz, eds, *The End of the Liberal Mind*.

2   Jan Cieński, *Start-up Poland: the people who transformed an economy* (Chicago: The University of Chicago Press, 2018).

3   Tomasz Zarycki, "Cultural Capital and the Political Role of the Intelligentsia in Poland," *Journal of Communist Studies and Transition Politics* 19, no. 4 (December 2003): 91–108.

4   Gil Eyal, Ivan Szelenyi, and Eleanor Townsley, *Making Capitalism Without Capitalists* (London: Verso, 1998); Marc Rakovski, *Towards an East European Marxism* (New York: St. Martin's, 1978).

5   David Ost, "The Politics of Interest in Post-Communist East Europe," in *Theory and Society* 22 (1993); Edwin Bendyk, "Do jakiej klasy społecznej nalezysz?" *Polityka*, April 23, 2013.

mechanisms to reward themselves. Szelényi argues that the cultural capital of the intelligentsia—both former mid-level party technocrats and opposition-oriented intellectuals—led many into key positions in the state and business, which meant their material status outpaced gains made by other groups. Szelényi suggests that intellectuals in fact created the capitalism from which they were now benefiting.

The communist system had itself produced this 'historical' group/class. György Bence and János Kis distinguished the political elite from intellectuals, the latter divided between enterprise managers and critical intellectuals. Managers sought greater autonomy to catch up with the political elite in terms of power and consumption, but ultimately "submitted" because subordination to the elite protected them from resistance from below, i.e., the workers.

World-systems theorists like Immanuel Wallerstein also focused on the triumph of a new technical class, suggesting that 1989 was actually a "continuation of 1968."[6] On the one hand, there was a new professional intelligentsia, brought into existence by the educational boom of the postwar period and the reorganization of labor. Alongside a "semiskilled stratum" of the working class who knew how factories were run. These emerged in 1968 in both West and East, Ost notes. Arrighi et al., meanwhile, compare France 1968, Czechoslovakia 1968, Italy 1969, and Poland 1970. In France, labor protest was tamed, but the professional intelligentsia "won" a transition to a new service economy. In Poland, however, protests led to nothing and after the 1970 workers strikes, the regime used concession and repression, neither of which managed to transform the economy or satisfy the new class, Arrighi notes. Eventually the movement could no longer be contained and governmental power had to be handed over to Solidarność: 1989 had begun.

Red Intelligentsia: The traditional role of the intelligentsia as a social group was reawoken in the 1970s via the so-called "Red Bildungsbürgertum" (intellectually and economically upper bourgeoisie, in contrast to the Kleinbürgertum, or petit bourgeoisie) as the Warsaw milieu around Michnik is described by Arndt.[7] This group opted in the 1970s to wage a struggle against

---

6   Giovanni Arrighi, Terence K. Hopkins, and Immanuel Wallerstein, "1989: The Continuation of 1968," *Review* 15, no. 2 (1992). Republished in *After the Fall*, ed. George Katsiaficas (New York: Routledge, 2001).

7   Agnes Anna Arndt, "Rote Bürger: Eine Milieu- und Beziehungsgeschichte linker Dissidenz in Polen (1956–1976)," (PhD diss., Freie Universität, Berlin 2012).

the communist authorities from a Leftist perspective. And it is here, ironically, that the problems start.[8] The post-1989 political landscape until 2001 and the electoral marginalization of UW saw these "Warsaw intellectuals" take leading positions in the government and the opposition. But their largely secular discourse framed on the one hand by "Shock Therapy," and on the other, by calls to lay the past to rest (including the "Thick Line"), was never broadly appealing enough to consolidate electoral support. Furthermore, the language of historical reconciliation also alienated a large chunk of the Solidarity movement that had wanted to "seize power" in 1989. In fact, the more Poland was forced to face up to past horrors, in particular inter-ethnic animosities in the 1930s and during the war, the more the Warsaw intelligentsia could be portrayed as "not one of us" in PiS's emerging nationalist/populist discourse.

The Committee for the Defense of Democracy (KOD),[9] which first appeared on social media in late 2015, in some ways recreated an intelligentsialed mass movement, but fizzled out precisely for that reason; it's constituent elements were socially and economically further apart than in 1976. The likes of Geremek and Mazowiecki, speaking on behalf of the workers, became a retro dream of the new Polish middle class in 2015.

"I think it is important to remember that the tradition that these liberal intellectuals represented has always been a minority one in Polish political culture because it lacked a broad social base," Robert Blobaum, author of *Anti-Semitism and its Opponents in Poland*, told me in 2018. "It reappeared briefly in the unique conditions of the late 1970s and 1980s in the anti-communist Left represented by Michnik and Kuroń."

Blobaum notes that this small group of privileged communist childrencum-dissidents-cum-democratic leaders—Kuroń, Michnik, Karol Modzelewski, Barbara Toruńczyk and others—played an out-sized role in the public sphere of the 1970s and 1980s. "But as soon as real democratic elections became possible, they became increasingly marginalized, returning to the space occupied by their predecessors earlier in the twentieth century," he went on. Likewise, many leaders of the 1968 student uprising had

8   See Jarosław Kurski, *Lech Walesa: Democrat or Dictator?* (Boulder: Westview Press, 1993).
9   The Committee for the Defense of Democracy (*Komitet Obrony Demokracji*, KOD) is a civic organization and NGO promoting European values, especially democracy, rule of law and human rights, founded in November 2015 by a group of citizens including Mateusz Kijowski, triggered by the Polish constitutional crisis of 2015. Kijowski left the organization in 2017 after being accused of appropriating 121 thousand złotys.

leftist views, following the spirit of the 1964 "revisionist" manifesto of Modzelewski and Kuroń; but liberal-democratic Poland obliterated the Leftist
aspects of March 1968. As Ascherson stated, an "ultra nationalist, highly
conservative, traditionalist party" moved in to fill the void. The new middle class,[10] as Ziemkiewicz observed,[11] was in fact more concerned about
new cars than ideas.

Workers of the World Disunite: A key question however remained: what
to do about the workers.[12] Elizabeth Dunn's study, based on ethnographic research in a Polish food-processing plant in the early 1990s, shows how class
formation—in the sense of deliberate efforts to create a managerial class and
a working class—was not something that just happened but was explicitly
made to happen. She notes how the new, private factory owners sought to
reshape a working class "bequeathed with reserves of dignity and self-confi-
dence into one that accepted submission and marginalization."[13]

Many dominant discourses in the mass media have blamed workers for
their own degraded circumstances and for society's difficulties.[14] "The voice
of the powerless and the poor rarely makes it through the accepted democratic procedures. Subalterns have to resort to radical methods if they want
to articulate their interests and are afterward accused of demagoguery. Then,
however, they are described as uncivilized and ignorant of the 'new deal.'"[15]

Dunn argues that this process of clarification in effect divided the post-
communist society into winners and losers. "And the former group defined
the modes of adaptation and criteria for evaluation. This division associated
attributes deemed by the dominant culture as positive with the West, capitalism and progress, and those qualities regarded as negative with the East,
communism and backwardness." Tomasz Zarycki suggests the "lumpenpro-
letarians" were accused of blindly following populist politicians. "This leads
us to suspect that struggle and resistance are themselves implicated in the

---

10   "Poland's Booming Economy Fuels Demand for Life's Luxuries," *The Financial Times*, December 30,
     2019; Jacek Kurczewski, "Poland's Perpetually New Middle Classes," *Transition* 3, no. 5 (1997): 12–14.
11   Rafał Ziemkiewicz, "A Newspaper or a Political Organ?" *Do rzeczy*, July 19, 2016.
12   Kazimierz Słomczynski and Bogdan Mach , "Dissolution of the Socialist Working Class in Poland,
     Hungary and the Czech Republic," *Sisyphus: Social Studies* 10 (1997): 93–117.
13   Elizabeth Dunn, *Privatizing Poland: Baby Food, Big Business, and the Remaking of Labor* (Ithaca, NY:
     Cornell University Press, 2004).
14   Wolfgang Streeck, "How Will Capitalism End," *New Left Review* 87 (May–June 2014): 50.
15   Buchowski, "The Specter of Orientalism in Europe," 467.

reproduction of culturally based class differences that are the necessary condition of inequality."[16] Signs of solidarity epitomized the "harmful capital of the backward and play a part in the process of their segregation, and in crafting the image of their social and cultural inferiority."[17]

Zarycki claims that the workers who went on strike in 1980 improved their economic chances by framing their demands via intelligentsia-based values such as freedom and autonomy. In the post-communist period, capital rather than the state controlled economic resources and was no longer swayed by moral appeals. In effect, the traditional values historically articulated by the intelligentsia no longer brought them rewards, he argues. Workers thus became denigrated as "losers" who deserved their economic disadvantage. Those able to improve their economic situation did so after 1989 because they had bargaining power due either to skills or collective action and strong unions. Interestingly, as Wielisława Warzywoda-Kruszyńska argues, "one can find hardly any explanation identified with the Marxist tradition, which sees unemployment and poverty as generated by the core dynamics of class exploitation in capitalism."[18]

The inheritors of the revolution were "the nationalists, the neoliberals, the ambitious entrepreneurs and the Eurocrats," Alison Stenning argues.[19] Post-communism has been marked by a denigration of workers,[20] she claims, "manifested not only in their demonization but also in blaming them for the woes of society and articulation of a desire that society be reordered to reward non-manual labour." Working class communities in Poland were portrayed as hopeless, aggressive, miserable and pathological, Stenning goes on.[21] They are made out to be "feckless, dependent and passive men (predominantly) who form tribes and wage war with 'traditional society,'" she suggests. In promoting

---

16 Michael Kearney, *Changing Fields of Anthropology: From Local to Global* (Lanham: Rowman and Littlefield Publishers, 2004).

17 Tomasz Zarycki, "Class Analysis in Conditions of a Dual-Stratification Order," *East European Politics and Societies* 29, no. 3 (2015): 711–718.

18 Wielisława Warzywoda-Kruszyńska, Document 36: Long-Term Unemployment and Hardcore Poverty in a Polish Industrial City (Sofia: UNESCO-MOST, 2000).

19 Alison Stenning, "Where is the Post-Socialist Working Class?" *Politics and Sociology*, December 2005.

20 Stenning, "Where is the Post-Socialist Working Class?" See also: Barbara Einhorn, *Cinderella Goes to Market: Citizenship, Gender and Women's Movements in East Central Europe* (London: Verso, 1993), and David Kideckel, "The Unmaking of an East-Central European Working Class," in *Postsocialism*, ed. C. Hann (London: Routledge, 2002), 114–132.

21 Stenning, "Where is the Post-Socialist Working Class?"

a particular form of capitalism, the transition agenda adopted discourses of enterprise, consumption and individualism and those who were once seen as heroes of socialist labor saw their position usurped by new "heroes of free market ideology."[22] The similarities with tropes of "ghettoes of the workless and hopeless" and newer constructions of "chav" culture were marked, and another example of the Westernization of the post-socialist world.

Stenning proposes that the place of the post-socialist working class can be explained by a combination of wider social and economic shifts—the "end of work," the rise of identity politics, and "individualization." Katarzyna Rukszto adds that central to the project of transition was the "creation of a new model of citizenship," which combined the characteristics required of contemporary capitalism with a "romantic portrayal of the patriarchal family, Catholicism and capitalism."[23] In combining these two, the enterprising and middle-class citizen was seen to represent a historical continuum from the pre-socialist past, interrupted only by the aberration of socialist industrialization, she argues.

Whatever Happened to Solidarność? After 1945 regime trade unions became the key element of workers' organizations, the goal being to make unions an instrument of the PZPR, a strategy that failed—rather obviously—in 1956, 1970, 1976 and then in 1980–81, with the foundation of the Independent Self-governing Trade Union "Solidarity" (NSZZ Solidarność) in August 1980, a mass organization with almost 10 million members. During Martial Law (December 13, 1981 until June 1983) Solidarność was banned and in 1984 the 'All-Poland Alliance of Trade Unions' (OPZZ) was set up as an umbrella organization. After 1989, OPZZ remained the strongest trade union federation, but like all other trade unions it saw a decrease in membership, at about only 2 million by 2001 and less than 750,000 members by 2007. From 1982 until 2005 the overall degree of unionization fell from 80% to below 14%, making Poland one of the EU-countries with the lowest degree of unionization. Solidarność sympathized with conservative parties of the national catholic right-wing, whereas OPZZ tended towards alliances with the post-communist Left.

---

22 Lewis Siegelbaum and Daniel Walkowitz, eds., *Workers of the Donbass Speak* (New York: SUNY Press, 1995).

23 Katarzyna Rukszto, "Making Her Into a 'Woman': The Creation of Citizen-Entrepreneur in Capitalist Poland," *Women's Studies International Forum* 20, no. 1 (1997): 103–112.

The Peasants Not So Revolting After All: Another fascinating and large-ly unreported or misunderstood feature of post-communist Poland was the role of the rural population. As Chris Hann argues, "social anthropology no longer found the European countryside very interesting after half a century of the Common Agricultural Policy and the eastern expansion of the EU."[24]

> The traditions established by Bronisław Malinowski have been modi-fied—watered down, one might say. Europeanists nowadays, like anthro-pologists in other regions, are likely to do their fieldwork at multiple sites. The action seems to be with migrant workers, the unemployed, urban so-cial movements, the state, English-speaking NGO activists ("civil soci-ety")—everywhere except in the countryside![25]

A few anthropologists have sought to rethink the concept of "the peas-ant" by investigating "post-peasant populism" in Central Europe or by link-ing "post-peasant futures" to new theoretical agendas concerning identity and value on a global scale, Hann argues.

He proffers an interesting theory that the dictatorship of the proletariat in the communist era was, paradoxically, relatively successful because it in-creased the importance of household commodity production in the country-side, "which in turn was the key element in a significant redistribution of na-tional income in favor of the former peasantry." He suggests that post-1989 the reversal of this was a key factor behind not only economic dislocation but also political disaffection in the rural sector.

> I was also rather surprised to find that the peasants I lived with in the Beskid Hills had very little sympathy with the Solidarity movement, which erupted soon after I had begun my fieldwork. The alliance of intel-lectual dissidents, blue-collar workers, and the Roman Catholic Church, about which I had read a great deal in Britain, did not impress my vil-lage interlocutors at all. To my surprise, even the Church was sometimes

---

24 Juraj Buzalka, *Nation and Religion: The Politics of Commemoration in South-East Poland* (Berlin: LIT, 2007); Edward W. Wynot, "The Polish Peasant Movement and the Jews: The Polish Peasant Movement and the Jews, 1918–39," *Nationalities Papers* 15, no. 1 (Spring 1987): 71–89.
25 Chris Hann, "Still an Awkward Class: Central European Post-peasants at Home and Abroad in the Era of Neoliberalism," *Praktyka* 3, no. 9 (2013): 177–198.

criticized, for anticlericalism ran deep; only the newly elevated Pope, formerly Archbishop Karol Wojtyła (later John Paul II), was a genuinely unifying figure.[26]

---

26 Chris Hann, *A Village Without Solidarity: Polish Peasants in Years of Crisis* (New Haven: Yale University Press, 1985); Maria Halamska, "The Polish Countryside in the Process of Transformation, 1989–2009," *Polish Sociological Review* 1, no. 173 (2011): 35–54; George Kolankiewicz "The New 'Awkward Class': The Peasant-Worker in Poland," *Sociologia Ruralis* 20, no. 1–2 (1980): 28–43.

Chapter 7

An Imported Middle Class?

Given this context, the importation of external capital—social, intellectual, financial, political—after 1989 was a crucial factor in reclaiming Poland from "the East." The Sachs/IMF plan was based on immediately stemming the hyper-inflationary spiral and the longer-term goal of creating mechanisms for injecting capital and know-how into Poland. Capitalism's need for a middle class was thus clearly a key goal of the transition. A buffer and a conduit were needed. Post-war British Poles[1] had a certain social status, human capital that was clearly in short supply in 1989 in Poland, hence one might think it was a perfect fit.[2]

But was it? Danièle Joly suggests the Polish exile community in the UK in the post-war period represents an example of an "Odyssean" type of refugee, whose main point of reference was the structure of conflict in their society of origin, hence anti-communism lay at its core.[3] However, as Agata Górny and Dorota Osipovič show, second generation British Poles had deeply internalized some of the ideas inherited from their parents, including a strong sense of symbolic ties with Poland as an ethnic homeland, but in contrast to their parents did not have the intimate ties with what Stanisław Ossowski called the "private homeland" in Poland.[4]

---

1   Agata Górny and Dorota Osipovič, *Return Migration of Second-Generation British Poles,* March 2006, Centre of Migration Research Faculty of Economic Sciences Warsaw University; Keith Sword, *Identity in Flux: The Polish Community in Britain* (London: SSEES, 1996).

2   Edward Kołodziej, "Emigracja z ziem polskich od końca XIX wieku do czasów współczesnych i tworzenie się skupisk polonijnych," in *Emigracja z ziem polskich w XX wieku,* ed. A. Koseski (Pułtusk: WSH, 1998), 11–24.

3   Danièle Joly, "Odyssean and Rubicon Refugees: Toward a Typology of Refugees in the Land of Exile," *International Migration* 40, no. 6 (2002): 3–23.

4   Stanisław Ossowski,"Analiza socjologiczna pojęcia ojczyzny," *Dzieła* 3 (Warsaw: PWN, 1967), 201–26.

Górny and Osipovič note that ideological reasons were widely mentioned as a factor in the re-migratory decisions made by many Anglo-Poles after 1989.[5] But, despite exiles' strong anticommunist views, when the political change took place in 1989, it was greeted by the London diaspora establishment with a certain suspicion. It was difficult for exiles to accept any compromises that the opposition was prepared to make with the ruling communists, and only when the free presidential elections in Poland were won by Lech Wałęsa in December 1990 did the president of the Polish Government in Exile, Ryszard Kaczorowski, make his way to Poland and hand over the presidential insignia to the newly elected president during a ceremony at the Royal Castle in Warsaw.

Britain's Foreign Reporter in Poland: This section drifts in and out of what is directly knowable, to what is surmised, to poetic license, all in the pursuit of sketches that may be intuitively pointing in the right direction, if not always backed up by hard evidence. *The Captive Mind* by Czesław Miłosz was an inspiration here. I'd like to add Gombrowicz, but can't really crowbar him in. Let's leave it as admiration for his absurdist sensibilities. But *The Captive Mind* seems ripe for shameless imitation. The book tells of a Mongol Empire that conquers Poland and introduces Murti-Bing pills as a cure for independent thought. Not that I would accuse my fellow journalists of being anything other than independent thinkers. They trade in facts; the best money can buy. As one American bureau chief told me, "markets are like gravity... They are, like, natural, inevitable and everywhere at all times." One could easily get the weird sense that he had read Francis Fukuyama at face value.

English-Language Media Hierarchy in Warsaw

The Brahmins: Chris Bobinski and Applebaum[6] probably stand out.[7] Star names, the latter a Pulitzer winner and the former "proper pucker," as one old

---

5   Agata Górny and Dorota Osipovič, "Return migration of second generation British Poles," *CMR Working Papers,* no. 6/64, March 2006

6   "Polish Journalist Slams Washington Post Columnist Applebaum," *Polish Radio-the news.pl,* November 21, 2016; Marek Ostrowski, "Sikorski & Applebaum: Polska znika. Nie wystarczy maszerować, trzeba się zaangażować," *Polityka,* December 13, 2016; Joy Lo Dico, "The Sikorski Set: The Polish Foreign Minister has Locked Horns with Cameron—But Their History Goes Back to the Bullingdon Club," *Evening Standard,* June 26, 2014.

7   An Anglo-Pole living in Warsaw and with connections in the political world, told me his version. "They may think they are special but in reality they don't measure up. Sikorski is a chancer with a dodgy

Polish-Brit in Warsaw told me. Players all, well in the thick of it, married to biggish hitters in the political sphere and the think-tank/NGO circuit, and well-connected in Brussels, London and Washington. Not afraid to tie their colors to masts, Applebaum and Bobinski were both unashamedly anti-PiS and Russo-skeptic. One-time foreign minister, Sikorski, Applebaum's husband, was a hawkish figure within NATO and the EU calling for harsher anti-Russian measures after Moscow occupied eastern Ukraine in 2013–14. They are also quite big in the UK and US, unusual for big fish in the little Polish pool. The dream couple may have epitomized a new class, one yet to be fully made, teleological in its aspiration, backward-looking in its inspiration, harking back to before the fish had been liquidized to make the fish soup. A kind of post-modern retro gentry. Under the veneer of liberalism lurked a worldview closer to social Darwinism.

A vignette of the habitus of this group was served at the World Economic Forum in Davos in January 2020, when, during one of the press conferences, Duda used the expression "you can't make an omelet without breaking eggs."[8] Applebaum pointed out that these words had been used by Walter Duranty to justify the murder of kulaks by Stalin. "Of course, we know that not everyone is happy with the development we are achieving in the Three Seas region. But that's ok. As one saying goes: you can't make an omelet without breaking eggs," Duda said at The Financial Times panel at the Polish House in Davos. Applebaum wrote on twitter: "The President of Poland uses the phrase popularized by Walter Duranty, who used it to justify murdering kulaks —'you can't make an omelet without breaking eggs'—to justify unpopular government reforms." It was a performative demonstration of symbolic power, of course. This, Davos and all it stands for, is my terrain, not yours. It is a minor footnote in a bigger story, but indicative of the pettiness, spite and personal vitriol that peppered much of this cultural-political terrain.

Bill and Ben, the History Men: In the grand sweep of Polish history, historians like Norman Davies will have a decent footnote, there is no doubt. Davies's history of Poland, *The Heart of Europe,* published in the 1980s was

---

accent... did he get his degree? Once Sikorski was in PiS, but jumped horses. Also quite disparaging about ordinary Poles. He is deluded or the people around him don't tell him the truth. Rostowski taught at a polytechnic and his qualifications for the job he had are dubious. Yes, he went to Westminster School but he's not someone you would invite to your dinner table in London. Chris is a gentleman."

8   Anne Applebaum krytykuje słowa Andrzeja Dudy z Davos, January 24, 2020, *Wprost*

a monumental work and one that was possible at the time only outside of Poland, hence its critical importance in sustaining at least some semblance of continuity in Polish historiography and a sense that communist Poland was not where Poland began and ended, both for those inside and outside. Garton Ash, likewise, with car trunks full of samizdat or research papers, jeans or copies of *The Economist*, or simply visiting and keeping lines of contact of open to Poland, also deserves a footnote or two. Premiership no doubt. TGA, as friends apparently call him, and Christian's dad, Norman Davies, are no doubt the source of many careers at *The Guardian, The FT* and elsewhere, for ex-students, friends and colleagues alike. Unquestionable authorities, both as authors and sources. But a little far removed from Poland "as it is lived." Romanticized and abstract, Poland will always be more a noble cause than a real place. In the playoffs for promotion are Ben Stanley and Stanley Bill.

Lawrence of Arabia-Syndrome: Good chaps, "one of us."[9] Earnest and plummy. Fast-lane, high-flyers. First parachuted into Warsaw, then Moscow, maybe Paris, later Washington. Generally, the most open to discuss ideas and questions. Not scared of being asked about their ideas and debating them in public. But generally lacking in experience and perhaps rather one-sided and deferential to the "natural leaders," namely those in business with whom they have strong ties. Likewise, "The Posh Girl" who would rather be in Paris, but this will do... for now.

The Oxford Link: *Guardian* writers who are in with the opposition. Garton Ash–Norman Davies; we all need our sources, right? And the best contacts are often family or family friends. Nice, but amused and slightly, ever so slightly, superior. A bit gauche, other worldly, but with sometimes surprisingly bright insights. Generally, though playing a role. Like the brahmins, but a rung or two down the ladder.

---

9   As a *Financial Times* reporter in Warsaw told me: "I agree that some commentators came at PiS with an ideological bias. But that's the job of commentators. In terms of reporters - for sure, all newspapers have an ideological bent, but I don't think that stating facts such as how paying 500 zloty per child will inflate the deficit, or how TVP's subject matter and editorial line has changed is incorrect or unfair. And I for one don't think PiS was belittled or ignored. Quite the opposite—and the party, in my experience, recoiled from greater scrutiny, especially foreign. An interesting angle for you to explore perhaps would be how PiS's dislike of engagement with outside voices helped assist the potentially maligned version of their rule some say exists in the international media."

The Mavericks: Individualists, eccentrics and ex-child geniuses snapped from obscure Polish poverty and recruited as foot soldiers of the British ruling class's relentless claim to be fair and meritocratic.

The BBC: In the top league by virtue of who they work for. Probably closely tied into the networks linking Warsaw espionage and journalism in the early 1990s. Warsaw was after all known as a little playground for spies in the 1980s, the Soviet's weak point, Polish communists not really in control. The place crawling with spooks, ex-spooks, wannabe spooks, old time communist-watching journalists and the new breed of journalist-adventurer. The Soviet Union was collapsing and then collapsed, drawing back to Moscow many old-timers and sending in new blood, uncertain of who was who here and there. The young journalists who had come to watch communism start to unravel in 1988 and then stayed to report for *The Observer, The Economist, The Financial Times* and *The Telegraph* rubbed a lot of shoulders with British embassy "staff."

Division Two

The "Game-Changers": Poland has bad or zero PR, they say, but we can change that. Usually once part of the Left, idealists who went over to the other side. "When the difficult questions are asked, where is the Left," as a Reuters reporter said. Then there's the plethora of English-language websites that have cropped up since 2016, most state-owned or state-funded and rather obviously so. Polish versions of RT. A bit perhaps like how news might have looked had communism simply morphed into hybrid democracy or Chinese-style capitalism, rather than collapsed in Poland 30 years earlier.

Disclaimer: I would probably place myself in the lower half of the second or upper part of the third leagues.

The New Ideology: The more egregious examples of what may be called quasi-colonial reporting have been many and varied since PiS came to power in October 2015, but a few structural strands run through the narrative body. *The Financial Times, The Economist* and *The Wall Street Journal* tended to bemoan PiS's apparent market illiberalism (taxes on banks, supermarkets, higher spending on welfare), and concur with warnings from ratings agencies. The rhetorical devices used indicated what we would be fed: "hard-right," "xenophobic," "nationalistic." This journalism was above the fray, merely observing and noting, and soberly analyzing. The virtues of liberal democracy are a given, in theory and in practice, in the abstract and sought-after future.

On the social wing of the liberal critique of PiS, meanwhile, one saw Poland's favorite foreign historians Norman Davies and Garton Ash fretting about Poland falling back into bad old ways. Poland in some subtle ways became a child again in the eyes of worried parents, a place seen through idealized lenses, as if PiS were somehow a symptom of a collective pathology, not as an expression—however clumsy—of an actual living organism. This apparently "other" Poland, like the "other" UK after Brexit, was a relic of the past, a place of backwardness, of failure. Rarely did reporters take the time to glimpse into this world, unless through heavily loaded eyes—via a mixed bag of labels used loosely and often interchangeably: the transition's losers, the marginalized, rural, populist, Catholic, nationalist, backward, elderly, provincial, Polska B. These labels were rarely explored.

The Other, as it were, thus worked both ways: if PiS divided the world into Us and Them, then the expat media pack tended to divide Poland into those with PiS and those with Us. Of course, the things the Western reporter would see and write down are ostensibly "true," objectively reported and widely agreed upon. Suggesting that PiS was a more complex beast and that Polish society—like all others—was not amenable to simple dichotomies did not preclude the possibility that what they reported had some truth to it.

But media coverage was likely to focus on Poland only when it represented "news." That may sound like an oxymoron. Things need to happen after all for news to be news, hence the name. But news is a commodity that needs constant refurnishing with people and events, and discursive borders need to be policed. And while PiS is of course easily demonized, the machinery of demonization still needs to exist, and its narrative wheels oiled. Stepping outside the borders of the hermeneutics of owners' and editors' ideological predelictions is a dangerous business, and one that many reporters neither want nor often contemplate doing. Mainly this is because the ideology is so deeply buried, either knowingly, or in most cases, not, in what Stuart Hall calls the hierarchy of credibility.[10]

---

10 Stuart Hall, *Encoding and Decoding in the Television Discourse* (Birmingham: University of Birmingham Centre for Contemporary Cultural Studies, 1973); Klaus Schoenbach, "Trap Effect," in *The International Encyclopedia of Communication*, ed. Wolgang Donsbach (Malden: Blackwell, 2008), 5176–5178; Philo C. Wasburn, *The Social Construction of International News: We're Talking about Them, They're Talking about Us* (Westport: Praeger, 2002).

Explanation of the Polish case was complicated by the fact that the heartland of liberalism, North America and Western Europe, was undergoing a fierce struggle along several key cleavages at the same time: market versus social liberalism, national versus international liberalism, rule-based versus libertarian liberalism. Indeed, the broadsheet section of the British media was confused in late 2019, infighting over very British ideological predilections as Brexit raged. The British middle classes were split along quite traditional party political lines:[11] *The Daily Telegraph* and *The Times, The Financial Times* and *The Economist*, all Tory papers but split over Brexit; and *The Guardian* and *The Independent*, nominally on the Labour or LibDem side, but less split on Brexit. The British media was thus, in effect, caught in two simultaneous dialectical relationships with the reality of a bitterly divided discursive environment, one in the UK and another in Poland. *The Telegraph* and *The Daily Mail* supported the new governments in Warsaw and Budapest—not necessarily because they endorsed their policies, but in line with their traditional Euroskepticism and because they saw them as allies against the EU. They expressed their contempt for the EU either explicitly or implicitly, but the point was always to make the EU seem like a hysterical imperialist bully, and the Polish and Hungarian governments like honorable independence fighters. *The Guardian*, on the other hand, while it condemned the new policies as anti-democratic, typically saw them as deviations from a standard Western path of development.[12]

Post-Post-Truth? In the week before the second round off the presidential election in early July 2020, the two remaining candidates chose their favored television channels to debate the other. Trzaskowski chose TVN and Duda TVP, state tv. Neither appeared with the other on the other's channel. If anything summed up the divisive nature of Polish politics in 2020 this was probably it. Foreign journalists like Christian Davies in *The Guardian*, obliged to write something, wrote about it. And fair enough, in itself it was interesting and indicative of something wider and deeper going on. But when writing news about how news is so discursively weaponized, the journalist is in

11   See Ed Jones, "Five Reasons Why We don't have a Free and Independent Press in the UK and What We can do About It," *OpenDemocracy*, April 18, 2019.

12   Ian Fitzgerald and Rafal Smoczynski, "Anti-Polish Migrant Moral Panic in the UK: Rethinking Employment Insecurities and Moral Regulation," *Sociologický Časopis/Czech Sociological Review* 51, no. 3 (2015): 339–361.

danger of stepping into an area of meta-news, where they are in a sense actually commenting on their own role in the process. It was already clear, for example, that *The Guardian* had decided to take a high moral stand against PiS and would 'campaign' in its own small way against the "descent into illiberalism." But perhaps that was precisely the trap PiS, as Farage and Johnson in the UK, and Trump in the US, had set. To undermine the notion of balance, of a realm of news as fact, they coaxed the existing unbiased ("mainstream") media into revealing its hand, show where it *really* stood. Or, alternatively, if it stayed true to its journalistic code, by not showing its hand, it also provided a conduit for the spread of nonsense, vitriol and often hate speech. Reporters, after all, are obliged to write, simply, firstly what happens and who said what. It is a complex, difficult and unenviable job when the sides are so far apart.

Part III
A Reporter's Voice

Chapter 8

Election-Year Issues

The following sections each look at selected issues up to and during election years 2019 and 2020. The pieces are mainly reworked articles written for *Forbes, Politico, Deutsche Welle*[1] and others during this period, and as such retain much of the original journalistic style, with some—though not exhaustive—footnotes used. This is not an attempt to explore all themes or all avenues for exploring them but aims to offer a glimpse into how some of the main fronts in the discursive battle were framed and contested.

1. Playing the Race Card

In March 2018 the events of March 1968 in Poland were commemorated, with many drawing parallels between the two eras, reheating questions of PiS's relationship to issues of racial and ethnic Otherness. While "1968"[2] and "2018" did not denote exactly the same thing, some similarities were striking: a virulent form of Polish nationalism reinventing itself within a ruling party, as a more liberal and secular strand in Polish political culture stumbled; the cynical political use of 'the Other'—in 1968 Jews, in 2018 Muslims—was combined with an international crisis—then the aftermath of the Six Day War in Israel and the Cold War, in 2018 the Syrian and the refugee crisis and the emerging new age of international relations—to create the conditions for

---

1   Jo Harper, "PiS Picks LGBT Battleground in Poland," *Forbes*, March 24, 2019; "Polish Right Goes Left on Health," *Politico*, February 10, 2016; "Poland's Extra-Parliamentary Opposition Stresses Need for Civil Society," *Deutsche Welle*, January 16, 2016.

2   March '68 started out as a student protest action against the government, coinciding with the events of the Prague Spring in neighboring Czechoslovakia. In its wake, at least 13,000 Poles of Jewish origin were forced to emigrate.

what was in 1968 an attempt at a hardline coup, and in 2018 what many called the dismantling of democracy and the post-1989 settlement.[3]

"We can trace the origins of today back not to 1968 but to the rise of Polish nationalism, that is the Endecja, in the 1890s," Michael Steinlauf, Professor of History at Gratz College in the U.S., told me. "There is stunning continuity from then to now," he added. "From Dmowski to Kaczyński there is a straight line through the interwar period, the war, communism and after. This continuity is the most amazing aspect of modern Polish politics," he goes on.[4] "The interwar ONR [the quasi-fascistic National-Radical Camp] is back!" Historian Marta Petrusewicz said this can even be traced back to the 1830s, to the "Praca u podstaw" (back to basics) "proto-Positivism" that started after the defeat of the anti-Russian November insurrection.

"It would be completely wrong to say that 1968 and 2018 are the same thing," Michael Schudrich, Poland's chief rabbi, told me. "But there are noises of a similar tone and much of what you suggest has validity," he added.

'The main change from the ONR period is the apparently diminished role of anti-Semitism with PiS. I say apparently because it's still there under the surface," Steinlauf noted. "But we should be careful when drawing parallels between what is still a democratic state and what was then a dictatorship," Konstanty Gebert, a Polish-journalist and academic, told me.

"But the danger is of course that those who don't stand up for the prominent place of Catholicism and its symbols in the public sphere and advocate instead a civic-secular Poland, are turned into 'Jews,'" Zubrzycki argues.[5] The

---

3   Perhaps the most infamous articulation of this conspiratorial interpretation of Poland's past is Dorota Kania, Jerzy Targalski, and Maciej Marosz, *Resortowe dzieci* (Warsaw: Fronda, 2013). For an example of the presentation of the leader of the Solidarity movement as a communist agent, see Sławomir Cenckiewicz, *Wałęsa: Człowiek z teczki* (Poznań, Zysk, 2013).

4   Michael Steinlauf, *Bondage to the Dead: Poland and the Memory of the Holocaust* (Syracuse: Syracuse University Press, 2006). PZPR First Secretary Gomulka had been accused in the late 1940s, of nationalist deviation, removed from power and arrested. In 1956 Gomulka returned and faced a leadership divided into two factions—reformist Puławy and Natolin, whose members had spent the war in Poland. The 1960s saw a new force appear, the Partisans, combining nationalism and communism, under the leadership of General Mieczyslaw Moczar, who accused Gomulka of supporting "Muscovites." Gomulka succumbed, denouncing the activists as "Zionist agents."

5   Geneviève Zubrzycki argues that civic nationalists see the recognition of that legacy as a tool to build an open society. This she argues is part of a plan to "soften, stretch, and reshape" the symbolic boundaries of Polishness that the Right has sought to harden and shrink. Michael Meng refers to this process as "redemptive cosmopolitanism," while Katrin Steffen argues that the "symbolic Jew" appeals in different ways to existing patterns of thought, ranging from Jews as communists or capitalists, to dissidents or Zionists. 'The result is a Judaization of the rejected 'Other,'" she argues.

notion that Jewishness can provide a kind of proxy for a liberal, plural, civic and secular Poland, Poland is said by the conservative Catholic Right to be ruled by "Jews"—symbolic Jews—who must be neutralized, she added. "Poland is thus host to the apparently curious phenomenon of anti-Semitism in a country with very few Jews," Zubrzycki said. "Jews are non-threatening and available to be filled with one's fantasies: nightmares or dreams depending on one's political orientation," she added.

Kaczyński had in fact been critical of anti-Semitism in Poland. "Yes, that is the case, but in the tropes used there is a very clear link between Islamophobia and the Polish anti-Semitism of 100 years ago," Gebert said. "PiS in its statements is totally not anti-Semitic, but when it comes to actions it does nothing. Poland has become a nastier place and PiS is not lifting a finger," he added.

"PiS itself is not overtly anti-Semitic," the U.S.-Polish historian Jan Gross told me. "But by association with Radio Maryja and Nasz Dziennik it feeds on associations with anti-Semitic rhetoric. The language used about the refugees is sinister, these strangers in our midst that carry disease."

The refugee crisis after 2014/15 was often presented in the Polish right-wing press as an Islamic invasion of Europe, with headlines using words like "raid," "conquest" and "penetration." At the same time, Western Europe was described as a culture dominated by Leftist influence, in which Christian values, tradition, and family had been undermined. For example, the cover of Polish weekly *wSieci* went viral in February 2016 when it showed a half-naked white woman wrapped in an EU flag, defending herself from male hands of a dark complexion. The caption read, "The Islamic Rape of Europe."

In 2015, anti-migrant rhetoric certainly helped PiS cement its identity among core voters and of the more than a million refugees who arrived in Europe the Polish government agreed to take in a tiny number. PiS was also heavily critical of the obligatory EU allocation system.[6]

"I am not sure if Muslims have taken on the role of Jews, but one can argue that 'the other' is definitely now Muslim," said Katarzyna Górak-Sosnowska, a professor specializing in Islamic studies at the Warsaw School of Economics. "And it is a strange, distant other. So, from the perspective of

---

6 Foreign Minister Witold Waszczykowski said in November 2015 that Syrian refugees arriving in Europe should form an army that could be sent back to liberate their home country, "instead of drinking coffee in the cafes of Berlin while western soldiers face [IS]. Jon stone, "Syrian refugees should be trained into an army to fight Isis, Poland's foreign minister says," November 16, 2015, *The Independent*.

de-humanizing Muslims we could say that they have taken the place of Jews, but Jews have been there in Polish culture, while Muslims are still alien to it," Górak-Sosnowska said.

The issue of restitution of pre-war property owned by Polish Jews in Poland became an election issue for the far-right in 2019 and PiS entered the discursive fray. Restitution claims "are a big threat," to Poland, said Krzysztof Bosak, MP from the hardline nationalist Confederation Liberty and Independence Party in early 2020. "We believe we need to strengthen legal protection of Polish property as we fear behind-the-scenes negotiations pertaining to restitution claims," he went on. Kukiz'15 had just floated a bill that would restrict restitution lawsuits by Jews over property confiscated or stolen during or after the Holocaust. In May 2019, to coincide with Israel's Holocaust Remembrance Day, parliament debated a bill proposed by Kukiz'15 MPs, which was aimed to "prevent demands for Polish property [in cases] without heirs" and thwart "frivolous suits over property."[7]

Just days ahead of the May 26 European Parliament elections, Kaczyński said: "Poland has no obligations resulting from the war, neither legally nor morally." He said Poland should be the one receiving compensation. "Some countries west of Poland owe us hundreds of trillions of euros or more," Kaczyński said, addressing Polish reparations demands towards Germany. "If we reach a situation in which Poland pays compensation for World War Two, it would be a victory for Hitler. As long as our party is in power it will not happen," Morawiecki said.

2. When a Man Loves a Woman

Ahead of the 2019 parliamentary elections, PiS threw its weight behind a campaign to marginalize Poland's LGBT+ community, countering what its officials called "Western LGBT ideology." The issue seems to have been bumped up the list of campaign priorities, replacing anti-immigrant rhetoric. Kaczyński warned, "Hands off our children!"—implying that "LGBT+

---

7   When the Red Army entered Warsaw in January 1945 over 90% of the city's dwellings had been destroyed by the retreating Germans. Poland was one of 47 countries to sign the Terezin Declaration on Holocaust Era Assets and Related Issues, but the country never followed up with legal regulations. An estimated 170,000 private properties held in Poland were wrongfully seized from Jewish victims of the Holocaust and nationalized by the communist government. The communists' so-called Bierut Decree of 1945 remained in legal force.

ideology" threatened the morality and health of young Poles. PiS was clearly in part paying back the church for its assistance in galvanizing support at the 2015 election, via organs such as Radio Maryja. According to both PiS and advocates of LGBT-free zones such as Ordo Iuris, "LGBT+ ideology" was a foreign (Western) imposition on Polish Christian culture and morality.[8]

After Warsaw's mayor Trzaskowski signed a declaration to support LGBT+ people in February 2019, several towns declared themselves "LGBT-free zones." The mayor had advocated integrating sex education and LGBT+ issues into school curricula, in accordance with World Health Organization guidelines.[9] A PiS campaign advert depicted an umbrella with the party logo protecting a family from rainbow rain. *Gazeta Polska* announced it would distribute "LGBT-free zone" stickers. The stickers featured vertical stripes in rainbow colors crossed out by a thick black x. The paper's editor, Tomasz Sakiewicz, argued, "Freedom means that I respect your views and you respect mine. We oppose only the imposition of views by force. Being a gay movement activist does not make anyone more tolerant."

Poland was ranked among the most restrictive countries in Europe in terms of LGBT+ rights.[10] In December 2019, the European Parliament adopted a resolution on discrimination and hate speech against LGBT+ people, including LGBT+-free zones.

This struggle played out across various forms, one of which was the formal cultural sphere. A film, for example, depicting Polish clerics as corrupt and pedophiles broke Polish box office records in 2019. *Kler* (Clergy), by Wojciech Smarzowski, featured an alcoholic priest who encourages his lover to have an abortion. Its release came a few weeks after a landmark court decision in Poznań against a religious order, where the judge ruled it bore responsibility for the fate of a girl, then 13, who had been repeatedly raped by one of its

---

8   Ordo Iuris has advocated for a near-total ban on abortion in Poland and is part of a wider international "pro-family" movement which coordinates to promote legislation that criminalizes abortion and undermines LGBT+ rights, among other things, according to BIRN's 2018 investigation.

9   Paweł Rabiej, the deputy mayor of Warsaw, likened it to the Nazi-era. "German fascists created Jew-free zones," he tweeted. See: *Rzeczpospolita*, August 6, 2019: 'RPO o „Strefie wolnej od LGBT": Polsce grozi dyskryminacja na rynku usług.'

10 Poland was second to last out of 28 EU states when it comes to equality and non-discrimination, according to Rainbow Europe, an organization linked to the International Lesbian, Gay, Bisexual, Trans and Intersex Association. Gay marriage is illegal in Poland and homosexual partnerships are not legally recognized. Whereas 41% of Poles said in a 2001 survey that being gay should not be tolerated and was not normal, that number had dropped to 24% by 2017, according to state pollster CBOS.

priests. *Gazeta Polska* reproduced the film poster on billboards across Poland with the images of "national heroes" including Father Jerzy Popiełuszko, who was murdered by communist security services in the 1980s, and Father Maximilian Kolbe, who volunteered to die in place of another inmate at Auschwitz. The poster read: *"The clergy: our treasure in the fight against Nazism, communism, LGBT and Islamists."*

Another film shown a year earlier, a documentary about children who had been sexually abused by priests, was viewed by 11 million people within three days. *Tell No One*, made by brothers Tomasz and Marek Sekielski, showed sexual abuse victims speaking on camera and confronting their former abusers. "A mental revolution is happening in front of our eyes. Victims are being called victims and perpetrators called perpetrators," Sekielski told the weekly magazine *Polityka*. After the film's release, the Catholic Church suddenly changed its tune, apologizing to abuse victims. Roman Catholic Archbishop of Gniezno and Primate of Poland Wojciech Polak even thanked the two brothers for their courage.

Meanwhile, Kaczyński hinted that child sex abusers would face tougher punishment, saying: "Anyone who is responsible for children will face especially harsh penalties, whether that is a priest or a celebrity. We want to be uncompromisingly strict. But do crimes by priests mean we can now attack the Church in its entirety? And insult all Catholics? No!" Morawiecki soon after announced tougher laws on abuse, with child sex abusers facing up to 30 years in prison and the statute of limitations scrapped for such crimes.[11]

"Genderism": The notion of "gender" itself had earlier become a fault line in the Polish version of the "Culture wars." The term, of course, functions in a double dimension, as an academic concept, and in an "opaque" form.[12] Urszula Chowaniec explains how the Church spoke of 'gender' as a concept that was 'deeply destructive' to 'the person, inter-human relations and all social life' and they believed to be rooted in Marxism or neo-Marxism.

---

11   Hours before a summit opened in the Vatican in February 2019 on pedophilia in the Catholic Church, three activists pulled down the statue of Henryk Jankowski, "Solidarity's Priest," in Gdańsk. Jankowski was a close aide to Wałęsa during the Gdańsk shipyard strikes in 1980 headed by the Solidarity movement.
12   The book by Maciej Duda exemplifies and describes well the whole phenomenon of the language manipulation in the church, politics, and sometime academic debates. Maciej Duda, *Dogmat płci. Polska wojna z gender* (Warsaw: Wydawnictwo Naukowe Katedra, 2016).

Some less extreme members of the Polish Church spoke out. Piotr Muchar-ski, chief editor of the Kraków-based Catholic weekly, *Tygodnik Powszechny*, for example said: "Gender Studies have been taught at Polish universities for years and no one until now has questioned this."[13] The Polish government's Equal Rights Plenipotentiary, Agnieszka Kozłowska-Rajewicz, said no pro-grams spreading anti-family material existed in Polish schools and accused the bishops of inventing the term "gender ideology" as an "imagined enemy." Meanwhile, a group of Warsaw-based professors said the Church's campaign risked "endangering freedom of research," and another group wrote to the Pope,[14] complaining that blaming gender studies as a source of family crisis was a "witch hunt." A leading Dominican, Father Maciej Zięba, questioned the wisdom of denouncing "gender" when most Poles had never heard the term.[15] Publications summarizing the last two decades of feminist thought in Polish academic circles also appeared.[16] Chowaniec suggests that the threat was constructed as being against "our children" and the "our" plays an impor-tant rhetorical role. The very structure of the phrase, "our children" is, in fact, an ideological appropriation of children, she argues.

3. Don't Shoot the Messenger!

Krzysztof Dzięciołowski argues that the 2010 Smoleńsk disaster proved a po-tent catalyst for the resurrection of an anti-"liberal media" backlash in Po-land.[17] It allowed the far-right—and PiS—to reopen or reheat old conspira-cy theories. So, perhaps, it was unsurprising when in December 2015, the PiS government passed a new law which allowed the government to take more direct control over public media. In the following weeks about 200 journal-ists were fired or forced to quit, many denounced as unpatriotic, un-Polish or

---

13 See Jonathan Luxmoore, "Polish Church Declares War on Gender Ideology," *Our Sunday Visitor Newsweekly,* January 29, 2014.

14 Luxmoore, "Polish Church Declares War on Gender Ideology."

15 Luxmoore, "Polish Church Declares War on Gender Ideology."

16 German Ritz, Magdalena Hornung, Jędrzejczak Marcin, and Tadeusz Korsak, *Ciało, płeć, literatu-ra: prace ofiarowane Profesorowi Germanowi Ritzowi* (Warsaw: Wydawnictwo Wiedza Powszechna, 2001).

17 Based on interviews with six leading Polish journalists—three from liberal media outlets (*Gazeta Wyborcza, Polityka Weekly* and *Onet.pl*) and three from conservative outlets (Wnet Radio, *Sieci Week-ly* and Belsat TV)—Dzięciołowski's report describes how the right-wing press became highly visible and partisan after the 2010 crash.

disloyal to the ruling party.[18] According to the Association of Journalists, 225 journalists left public media during 2016, due to either layoffs or resignations.

After PiS came to power in 2015 it also frowned on advertising by state-owned companies to media outlets critical of the government, throttling several independent print media outlets, such as *Gazeta Wyborcza, Polityka* and *Newsweek Polska*. Two privately-owned TV channels, Polsat and TVN also faced a choice of either having to support the government or seeing their business interests damaged. Polsat, owned by Zygmut Solorz—who had several business interests that could be affected by government regulations—had already moved to a pro-government position before the elections. Other foreign-owned media outlets, such as Germany's Axel Springer which owned the online platform Onet and local papers, were also affected. A week before the 2019 parliamentary election PiS said it wanted to regulate the status of the country's journalists, and to create a "new media order."

The Special Case of Gazeta Wyborcza: From 2015 to 2020, *Gazeta Wyborcza* received 55 legal threats, including civil defamation actions and alleged infringement of personal interests by a number of actors, including Kaczyński, the state television broadcaster, Telewizja Polska, and state-owned company KGHM Polska Miedź. Each threat was in relation to articles published in the newspaper or on the outlet's website, including coverage of a re-privatization scandal in Warsaw, the quality of COVID-19 face masks bought from China, and a business relationship between the PiS leader and an Austrian businessman in relation to the construction of a skyscraper for a company associated with the ruling party.[19]

All government offices and state-dominated firms were forbidden to advertise in the paper, while private firms hoping for government contracts were warned that their practices in this regard would be watched. Income from ads declined by 25% in the first year of PiS power, causing *Gazeta Wyborcza* to announce layoffs and cutbacks.[20] The paper sold about 450,000 copies in 2005, 190,000 in 2015 and by 2019, 91,000.

---

18 According to a poll from market research institute Ipsos, 51.6% of Poles believed that TVP was not fulfilling its mandate. In the 2019 edition of the World Press Freedom index, Poland was in 59th place among 180 countries, down from 18th place in 2015.

19 European Centre for Press and Media Freedom (ECPMF), *The Media Freedom Rapid Response Supports Gazeta Wyborcza in Poland*, July 6, 2020.

20 Adam Michnik, "Adam Michnik: zmiana władzy straszliwie walnęła 'Gazetę Wyborczą' po kieszeni, nie stać nas na oddziały regionalne i korespondentów," *wirtualnemedia.pl*, November 23, 2016.

Fearing government attempts to close the paper, George Soros was invited to buy 11% of its publisher's shares in June 2016.[21] Not coincidentally, PiS soon after began ratcheting up its campaign against "foreign intervention" in the Polish media market. Opposition TV stations still operated but were facing similar pressure.

After the fall of communism in 1989, Kaczyński said *Gazeta Wyborcza* disseminated "liberalism, anti-traditionalism, anti-Catholicism" and was "against the very notion of the nation." He accused Gazeta of using the "pedagogics of shame," referring to the "destruction of Polish national pride," such as the role of Polish collaborators in the Holocaust. The history of antipathy between Kaczyński and Adam Michnik, the original editor in chief of *Gazeta Wyborcza*, goes back a long way.

PiS also had its foot soldiers in the rightwing press. A few passages from Rafał Ziemkiewicz writing in *Do Rzeczy* illustrate this.[22] "It appears that the lack of capabilities held by the politicians they support has finally irritated the editorial team [of GW] to such an extent that it has decided to take matters into its own hands and it has in fact become a political party," Ziemkiewicz wrote. "It is not difficult to find out that it is aimed at making Poland secular and moving to the Left as far as possible, as is the case in Western Europe. Michnik's paper was trying to do this from a cross-party, meta-political position from the start. Wyborcza regarded its primary task as being to reconstruct the Polish mentality, to 'raise' Poles so that they may become 'modern Europeans. Gazeta Wyborcza was the voice of a group of the enlightened, standing higher morally and ethically, however, willing to accept the masses inspiring to become a part of the elite, provided that the applicant has passed a test of being different in a beautiful way. New power elites of a cunning, post-colonial nature have gradually been created. They pay little attention to any form of absolving themselves from 'European' fairness, because they were more impressed by 'posh cars' than gaining the recognition of intellectuals."

---

21 Billionaire George Soros in early 2019 teamed up with Agora—in which he owned a 16% stake—in a bid to buy Eurozet, owner of several radio stations including Poland's second largest, Radio Zet, through the intermediary of Czech company SFS Ventures. Fratria, the publisher of the pro-government weekly *wSieci* and owner of several rightwing news websites, including *wPolityce*, PMPG Polskie Media SA—the owner of the weekly *Do Rzeczy* and *Wprost*, and businessman Zbigniew Jakubas, also wanted to buy the company.

22 Ziemkiewicz, "A Newspaper or a Political Organ?"

The tone of the piece was quite aggressive, but it touched a nerve. *Gazeta Wyborcza* didn't do itself or the anti-PiS "coalition" many favors at the start of the 2019 campaign with a poorly timed expose that appeared to show Kaczyński taking a bribe.[23]

In the week before the second round of the presidential election, I spoke with the investigative journalists, Agata Kondzińska and Iwona Szpala, at *Gazeta*'s Warsaw headquarters. They were scathing of PiS, of course, but also less than positive about Biedroń and Trzaskowski. The paper, they said, was committed to "democracy," and that meant it was likely to be closer to PO, but "we support no party." Brave souls and fighting the good fight, but not really a massive endorsement of the anti-PiS coalition.

4. Still the Economy, Stupid!

PiS had an impressive economic record up to the 2020 coronavirus crisis. There had been fears expressed in the non-PiS media mainly that the party's plans would lead to a deterioration in public finances, but this didn't materialize. PiS had somehow cobbled together a winning brand, with doses of economic redistribution, social conservatism, and patriotic rhetoric. "Good times for Poland" was PiS's main slogan in October 2019. "Restoring the dignity of the Polish family," "Helping regular Poles," and a "Poland that does not apologize for itself," were not far down the list. PiS had been accused of propagating a form of economic nationalism,[24] which broke from economic liberalism and instead wooed voters through offering a series of state-led social welfare policies. PiS branded itself the creator of a "Polish welfare state" and its election manifesto rejected "the rules of neoliberalism." In fact, as Gavin Rae argues, the macroeconomic strategy of the government remained essentially the same as that which came before—maintaining an open economy with low taxation and regulations for businesses and using EU funds

---

23 "The paper published a secret recording in which Kaczyński was heard discussing a big construction project in Warsaw in July 2018, appearing to suggest his personal political favor could influence the project." See: *Euractiv*, January 30, 2019, "Fallout from the Kaczynski Twin Towers Scandal."

24 Kaczyński claimed that Poland's economy would catch up with Germany's by 2040. This is a common theme of his political schtick, namely Germans thwarting Polish ambitions down the ages. Kaczynski claimed that by 2033 Poland will reach the EU GDP per capita average and in 2040 catch up with Germany. Given that Poland's success is in large part also a product of its close economic ties with Germany and EU funds largely underwritten by Berlin since 2004, perhaps the claim requires some unpicking.

to sustain public investment. PiS also didn't make any attempt to raise investment in key productivity-enhancing areas and labor productivity generally kept pace with the surge in wages. As Rae argues, in fact the Catholic Church influenced the social policy of PiS, with the PiS government prioritizing spending on family benefits, and not, for example, on building preschools or developing childcare in workplaces, hence the burden of childcare was further placed on the family, most particularly women.

5. History: War and PiS

PiS placed rethinking how both Poles and the rest of the world perceive Poland high on its political agenda after 2015. Minister of National Education Anna Zalewska, for example, declined to acknowledge that some Poles had been perpetrators of the murders in two of the most infamous cases: the burning of 300 people in a barn in Jedwabne in 1941, and the Kielce pogrom in 1946. Instead, the role of the Germans was emphasized (Jedwabne), as well as that of the communist authorities (Kielce).

In 2017 PiS called for criminalizing the use of the term of "Polish concentration or death camps." PiS also publicly scorned Jan Gross for his accounts of Poles killing Jews in the war.[25] The Museum of the Second World War in Gdańsk was another case in point. "This is a museum almost entirely created by the Germans. The Polish identity has been erased," Kaczyński said of the museum, which opened in April 2017. In October 2017, PiS dismissed its director. "I think patriotism is something good in Poland," said the new PiS-selected director Karol Nawrocki. "Does Gdańsk want to be part of Germany?" asked PiS-linked weekly *wSieci* on a cover featuring the city's mayor, her murdered predecessor and Nazi imagery. It claimed the city, an opposition stronghold, was "at war with Poland" and "cultivating its German roots."

The minister of culture, meanwhile, also accused of attempting to wrest control of the European Solidarity Center in Gdańsk.[26] As the PiS MP

---

25 Jan Grabowski, *Hunt for the Jews: Betrayal and Murder in German-Occupied Poland* (Bloomington: Indiana University Press, 2013). Grabowski argues that Poles living in the countryside served as enthusiastic accomplices to the Nazis and that many Jews who had managed to survive the ghettos and escape transports to the death camps eventually lost their lives only because they were turned in by their Polish neighbors. His findings corroborate those of Gross's "Neighbors" and "Golden Harvest."

26 In 2008, during a parliamentary session Kaczyński proclaimed that the museum should portray the "Holocaust that affected the Poles." In April 2016, Minister of Culture Piotr Gliński announced un-

Dariusz Piontkowski stated: "It is our right that museums built in Poland should portray the Polish perspective." The debate, he said, revolved around "whether the museum should be a cosmopolitan one in which British and American historians tell us how we Poles should conceive of the Second World War."

His use of the term cosmopolitan is interesting. In the Soviet Union and the state-socialist satellites of Europe, the term was used as an accusation against ideological opponents; in the Stalinist vocabulary of defamation, it became a synonym for "imperialistic" or "Jewish," or "Zionist." As spokesperson for the advisory board, Norman Davies said the government's actions were "Bolshevik" and "paranoid" in style: "The Law and Justice government does not want a bunch of foreign historians to decide what goes on in 'their' museum."

The idea of the "Accursed Soldiers" was another flash point. The name "Accursed Soldiers" (żołnierze wyklęci) was taken from a book by Jerzy Śląski and the late President Lech Kaczyński propagated the idea. To explain the Smoleńsk crash PiS politicians claimed that the victims of the fatal crash had been "killed in action," with talk about explosions on board the presidential airplane and of Tusk's "moral responsibility" for the crash.

Memory Laws: Poland is not unique in Europe when it comes to seeking to protect its historical reputation, Uladzislau Belavusau argues.[27] Poland's 2016 "De-Communization" law and the 2018 law on historical expression introduced changes to the Act of the Polish Institute of National Remembrance (IPN) were the main focus.[28] Under the 2016 law, local authorities

---

expectedly that the new institution would be merged with the Museum of the Second World War under this new name. One of the first responses to these plans came from Paweł Adamowicz, the mayor of Gdańsk, who threatened that if the museum were amalgamated and its name and mission statement changed, the city would revoke the building plot, which it had donated free of charge. Gliński back-pedaled.

27   The German Criminal Code prohibits "insulting or maliciously expressing contempt toward Germany or one of its states." Article 423 of the Slovak Criminal Code provides criminal liability for defamation of the "nation, its language or any race or ethnic group" and a parallel provision is found in Article 355 of the Czech Criminal Code. According to a 2017 OSCE report on insult and defamation laws, "[a]t least 14 OSCE participating states have criminal laws prohibiting insult of the state." citations

28   Uladzislau Belavusau and Aleksandra Gliszczynska-Grabias, eds., *Law and Memory: Towards Legal Governance of History* (Cambridge: Cambridge University Press, 2017); Aleksandra Gliszczyńska-Grabias, "Calling Murders by Their Names as Criminal Offence—a Risk of Statutory Negationism in Poland," *Verfassungsblog*, February 1, 2018; Volha Charnysh and Evgeny Finkel, "Rewriting History in Eastern Europe: Poland's New Holocaust Law and the Politics of the Past," *Foreign Affairs*, February 14, 2018.

were obliged to rename locations that propagated communism as defined in the law and according to a list prepared by the Institute of National Remembrance, an institution that was created in 1998 to specifically investigate the crimes of the Nazi and Soviet regimes. At the beginning of 2018, Poland found itself at the center of a scandal stemming from the 2018 law. The argument of the Polish government that all Western European countries have been legally protecting the memory of the Holocaust in the same way is "at best misleading," Belavusau argues.[29]

6. Brussels or Death

The constitutional crisis's first stage started one month after the government took power, in December 2015, and revolved around the Constitutional Court. It resulted in a large-scale reshuffling of constitutional judges. Of the 15 seats, 13 were appointed by the new government, two of which were former members of the Sejm who had served as MPs for PiS. The second phase revolved around the Supreme Court and the judicial system as a whole.

One of the most contentious elements of the reform program was the establishment of a new Supreme Court chamber to conduct disciplinary actions against judges. The new chamber was appointed by an overhauled National Judicial Council (KRS), the body that nominated judges and decided how the courts were run. The majority of its members were selected by parliament, rather than the legal profession, as had previously been the case. After 2015 PiS also waged a campaign to fill the Constitutional Tribunal and the KRS and sought to do the same to the Supreme Court, lowering the mandatory retirement age for judges and subordinating those left to two new chambers. The method was quite old school: the PiS government was rooting out, relocating and demoting political critics in the name of judicial reform. In 2016, the roles of justice minister and prosecutor general—which had been separated in 2009—were merged in the person of Ziobro.

PiS's efforts to silence, persecute and fire judges not aligned with its political program became even more blatant after the parliamentary elections in

---

29 For explanation on the relation between memory laws and claims to protect public security, see Maria Mälksoo, "Memory Must Be Defended: Beyond the Politics of Mnemonic Security," *Security Dialogue* 46, no. 3 (2015): 221–237; Anna Wójcik, "Memory Laws and Security," *Verfassungsblog*, January 5, 2018; Wojciech Sadurski, *Poland's Constitutional Breakdown* (Oxford: Oxford University Press, 2019).

2019 when judges became liable for prosecution for complying with rulings issued by their own supreme court. The government was accused of seeking criminal proceedings, for example, against Jozef Gacek, a prosecutor who, PiS claimed, had failed to go far enough in investigating the 2010 Smoleńsk airplane disaster.

Meanwhile, although the prosecution service was not perfectly independent before PiS took power, it had never been politicized "with such force, with such power, and on such a scale," Krzysztof Parchimowicz, a public prosecutor, told *Foreign Policy*. In October 2019, Parchimowicz was taken into disciplinary proceedings to answer charges of insubordination. The government's opponents argued that the new measures, which they dubbed a "gagging law" (*ustawa kagańcowa*), undermined judicial independence by attempting to intimidate critical judges so that they ruled in line with the ruling party's expectations. They also warned that the law could lead to Poland being excluded from the EU, so-called "Polexit," as its provisions violated the terms of European treaties by undermining the primacy of EU law.

PiS's Defense: The government's supporters argued that reforms were needed because Polish courts were too slow, inefficient and tolerated frequent irregularities and corrupt practices. They argued that the judiciary had been expropriated by an entrenched, and often deeply corrupt, postcommunist elite, which then co-opted a new legal establishment that perpetuated its legacy.[30]

Following mass protests in the summer of 2017, Duda vetoed some of the reforms, but his revised version was close to the government's original proposals; the main change was a guarantee that parliamentary nominees to the national judicial council would be elected by a qualified three-fifths supermajority. The official rationale was threefold. Firstly, according to Morawiecki, there was a historical justification: *"In 1989... the judiciary from the communist times became the judiciary in the new Poland. The same judges who had sentenced my brothers in arms... were building 'independent' and 'objective' judiciary of the III Republic of Poland during the 1990s,"* Morawiecki told the New York University School of Law on April 30, 2019. Secondly, he highlighted that there was a need to change the way in which judges were selected, because the old method which delegated most of this power to the judiciary was not well equipped to

---

30   Chelsea Michta, "The Struggle over Poland's Judiciary is also About History," *CEPA*, April 17, 2020.

deal with corrupt members. The third argument called for a more politicized selection to improve the "appallingly low" quality of the judiciary.

7. Culture: Reaching for the Revolver

Two days before the 2019 parliamentary election, Olga Tokarczuk won the Nobel prize, was acclaimed abroad and attacked by PiS at home.[31] A week before this, Kaczyński had lashed out against the country's "cultural elites." Writers and filmmakers must not reopen the country's national wounds or remind the public of the darkest chapters of the country's history, he said.

At the beginning of 2020, PiS-supporting Piotr Bernatowicz assumed the top job at one of Poland's most internationally renowned institutions, the Ujazdowski Castle Center for Contemporary Art in Warsaw. The ministry of culture also fired directors whose views it deemed too progressive: Paweł Potoroczyn, who had run the Adam Mickiewicz Institute since 2008, was fired in 2016. The director of the institute's Berlin branch, Katarzyna Wielga-Skolimowska, was also let go in 2016 for programming that the government criticized as too focused on the Holocaust. Poland's national art gallery (Muzeum Narodowy) in 2019 removed a video installation featuring a human interaction with a banana. People took to the streets with bananas to protest censorship.

8. Between Iraq and a Hard Place

The International Liberalism that had been heralded by Tony Blair and Garton Ash (among others) in the 1990s dragged Poland into its orbit when Warsaw joined NATO in 1999 and applied for EU accession a year later. Its first test of loyalty was the U.S.-led war against Iraq in 2003. Poland has since been caught between its alliance with the US and its more EU-phile instincts. The rise of PiS saw the former flower at the expense of the latter, leaving Warsaw in a somewhat hard place.

---

31 For a few minutes after Tokarczuk's win had been announced, Polish public television TVP did not mention her name. Her picture appeared on the screen of TVP Info, the public news channel, along with the headline: "Pole Awarded Nobel Prize." Tokarczuk was on the Polish Ministry of Culture's informal "blacklist," and it may be that in the minutes after the announcement of her award, the TVP Info editors simply did not dare mention her name.

Foreign issues in 2019 and up to the impact of the coronavirus in March 2020 provided a discursive wardrobe full of villains and heroes, good history and bad history to be brought out, paraded and discarded when needed by PiS. That is not to say threats were not real. The Nord Stream 2 pipeline, for example, excited a phalanx of Polish nightmares, from the eighteenth century partitions via the 1939 Ribbentrop-Molotov Pact to the present day. And climate change goals set out by the EU were also real enough. But bashing the EU, or being bashed by it, a victim of Brussels' overweening powers or a bastion of a new Europe based on traditional Christian values, or both, PiS knew its constituency. As with the party's determination not to talk to the foreign press, not to seek to spin its position or curry favor, the significance for PiS's core electorate of being seen to be in conflict with Brussels was not lost: we are with you, not them. PO is with them, is one of them.

As the EU faced crises, from Brexit, to Italian debt, to France and Germany's perennial struggle with each other and their southern European neighbors, Warsaw and Budapest provided another fault line that Brussels could not ignore, but could also not fully deal with without upsetting the fragile equilibrium within the bloc. Where PO had been close to Berlin and sought to move closer to Brussels, in particular after Tusk's rise, PiS pursued a far more Atlanticist line, with support for Britain's "right to choose" within the EU and for U.S. belligerence against Russia, but also its trade scraps with Berlin and Paris.

The EU—A Transactional Affair: Some in Brussels, and others, were asking in 2019 if the EU could be faced with death by a thousand cuts, a de facto reassertion of national member states' sovereignty, with Poland joining the UK and Italy in a growing group of malcontents. Tusk, for example, warned that PiS could push the country towards Polexit. Brussels was so concerned about Poland's anti-democratic trends that it invoked Article 7 of the EU treaty for a potential breach of obligations as a member of the bloc. Sanctions on Poland also required a unanimous decision of the European Council, where Hungary and Romania repeatedly said that were such a Council vote to occur, they would veto sanctions.

On April 30, 2020, the European Commission launched a legal case against Poland for what it considered an attempt to muzzle judges. It was the fourth case it had forwarded against Warsaw since the PiS government began instituting judicial reforms. Three days before the October 13, 2019 election the Commission announced it was referring Warsaw to the European Court of Justice over its disciplinary regime for Polish judges.[32]

EU budget negotiations stalled in late 2019 as the rifts between countries in the North and South of the now 27-member bloc and between East and West widened further. The so-called Frugal Friends (the Netherlands, Austria, Sweden and Denmark) wanted to lower the new seven-year budget in the budget period that expired at the end of 2020. European Council President Charles Michel's compromise was rejected by both sides. A second key question was how to fill the €75 billion funding gap created by Brexit. Britain had been the second-biggest net contributor to the budget after Germany, at around €9.2 billion per year. To help fill the Brexit gap, the Commission had also proposed ending rebates on budget contributions that many of the net payers were getting. Germany, the Netherlands, Austria, Denmark and Sweden all had their own rebates and wanted to keep them.

A third issue was cohesion and agriculture funds, which together took up over 60% of the budget. The Commission proposed €41.3 billion for cohesion funds in the 2021–2027 period, down from €63.4 billion for the 2014–2020 period. The overall net cut in cohesion funds would be around 12%, although some member states stood to lose up to 24%. Michel's proposal would adjust that by diverting money from richer to poorer regions. According to the European Commission's proposal, the Czech Republic and Hungary would get 24% less for cohesion policy than in the 2014–20 period, Poland 23% and Slovakia 22% less. Michel also included €7.5 billion new money to fund the greening of the economy. To get reluctant countries like Poland on board, the EU made expensive promises to help emissions-heavy regions adjust, in the Just Transition Fund.

PiS Puts its Case: "Negotiating a budget deal is not a purely arithmetical exercise. Rather, it must be a translation of political priorities into a financial framework," Morawiecki wrote in an opinion piece in *The Financial Times*. Morawiecki argued that there was a strong relationship between gross contributions of EU member states and the benefits they accrue from the single market. He gave the example of the Visegrad Group (V4) countries, comprising the

---

32   Under the law Polish judges can be investigated and sanctioned for their court rulings. Announcing the decision to go to court, the European commission said the law did not "guarantee the independence and impartiality of the disciplinary chamber of the supreme court." It added: "Judges are not insulated from political control and thus judicial independence is violated." citation

Czech Republic, Hungary, Poland and Slovakia, which in 2010–2016 received net funds from the EU of 1.5–4% of their GDP. However, the outflow of dividends and property incomes from V4 to investors located in 15 countries of the "old" EU was 4%–8% of the V4 countries' GDP in the same period. Tenders for investments in Poland co-financed from EU funds, for example, often went to Western companies, many of which sent profits back home via dividends to non-Polish shareholders, he said. By joining the EU Poland also became a large consumer market on the doorstep and a place for cheap production of auxiliary industries serving the German market. And perhaps above all, Poland saw a mass emigration and brain drain to countries like the UK.

For the first time, a new tool was to be introduced into the EU budget designed to make sure EU money was spent correctly. Denmark, Finland, France, Germany, the Netherlands and Sweden said they would veto any framework if it did not link the distribution of funding to respect for the rule of law. Commission Vice President Jyrki Katainen warned Poland against treating the EU as a "money machine." The Commission had earlier in the year proposed cutting about one quarter of Poland's funding in the 2021–2027 budget as a starting point for talks.

Energy and Insecurity: In early 2019, Poland announced that the country's state gas company PGNiG had signed a 20-year deal for liquefied natural gas (LNG) deliveries from the US and that it would be spending €200 million buying into a long-term project to deliver gas from Norway. Warsaw also said it would not be extending its 22-year gas deal with Russian gas firm Gazprom in 2022.

Meanwhile, the Russian-led consortium building the Nord Stream 2 gas pipeline from Russia to Europe continued. The €11-billion project came under attack from Washington and several Eastern European and Nordic countries, although some pro-Russian eastern members of the EU, including Bulgaria and Hungary, had few such worries. Under EU law, ownership of gas transmission infrastructure had to be separate from that of the commodity itself. However, Germany—whose firms were heavily invested in the project—sought to exempt Nord Stream 2. Berlin had claimed for years that the pipeline was a purely commercial endeavor. But then in April 2018, at a meeting with former Ukrainian president Petro Poroshenko, Merkel recognized for the first time that the political factors surrounding Nord Stream 2 also had to be taken into account.

The pipeline had polarized debate in the EU, between the bloc and the US, and added to ambiguous EU-Russian relations. Poland's former foreign minister, Witold Waszczykowski, suggested in 2017 that the pipeline was another way for Berlin to punish his country over its alleged reluctance to change course on domestic judicial reforms that Brussels deems anti-democratic. Washington threatened to introduce sanctions against European energy companies participating in the project and said it could carry "reputational costs" for those involved.

Poland, Trump, NATO and Russia: Tensions had been building after Russia's annexation of Crimea in 2013 and the West's imposition of sanctions; but the collapse of a US-Russia brokered ceasefire in Syria and Washington's accusations that Moscow has been using cyberattacks to disrupt the US presidential election saw already-fragile relations worsen.

To make matters worse, Putin started to cast the Molotov-Ribbentrop Pact as a move the Soviet Union had been forced into by Western leaders' alleged collusion with Hitler at the time of the 1938 Munich agreement. In December 2019, Putin blamed Poland for the start of World War Two, "Poland assumed the role of instigator" and "Poland and Germany acted together." In a meeting with the Defense Ministry on December 24, he proclaimed that the Polish ambassador to Nazi Germany in the 1930s was "scum" and an "anti-Semitic pig." That same day, the speaker of Russia's parliament publicly called for Poland to apologize for starting the war. In Russia, memories of World War Two had been used in an attempt to legitimize the invasion of Ukraine and annexation of Crimea. Putin compared the Ukrainian military's offensive in Donbas to the Nazi siege of Leningrad during World War Two.

Meanwhile, with defense contracts up for grabs among its mainly Eastern European members, NATO made good on its promise to bolster its presence in northeastern Poland and the Baltics. To justify such a move, NATO needed a threat, and in this case the old enemy, Russia, was seemingly ready-made. In October 2016, the Polish General Roman Polko, former head of the GROM military unit, claimed a "Russian invasion" of the Baltics was inevitable "in the nearest future." Warsaw said it planned to raise its military spending to 2.5% of GDP by 2030, replacing old Soviet equipment with modern armaments that could counter the threat from Russia. Under the program, Poland planned to spend at least 83 billion zlotys on new weapons and military hardware and to buy the US Army's Patriot surface-to-air missile defense system, in what was clearly a response to Russia's deployment of nuclear-capable missiles to Kaliningrad. The deal could reportedly be worth $5.6 billion.

France, Forks and Fighters: When Central and Eastern Europeans backed the US invasion of Iraq in 2003, French President Jacques Chirac said they had "missed a good opportunity to shut up."[33] Several years later, Polish Deputy Defense Minister Bartosz Kownacki, as the dispute over the Caracal defense helicopter contract descended into a bitter row, claimed that Poland had taught the French how to use forks.[34] Seemingly innocuous, sometimes petty squabbles have larger consequences.

French President Emmanuel Macron visited Poland in February 2020, offering Warsaw "a chance" to end its isolation within the EU. But immediately following the visit, Duda signed the so-called "muzzle" law that empowered the government to punish judges for acting independently. The signals were clear.

When Poland announced in April 2015 that it would enter exclusive negotiations with Airbus to purchase fifty Caracal helicopters for three billion euros, Paris was enthusiastic. After winning the Polish elections in October 2015, PiS criticized the previous Polish government's decision. In October 2016, following more than a year of negotiations on offset terms, and a few days before an official visit by then French President Francois Hollande, Warsaw ended the talks. The same week, it announced the purchase of Sikorsky Black Hawks. The "Caracal Affair" was a watershed in Polish-French relations and appeared to open the door to integrating Poland into Airbus. Hollande's visit was cancelled and Poland's invitation to the Euronaval fair was rescinded. Macron advised frustrated climate change activists to "go demonstrate in Poland!"

In the run ups to the presidential election in June 2020, the daily *Dziennik* reported that defense-related talks would take place during Duda's visit to the US, in particular what had become known as "Fort Trump" and the

33 Eleanor and Michel Levieux, "The World; No, Chirac didn't say 'Shut Up,'" *The New York Times*, February 23, 2003.
34 The fork is sometimes said to have been introduced into France by King Henry III. Born to an Italian mother, Henry III was elected king of Poland and Grand Duke of Lithuania before ascending to the throne of France in 1574.

signing of an agreement on Warsaw acquiring an attack helicopter that would finalize the Polish Kruk program.

Climate Change: Poland was the only country not to sign up to the EU's goal of reaching climate neutrality by 2050. Commission President Ursula von der Leyen wanted the bloc to become climate neutral by 2050 and to reduce emissions by 2030 by 50% from 1990 levels. Poland opposed, with fraught talks on emissions reductions and the scale of financial compensation through the Just Transition Fund. From the beginning of negotiations, Poland made clear that its agreement was contingent upon receiving "significantly larger" funding from the EU budget to help with the costs of transition.

Part IV
A Lay Voice

Chapter 9

Diary of British Media Coverage of the October 2019 Parliamentary Election

This chapter deals with how the story of the Polish parliamentary election was told in the broadsheet British press in September and October 2019. It is deliberately narrow in focus, looking at *The Guardian*, *The Economist*, *The Daily Telegraph*, and *The Financial Times*. There are occasional pieces in the Right-of-center weekly *The Spectator* and left-of-center weekly *The New Statesman,* the Right-wing nationalist tabloid *The Daily Express*, and centrist *The Independent*. The British broadsheet press was roughly split along pro- and anti-Brexit lines, with *The Daily Telegraph* and *The Guardian* perhaps the most vocal and representative of the two positions, respectively.

The chapter focuses on how each news article frames a context, creates a stage, then peoples and scripts it. Who is chosen to speak, what questions are they asked? Who are the experts and who the ordinary folk? How are they described and presented? How are dominant theme(s) naturalized? Is there a pattern and sequence, semblance of some kind of narrative(s)? How do news and commentary interplay? Is there any leakage, overlap, clear directional pattern, or contradictions and outliers? The need to differentiate between news reporting, editorial and features is important, in particular recognizing how news language informs a certain way of understanding, which in turn is taken as accepted truth or fact to be commented on.

I decided to comment at times inside the selected texts, which are set out chronologically, and to use my "lay" voice, the one I might use to assess the text as if I were reading it for the first time or as someone with limited knowledge of Poland. This is intentional, and I hope offers some insights into how a reader, however unideal, might actually approach such texts. The insertion of some insights using CDA and other methodologies used in discourse analysis I hope also adds to the picture.

Part 1: Floating Frames

In the pre-election phase up to October 13, the emerging public discourse of both PO and PiS appeared to be placing them on two sides of what was increasingly being calling the "Culture Wars." But at his stage PO (the largest group in the Civic Coalition, or KO) appeared not to know where its best line if attack might lie. This period is therefore one of floating issues and gauging reactions, from the economy, to history, to religion/the church, LGBT+, 500+/minimum wage, the media and warnings about democracy at stake. British reporting was thus also caught up in the local mix, reporting the news, while also supporting a version of liberal democracy and hence opposition to PiS.

Meanwhile, Brexit was sitting center stage in UK politics, with the legislature standing up to the government of Theresa May. It was a period when Boris Johnson and the European Reform Group (ERG) was in the ascendant, with talk of proroguing parliament.

The interplay of an anti-EU discourse among the Rightwing press, with implicit acceptance of the strong man rule (The Daily Mail's 'blame the traitors' line, for example) and PiS thus occupying another symbolic role as a potential EU ally and a template of this new illiberalism. Many of the issues that had been brought up in the first four years of PiS's rule in Poland were center stage in UK debates over Brexit: the independence of the judiciary, the power of the legislature versus an overbearing executive, the independence of the media. It also took place in an atmosphere of increasingly vitriolic social media commentary and political violence.

UK press coverage of Poland and its election on October 13 was therefore to some extent a product of an internal struggle within the UK as much as a simple reflection of events as they actually happened in Poland. 'Poland' and the other 'populists' in the EU could either be held up as why a stronger EU needed Britain's continued input or why it should leave the Europeans to their own devices.

The European Commission's admonishment of PiS a week before the election, and the Nobel victory of the Polish writer Olga Tokarczuk in the same week couldn't have come at a better moment to undermine PiS in the eyes of world opinion. But, however sadly, perhaps also this provided PiS with another bone to throw to its more intransigent supporters.

September 18, 2019
The Daily Telegraph[1]

"Poland's ruling party pledges to double minimum wage and end country's 'post-colonial' reputation as a source of 'cheap labour.' (...) PiS portrays itself as a party caring for what it regards as the people left behind by Poland's economic progress since the end of communism in 1989."

Commentary: The term "left behind" carries a solidly pejorative set of semantic luggage. *The Telegraph* reader might get it, though: the "losers" are grumpy, well, because they lost. Not everyone can live in Tunbridge Wells, after all. This is followed by a juxtaposition of "economic progress" and "people left behind" as if they are not connected.

"Since coming into office in 2015 it has introduced several welfare schemes."

Commentary: "Welfare" had long become a loaded, weaponized, term, particularly for *Telegraph* readers.

"As part of its election campaign his party has called for a 'revolutionary improvement in the standard of living of Polish families,' bringing it up to a 'European level' within 10-20 years."

Commentary: Revolutionary is not a word your average *Telegraph* reader wants to read over his corn flakes.

"But experts point out that Poland is already moving away from the low-labour-cost economy that attracted much of the foreign investment into the country over the past 20 years."

Commentary: This is a somewhat mangled version of events and processes. The implication is clearly that markets, like gravity, always find some way of working. It is part of the Hidden Hand thesis that informs most journalists obliged to write about economics when they have very little idea about economics. Unemployment wasn't a political decision here, not something that was discussed, fought over and contested. It just happened, like the rain.

---

1   Matthew Day, "Poland's ruling party pledges to double minimum wage and end country's 'post-colonial' reputation as a source of 'cheap labour,'" *The Daily Telegraph Times*, September 18, 2019

"'But this is now changing,' Piotr Arak, director of the Polish Economic Institute, a Warsaw-based think-tank, told The Telegraph. 'You have demographics. Poland is getting older. This means wages are going to increase. The time of cheap employees in Central and Eastern Europe is ending.' (...) The government's plans to force the pace of change, however, have raised concerns amongst employers. (...) Lewiatan, a business lobby group, says the increases in the minimum wage could trigger inflation and lead to higher costs as the new wage levels hit the economy."

Commentary: There is a largely unexplained and unexplored post-colonial theme. Readers are expected to understand what it means, its historical context and its contemporary usage. Then we again face the poor "left behind" people. Two sources, both on the business side, are used to back up the implied assertion that PiS is not economically sound. There is no voice from PiS, from trade unions, from supporters of the idea. The possibility that PiS's idea might make sense is rather timidly floated by the expert on demographics, who tells us the natural order is moving in the direction of higher pay anyway, if the market is left to its own devices.

September 17, 2019
The Guardian[2]

"The populist rewriting of Polish history is a warning to us all. Estera Flieger is a journalist with Polish newspaper Gazeta Wyborcza. Thirty years after communism ended, Poland's past is again being manipulated for political motives."

Commentary: We, the readers, are given a front row seat for a *Gazeta Wyborcza* journalist to explain how populists are behaving like children. We are asked to understand that this also refers to how the communists before 1989 manipulated history. It's perhaps so obvious to the author that it simply goes without explaining. Populists are the bad ones, who cheat, take shortcuts and are unhealthy. Brits reading *The Guardian* will simply nod in agreement; we have our own populists at home, and we know what they can get up to. We are the adults and the populists are the children. We are morally superior, better, more in touch; we can take the truth, however painful it is.

---

2   Estera Flieger, "The Populist Rewriting of Polish History is a Warning to us All," *The Guardian*, September 17, 2019.

September 21, 2019
The Independent[3]

"Left-of-center parties have not always been marginalised from Poland's politics: as recently as 2001 the Democratic Left Alliance, the largest party in today's Lewica coalition, dominated the Sejm and led the country's government..."

Commentary: This sentence shows a rather alarming absence of historical awareness. The SLD was the postcommunists' party, a party that held power for eight of the first 16 years of post-communism. It was the direct descendent of the workers' party, or PZPR, that ruled for 40 years. The idea that it had any genuine social democratic idealism is a bitter irony of the transition in Poland. In fact, the whole idea of a left in a postcommunist country is one that requires a huge amount of unpacking. The transition to capitalism was in fact driven in large part by the acquisitive character of the old communist networks.

"A series of corruption scandals and the appeal of right-wing populist parties gutted their vote and has left them marginalized..."

Commentary: Treating the election as somehow simply about left-right choices, as if transposing the notion of Labour versus Conservative might work.

"Today the party relies largely on the 'residual' votes people associated with the former communist regime, a significant voting bloc."

Commentary: There is nothing here about the new left forces, Razem and Wiosna, about the Leftist part of the Solidarity movement, about trade unions, about how 'populism' stole much of the language of the Left.

October 1, 2019
The Financial Times[4]

"How Poland's wild ride out of communism remains an election fault line. (...) Leszek Balcerowicz and a group of advisers..."

---

3   Jon Stone, "Socialists set to make comeback in Polish elections next month" *The Independent*, September 21, 2019.
4   James Shotter, "How Poland's Wild Ride out of Communism Remains an Election Faultline," *Financial Times*, September 30, 2019.

Commentary: Who were these advisors and where did they come from? Do we not need to mention Jeffrey Sachs, IMF conditionality and other geopolitical forces at the time? Balcerowicz was a hate figure for many Poles in the 1990s. But we are told that, like during Thatcher's era in the UK, the costs of success are high.

"In the decades since, Poland's economy has almost trebled, and the country is in the grip of a multiyear boom."

Commentary: The individual brilliance of one-man triumphs?

"Yet Mr Balcerowicz's reforms remain a topic of heated debate."

Commentary: But wait, is our hero blemished?

"For many Poles, the transition brought opportunities that would once have been inconceivable..."

Commentary: The ungrateful sods.

"'A typical politician would have been afraid of protests. But I was most afraid that the dose of change would not be enough,' recalled Mr Balcerowicz..."

Commentary: Demonstrating the kind of technocratic logic for which he was in parts detested. Our hero displays the lack of empathy and understanding characteristic of a professor of economics educated in communist Poland and sent to the U.S. to study capitalism.

"The plan worked... But the chaos of Poland's transition also created losers."

Commentary: We are told the plan worked (hurrah), but, alas! Those losers again. 'Operation a success, patient dead' syndrome?

"On the left and in PiS, critics argue that the pace and extent of the reforms left too many people behind and allowed foreign investors to gain too much control over the Polish economy."

Commentary: I hear a "but" marching through the thickets.

"The focus on the growth of material inequality ignores the fact that the transition reduced the 'huge inequalities of power' that existed in the socialist dictatorship, he said (...) The decision to import foreign capital was both necessary, given that Poland lacked the domestic means to fund its economic reconstruction, and beneficial as it also led to a huge technology transfer..."

Commentary: We had no choice, guv.

"PiS, which melds deep social conservatism with big-state economics, has made an appeal to those who feel that they lost out in the transition a recurring theme in its four years in power, and many see its social spending programmes as the key to its dominance..."

Commentary: Losers always looking for excuses. The onus is on them. A certain passive-aggressive attitude. Social spending is a magic trick, an illusion. But never fear, like all illusionists, PiS will finally be found out, the truth will win out.

"Mr. Balcerowicz, however, is skeptical. He puts PiS's victory in 2015 down to the fluke that a coalition of leftwing parties narrowly missed getting into parliament, and the refugee crisis that PiS exploited to whip up fear among Polish voters. He attributes its continued success to a combination of economic good luck, relentless propaganda from the state media, and support from the church. No systematic forces working in Polish society..."

Commentary: The question asked by the author of whether the democratic institutions created during Poland's transition could have been better designed to withstand a government bent on removing checks on its power, betrays a real crisis of liberal idealism and a fearfulness that something fundamental is changing. If only we had better prepared for the barbarians with more gates and higher walls?

October 3, 2019
The Financial Times[5]

"Daughter of political dynasty woos Polish opposition. (...) On a campaign stop in a sparse village schoolroom—decorated with sagging balloons and pictures of caterpillars—Malgorzata Kidawa-Błońska, one of the leaders of Poland's opposition, has drawn an audience consisting mainly of the local rural women's association and a heckler who is slightly the worse for wear."

Commentary: "We" are inviting Malgorzata Kidawa-Błońska in for a chat, to sound her out, see what's she's made of. And to set the scene, we highlight what she is up against. Cue a drunk. In rural Poland?

"'I am here to mobilize you,' the prime ministerial candidate of the Civic Coalition tells the gathering in Przychody, in Poland's poorer east."

Commentary: We are in the dirty, wild, dangerous "East." Almost a war zone.

"While most of Ms Kidawa-Błońska's audience listen politely as she discusses local issues, she is soon challenged on her party's record. 'You've just come

---

5   James Shotter, "Daughter of Political Dynasty Woos Polish Opposition," *Financial Times*, October 2, 2019.

here now because you need support,' the heckler cuts in. 'Where were you 10 years ago?'"

Commentary: He's got a point. How our brave maiden handles this, we aren't told. Perhaps the man is ejected from the hall? We don't know.

"Opposition leaders hope more Poles will be wooed by Ms. Kidawa-Błońska's warmer manner and her political ancestry: one of her great-grandfathers was president in the 1920s, and another was prime minister."

Commentary: She's got some serious blood, perhaps even some breeding. Our brave reporters talked with a PO colleague:

"'She is a woman with great charisma, great charm, and she has those very unique roots,' said the unnamed politician. 'Her great grandparents were very important politicians...outside Warsaw we do not have that many who can do that.' (...) To underscore the soft-spoken Ms Kidawa-Błońska's non-confrontational approach—a rarity in Poland's febrile politics—the 62-year-old former parliamentary speaker's campaign bus is emblazoned with a picture of her hugging another woman, and the slogan: 'Co-operation, not quarrels.'"

Commentary: She's nice and that's nice.

"Crucially, Civic Coalition is also still dogged by criticism that it did not do enough for less well-off Poles, especially in Poland's east, during former prime minister Donald Tusk's two terms in office."

Commentary: Umm, yes, but isn't that the point?

"Joanna Sawicka, an analyst at Polityka Insight, says Civic Coalition has struggled to communicate its policies to voters. 'The program of the Coalition is very thin, they don't say what kind of state they would like to create. There is no diagnosis,' she said. (...) Others think the problem goes deeper and stems from a fundamental indecision over whether to try to beat PiS by winning back moderate conservative voters, or instead to try to consolidate Poland's liberal forces."

Commentary: PO had thin policies and didn't communicate them well? It seems odd that so much hope was then placed on the party and its candidate for prime minister.

October 5, 2019
The Observer[6]

"Family, faith, flag: the religious right and the battle for Poland's soul"

Commentary: This article moves the narrative explanation a step forward, if you like, by recognizing that, while:

"[T]he rightwing PiS party may be authoritarian and anti-LGBT, its welfare programmes have transformed the lives of low-income Poles."

Commentary: The good old *Observer* makes its way down south, to meet Augustyn Ormanty in Kalwaria Zebrzydowska, where:

"photographs with Pope Saint John Paul II hang on the walls."

Commentary: Well they would, wouldn't they?

"'It's unprecedented what is being done on social welfare,' he says. 'This has gone not just to families, the government is taking care of the disabled and the elderly too...PiS is fighting the good fight in the battle to defeat the secular liberal values that have corrupted western European nations and which are threatening to do the same in Catholic Poland.'"

Commentary: We are not sure he actually put it this way, but we see the picture through our reporter's eyes, and he reaffirms what we all agree, namely that secular liberal values are a good thing.

"PiS exploited Europe's refugee crisis in 2015. This time around, LGBT rights seem to have been chosen as a useful anti-liberal battleground..."

Commentary: Well, it never really went away and the rise of Biedron and Wiosna and the persistent criticisms of PiS during 2019 on LGBT+ issues were also part of the process.

"The atmosphere has turned toxic. Poland is bitterly divided between Catholic conservatives, who dominate small towns like Kalwaria and the rural areas, and secular liberals, who hold sway in the big cities such as Warsaw and Kraków. The old, the less-educated and the less-wealthy are more likely to vote for PiS. Wealthier Poles and the young gravitate to the liberal PO coalition or the leftwing United Left..."

Commentary: The boilerplate analysis, written circa September 2015 and repeated ad nauseum thereafter. It fits the "left behind" and "the losers"

---

6   Julian Coman, "Family, Faith, Flag: The Religious Right and the Battle for Poland's Soul," *Observer* special report on *The Guardian*, October 5, 2019.

narrative, the Brexit-inflected narrative that, well, progress comes at a cost and only the fittest survive. When this explanation is adopted, the list of grievances really just writes itself:

"[T]he independence of the Polish judiciary, public media, women's reproductive rights, corruption, a director of a museum removed, government's refusal to form a commission to investigate revelations of pedophilia in the church."

Commentary: But then something unusual happens. Our text departs from the script. It goes and speaks with Father Jacek Prusak, a Jesuit priest and professor at the Ignatian Academy in Kraków.

"Although 'a turbulent priest,' he is one of a small minority of clerics willing to challenge the hand-in-glove cooperation of church and state under the present dispensation. (...) 'They do not conform to traditional left-right divisions,' says Prusak. 'It's culturally rightwing and economically leftwing. The welfare policies can be seen as within the spirit of Catholic social teaching.' Nevertheless, religion, he says 'is being used as a weapon in PiS's culture wars. The party picks the aspects of church teaching that it prefers.'"

Commentary: One of the very rare thoughts on the concept of populism:

"According to the sociologist Radosław Markowski, 'populism is a lazy catch-all description of this. This is authoritarian clientelism.' (...) Also interesting is the voice of Piotr Janusiewicz, the PiS-backed president of the town council in Kalwaria. He says the impact of social spending has been 'decisive...Self-esteem has been restored to those people in need.'"

Commentary: Welcome, then, Ewelina Gastol, a 33-year-old nurse and mother of two small children, who lives in the village of Kryspinów, near Kraków. She says that the new money available has

"changed things for her and her husband, a fireman."

More, please. Then Magda Dropek, an LGBT+ activist, standing for election in Kraków. Running on the United Left slate.

"It has to be acknowledged that they are the ones who have given money to ordinary people. They have given dignity back to a lot of people who have been forgotten in the decades of economic transformation."

Commentary: Then we have a reference to the failures of the opposition.

"PO in particular faces a credibility gap. Why, when it ran Poland between 2007 and 2014—and the current president of the European Council, Donald Tusk, was prime minister—did it fail to deliver anything remotely similar?"

Commentary: Adding to the quasi-Keynesian narrative:

"The huge level of state spending appears to have boosted rather than damaged Poland's finances. Levels of private consumption have gone up significantly, fueling a stellar growth rate last year of 5.1%, which far outstrips the eurozone."

October 8, 2019
Financial Times[7]

"Poland's ruling party pledges big minimum wage rise to woo voters."

Commentary: And back to business and the business of effectively buying votes.

"Business leaders agree that Poland's economic model should rely less on cheap labour, but there are many questions whether raising the minimum wage will achieve this."

Commentary: Well, it's quite blatant, we know that business leaders' interests are the focus here.

"Poland's ruling PiS government is offering a sharply higher minimum wage if it wins re-election on Sunday—renewing its vote-winning platform of support for the poor but setting the country's businesses on edge."

Commentary: "The poor"? "Business on edge"? "The poor" is such a strange term to use, for several reasons. But there appears to be an intrinsic assumption here that there is somehow no structural connection between the interests of business and the plight of the poor.

"The conservative-nationalist party swept to power four years ago with a promise to dramatically expand public welfare spending. This time, it says the minimum monthly wage would increase. The party's leaders claim this will provide a fairer deal for workers and foment radical change in the model that has powered Poland's economy for the last three decades."

Commentary: "Workers" and the "poor," "a fair deal," "fomenting radical change" in what has been a success. Bring on the experts:

"According to Alicja Defratyka, senior analyst at Spotdata, the lowest wage will rise to about 60% of the average wage in 2023. 'For sure there will be inflation, some lay-offs (...) and also bankruptcies of some small companies, because they won't be able to pay the [higher] wages,' she said. (...) Other economists argue

---

7   James Shotter, "Poland's Ruling Party Pledges Big Minimum Wage Rise to Woo Voters," *Financial Times*, October 8, 2019

that PiS's plans would simply encourage companies in low-value parts of the economy to replace workers with mechanization."

Commentary: I am sure she did. But it does sound like a threat. The choices are clear and sensible folk will understand. Are we, the readers, being asked if there is no real need for change?

October 8, 2019
The Guardian[8]

"Poland's drift to right divides young male and female voters"

Commentary: A genderized Poland, again, a thread in the narrative that makes an intermittent entry. We start with Jolanta Banach, a leftwing candidate, who has noticed a recurring pattern, namely:

"[A] significant divide between young men and women in their political views, with men under 30 more likely to support nationalist parties and hold far-right views, and women much more liberal or leftwing in their outlook."

Commentary: We know by this time, a week before polling, that PiS is on course to win, the question being by how much. The first sentence draws us into a position of preparing ourselves to lose, but padding our disappointment with the knowledge that demographics, again, are on "our" side.

"The split manifests itself along many lines: countryside versus cities; the poorer east against the more affluent west (...) It was long thought that gender did not play much of a role, with PiS even drawing slightly more support among women than men in the 2015 elections..."

Commentary: By whom? Oh, I see, by Krzysztof Pacewicz, a columnist for *Gazeta Wyborcza*, again.

"Among women the most popular answer was the climate crisis, while among men it was 'gender ideology and the LGBT movement'"

Commentary: The normative aspect is clear: *The Guardian*'s job is to tell us Brits that Poles, or at least some of them, are as advanced as us. All we have to do is encourage those ones and all will be well.

---

8   Shaun Walker, "Poland's Drift to Right Divides Young Male and Female Voters," *The Guardian*, October 8, 2019.

October 8
BBC Online News[9]

"LGBT+ rights have become the single biggest cultural issue in Poland's election campaign ahead of Sunday's vote. In the eyes of Jarosław Kaczyński 's national-conservative party and the Catholic Church, those rights are a threat to traditional Polish families and values."

> Commentary: Frames the issue as expected, the lines set by PiS. It then equates LGBTQ and migrants:

"Mr Kaczyński likes to identify threats to Polish society - during the election campaign four years ago, he said Middle Eastern migrants might bring 'parasites and protozoa' to Poland. This time around, according to Mr Kaczyński, the threat comes from LGBT+ people and from Europe, where families can have 'two mummies or two daddies', he said."

> Commentary: The narrative is clear. But the story is following a well-trodden path, and one set by a combination of PiS's narrative and PO's decision to stand on this terrain.

"'Christianity is part of our national identity, the [Catholic] Church was and is the preacher and holder of the only commonly held system of values in Poland," he said. 'Outside of it we have only nihilism.' (...) Senior Catholic Church figures have gone further, most notably the Archbishop of Krakow, Marek Jedraszewski, who on numerous occasions has identified the 'LGBT lobby' and 'gender ideology' as the new threat to Polish freedom following the end of communism in 1989, calling it 'totalitarian' and a 'great threat to our freedom...'"

> Commentary: Jedraszewski again, the bogeyman. Then on to the ordinaries:

"In the beautiful, medieval city of Torun, birthplace of the astronomer Copernicus, chef Mariusz Godlejewski rejected the notion that he was a threat. During more than a decade living in Ireland, Mariusz married his long-term partner Bartosz before the couple returned to their homeland last year. Godlejewski believes it is only a matter of time before things do change but finds the tone of political debate depressing..."

> Commentary: We are invited to empathise with Mariusz. A tenderized Poland. Plays into both PiS's defence of Poland's 'good name' and the

---

9   Adam Easton, "Polish election: Leader targets gay rights as threat to society," *BBC News*, October 8, 2019.

western media's love affair with the Poland damsel in distress narrative.
Prepare the *nut graf*, with a touch of hope:

'Poland remains more socially conservative than many countries in Western Europe but attitudes to LGBT+ issues are changing.'

Commentary: Then the baddies. He's behind you. Booo!

"Underneath a statue of Copernicus in the city center, a small counter demonstration gathered before the equality march. There were several members of the far-right National Radical Camp, holding their green and white flags emblazoned with a falanga sword, which is associated with fascism. Organiser and teacher Radoslaw Duch said. 'We don't want to arrest them, we don't want to get rid of them. They have to be aware they are sinners. Me as a Catholic person, I want to show them a better path of their life,' he added."

Commentary: What a loser. A man, a failed man, an uneducated man. Poland deserves our sympathy.

October 10, 2019
The Guardian[10]

Editorial: The Guardian's view on Poland's election: church-sanctioned bigotry casts a shadow. (...) Pope Francis must despair of Poland. The church was a bastion of resistance to the communist regime, the country's identity is still bound up with its Catholicism, even as much of the rest of Europe secularizes at pace. The religious wing of a xenophobic, homophobic government. The Catholic faith is being used to bully and marginalize the vulnerable. Europe will face four years of grappling with the confrontational, illiberal politics of one of its larger member states. It shames the Polish Catholic church that it has given a theological stamp of approval to the kind of hateful bigotry which is nowhere to be found in the Christian gospels."

Commentary: An air of righteousness adds to the binary nature of the dialogue. *The Guardian* is wagging its finger at a foreign government. The onus is on them to explain why they do not abide by our rules. There is no recognition that our rules are not perceived as universal and unproblematic.

---

10   "Editorial: *The Guardian*'s View on Poland's Election: Church-sanctioned Bigotry Casts a Shadow," *The Guardian*, October 9, 2019.

October 10, 2019
The Guardian[11]

"Poland's election may be the dawn of a more tolerant future"

Commentary: Throwing the kitchen sink at LGBT+, accepting the terrain upon which the election campaign was set earlier in the year. Then we get wishful thinking.

"PiS' conservative anti-LGBT agenda is alienating moderate Poles. PiS's platform is to provide a strong Catholic moral foundation to a program of social benefits, and it has clearly paid off over the past four years. But this runs a risk of alienating more moderate voters. It has never pretended to be a party that works for everyone: instead it has identified a specific base of supporters and cornered their vote through smart, if occasionally cynical, campaigning and largely delivering on electoral pledges."

Commentary: Which parties don't do that?

"Schemes such as the 500 Plus child benefit package, offering 500 złoty (£103) each month for every child after the family's first, have genuinely improved the lives of people in parts of the country that previous Polish governments had stopped even paying lip service to, and have begun to more evenly distribute the country's growing wealth for the first time since EU accession in 2004."

Commentary: Yes, we arrive at the point after all.

"By contrast, a great deal of energy and positivity has been generated by the resurgent left, following campaigns by both the women's rights movement against a tightening of abortion laws and, more recently, the LGBT equality marches. (...) Razem's work deserves respect in a country where far-right Christian terrorists were recently arrested for planning bomb attacks on Lublin's equality march, and where Biedron himself has experienced various acts of homophobic violence. (...) Not that PiS will be worried (...) but therein may lie its ultimate downfall. The party's enormous success risks instilling the same kind of complacency that brought down its opposition four years ago."

Commentary: Wishful thinking again. But there is always 'the demographics.'

---

11   Stefan Bielik, "Poland's Election may be the Dawn of a More Tolerant Future," *The Guardian*, October 10, 2019.

October 11, 2019
The Guardian[12]

"'Cruder than the Communists': Polish TV goes all out for rightwing vote"
   Commentary: We dive straight in, with the headline and lead providing us with a well-trodden framing device.
"According to a program on national broadcaster TVP's news channel, the KOD protesters had a secret agenda guided by a hostile foreign power. The scenes on the street, it said, were a 'street revolt to bring Islamic immigrants to Poland' and backed by EU leaders as revenge for the refusal of PiS to accept migrants under a European relocation scheme. (...) Another program on the channel described opponents as 'defenders of pedophiles and alimony-dodgers.'"
   Commentary: Now for the explanation, namely, that PiS uses such language.
"Such language has been par for the course since PiS passed legislation to give itself direct control of the public broadcaster. (...) It has also repeatedly claimed the opposition is intent on impoverishing ordinary Poles by rolling back welfare programs and deliberately negotiating a less generous financial settlement from the EU."
   Commentary: We are asked to believe this is not the case, without evidence or context.
"An analysis of the content of TVP's flagship evening news program by Poland's Society of Journalists found that in the two weeks before the May European elections, of the 105 items about the polls, 69 items were focused on PiS, of which 68 were classified as positive and one as neutral. Every one of the 33 items about the opposition was negative."
   Commentary: Again, no context, no analysis. PiS believed the narrative needed to be changed, was explicit about that, and that was what it did.
"A study by the Council for the Protection of the Polish Language found that TVP was systematically portraying the ruling party in a positive light. Items relating to PiS routinely used words such as 'reform,' 'sovereign,' 'strong,' 'hero,' and 'patriotic,' while items about the opposition tended to deploy words such as 'shocking,' 'scandalous,' 'provocation' and 'putsch.'"
   Commentary: Yes, all true and all horrible, but why not use the same methodology to analyze the other side? "Business anxious," "the poor," "bribery,"

---

12   Christian Davies, "'Cruder than the Communists': Polish TV goes all out for rightwing vote," *The Guardian*, October 11, 2019.

"losers," etc. We hear the voices of clever chaps nodding to each other about how terrible it all is. Again, not much evidence to suggest the author recognizes the problem as it is seen by many on the other side, namely that a "liberal" agenda was propagated after 1989. True or not, it might be worth acknowledging it exists and perhaps even why.

October 11, 2019
The Financial Times [13]

"Kaczyński propels Poland's PiS towards victory (...) The veteran leader of Poland's ruling PiS party 'is an icon,' said Tadeusz Staniszewski, a retired policeman who had come to Płock to see Mr Kaczyński for the first time. 'He dedicated his whole life to Poland.'"

Commentary: Do we hear if he spoke in Polish, to whom, or if in English, was it translated, on the spot, there and then, were there other questions asked in real time?

"Since coming to power in 2015, Mr Kaczyński's party has clashed with the EU on numerous fronts, and provoked consternation at home and abroad by subordinating judges and prosecutors to politicians and turning the state media into a mouthpiece."

Commentary: So over-used it has become the truth. The "left-behind," again: "But the party has also won over many voters who felt left behind in Poland's rapid but wrenching transition to democracy with large welfare spending programmes, and others with its appeal to the country's deep-seated Catholic-infused social conservatism."

Commentary: The size and shape of welfare programs are all relative to the social contract a society chooses for itself. No?

"'[PiS is] a revolutionary party,' said Anna Materska-Sosnowska, a political scientist from the University of Warsaw, comparing the party's impact on Poland's state and society to a 'coup d'état.' 'This election is about(...) what kind of Poland we want, what vision of Poland we have.'"

Commentary: Yes, indeed it is. Please tell us what's on offer, without the binary template. But instead we get the usual "bad PiS" narrative:

---

13 James Shotter and Agata Majos, "Kaczyński Propels Poland's PiS Towards Victory," *Financial Times*, October 11, 2019.

"He launched into an attack on LGBT rights—which PiS has sought to portray as a threat to Poland's traditional family model, much as it used fear of refugees to whip up its base four years ago. (...) 'Kaczyński believed that there were many Poles, especially anti-communist activists, who were not rewarded for their fight for freedom,' said Igor Janke, a conservative author and commentator."

> Commentary: And he was right. With help from the *FT* and others. Then another journalist is brought in to speak:

"'There was a theory that what liberal elites did after 1989 was a 'Xerox modernisation' of Poland: that we just copied what was happening in the west without taking into account Polish specifics,' said Michal Szuldrzynski, deputy editor of Rzeczpospolita, one of Poland's main newspapers."

Part 2: "Some Losers"

Context: What was happening?

PiS had won the election, but narrowly lost its majority in the Senate. Britain heads for a No Deal Brexit as elections are called for December.

October 15, 2019
The Daily Telegraph[14]

"Biased State Broadcaster Left Polish Voters with Limited Choice in Election, Report Says"

> Commentary: Making an informed choice? It smells a little of closing the door after the horse has bolted.

"Poles voting in Sunday's general election had limited chances of making an 'informed choice' because of Poland's state-owned media, a leading intergovernmental organisation has said."

> Commentary: The selection of this story is interesting in itself. The bad loser syndrome. Experts rolled in:

"The report published by the Organization for Security and Co-operation in Europe (OSCE) adds weight to complaints that public radio and television have been

---

14 Matthew Day, "Biased State Broadcaster Left Polish Voters with Limited Choice in Election, report says," *The Daily Telegraph*, October 15, 2019.

reduced to the broadcasting arm of Law and Justice. (...) 'The distinct editorial bias of the media, especially the public broadcaster, and the absence of active oversight, adversely impacted the opportunity of voters to make an informed choice,' said the report."

Commentary: It's hard to measure, but one can almost hear the PiS rebuke being "scornfully" constructed as *The Telegraph*'s words are read. The world is unfair, the winners always write history, etc. And we move on to the boilerplate:

"Further accusations of bias could also add to concerns that the Central European country is back-peddling on democratic values under Law and Justice, which have been sparked by a judicial overhaul some consider a threat to the rule of law. This concern is articulated in places like this, that are read by people who, like the author, spend most of their time far away from the people that vote PiS."

Commentary: The underground discourses have gone mainstream, that is perhaps all.

"'Law and Justice is a danger to press freedom,' said Andrzej Krajewski, who co-ordinates a team monitoring public media for the Polish Journalists' Society. 'This reminds me of Martial Law journalism,' referring to the military crackdown on the Solidarity trade union in 1981..."

Commentary: The last word to an expert on the right side.

October 15
The Daily Express[15]

'The strong performance of the right-wing PiS party in yesterday's Polish general election has "disastrous implications" for the European Union, a political commentator has warned.'

Commentary: It is only *The Express,* but still worth a short mention. In the context of ongoing chaos over Brexit, the paper offers a glimmer of hope for the 'EU collapse' thesis.

"Piotr Buras, Head of the Warsaw Office of the European Council on Foreign Relations (ECFR) said: 'Europe cannot prevent Poland's or any other country's backsliding towards semi-authoritarianism, nor can it ignore the disastrous implications of such a scenario.'"

---

15   Ciaran McGrath, "EU Disaster: PiS Victory in Poland Election Delivers Massive Blow to Brussels," *The Daily Express,* October 15, 2019.

Commentary: Any other country? Any country in mind? And then the threat: "'However, if Brussels and other democratic capitals want to avoid a contamination of the EU system, they will have to apply the full range of its instruments to fend it off: including the infringement procedures against Poland before the CJEU, Article 7, rule of law conditionality of EU funds and support for civil society (...) 'Pawel Zerka, the ECFR's Policy Fellow and Senior Coordinator on European Power: 'High levels of support for PiS should not be interpreted as a sign that Poles have become nationalist or xenophobic. Rather, it reveals an effective party machine – and an ability of PiS to mobilise voters with policies based on direct social transfers. The opposition sought to frame this election around democracy, the rule of law and values of openness and tolerance.'"

October 14
BBC Online News [16]

Commentary: Template alert:
"PiS has been at loggerheads with the EU over reforms to Poland's judiciary and has also been criticised over its position on gay rights During its first term in office, the party put in place generous welfare programmes, boosting its support among poorer voters. (...) 'The PiS is finally taking care of the weakest, most vulnerable members of society,' Kasia, a 40-year-old psychologist working at a women's shelter, told AFP news agency after voting in Warsaw on Sunday. 'I've seen it first hand at work.' (...) Instead the party has reaped the rewards of its generous welfare scheme, which has benefitted millions of families. For the first time in years, it has proposed a balanced budget for next year despite economists' warnings that the scheme would ruin public finances:' exactly. 'PiS now has a reputation of a party that delivers on its promises.'"
Commentary: Template alert II:
'LGBT rights became the single biggest cultural issue ahead of the election. PiS – and the Roman Catholic Church - maintain that gay rights are a threat to traditional Polish families and values.'

---

16   Adam Easton, "A Party that Delivers: Poland Election: Ruling Law and Justice Party Win Poll," *BBC News*, October 14, 2019.

October 14, 2019
The Guardian[17]

"Rightwing PiS's grip on power weakened after it lost control of the upper house and failed to increase its majority in the lower chamber."

Commentary: So far, so good. It's not all lost. Then take comfort in the experts. "Stanley Bill, a senior lecturer in Polish politics at the University of Cambridge, asked: 'Could PiS's high-water mark have passed? Their second term is shaping up as a greater challenge than their first. Parliament will be trickier, with more parties to contest their policies from different directions.' He said the party risked 'losing momentum.'"

Commentary: Normative, wishful thinking.

"The worse-than-forecast Polish result marked a setback for eastern Europe's right-wing nationalists."

Commentary: Right-wing nationalists? A setback. Some setback. You can almost feel the deflated sense of doom across the page.

"PiS's political strategy was to combine a big increase in social spending in certain areas, made against the backdrop of a booming economy and record consumer confidence, with nationalist and traditionalist rhetoric and an uncompromising authoritarian political style that has exacerbated divisions in Polish society."

Commentary: Or redirected them. Is the economy just about luck? When PO was in government, was that luck too?

October 14, 2019
The Guardian[18]

"Election results give hope to opposition in Poland and Hungary. Analysts say tactic of cooperation against nationalist parties appears to be working."

Commentary: If it's working, why were they doing so badly?

"'It looks like this may be a small step in the right direction—but it's clear the

---

17 Jon Henley and Christian Davies, "Poland's Populist Law and Justice Party Win Second Term in Power," *The Guardian*, October 14, 2019.

18 Jon Henley, "Election Results Give Hope to Opposition in Poland and Hungary," *The Guardian*, October 14, 2019.

opposition still has an awful lot of work to do,' said Agata Gostyńska-Jakubowska, a senior research fellow at the Center for European Reform."

> Commentary: Someone obviously on our side. But again, is it wishful think-
> ing? And then our friend, the expert.

"Ben Stanley, a political scientist at Warsaw's SWPS University, said Sunday's
results suggested that when opposition parties 'work together and construct a
positive narrative, they can convincingly take on politicians who once looked unassailable...'"

> Commentary: A positive narrative is not how many would characterize the
> campaign. Enter Cas.

"Cas Mudde, a political scientist and leading populism expert at the University of
Georgia, said: 'In both Hungary and Poland the opposition seemed to understand
the fundamental challenge to liberal democracy they were facing. Strategic collaboration is crucial, particularly when the government party is gaming the system by, for example, controlling the media.'"

> Commentary: Again, defending but no vision of a future.

"The ruling party cast the election as a choice between a society of traditional Catholic values and a liberal elite that undermines family life, with critics accusing it of stoking homophobia and anti-LGBT sentiment... It was also rewarded
by poorer, mainly rural voters for the 70bn-zloty (£14bn) social and welfare programmes it has rolled out."

> Commentary: The notion is running riot that people can be bought. Tells us
> much about the mindset of the authors and their readers. And then the
> magic media trick:

"'The party had not been altogether successful in walking the tightrope between
keeping its base happy and not alienating floating voters,' he said. 'Both the blatant TV propaganda and the anti-LGBT campaign will actually have ended up putting some people off, and the net result is that PiS does not look like it will be able
to govern in the same way that it has until now,' Stanley said."

> Commentary: PiS won more votes than before and the notion of floating
> voters is so very UK.

"'This idea that has held sway for so long in Poland and Hungary, that the other side
has complete control of the discourse and all we can do is wait for them to make a
mistake, looks like it may no longer apply.' (...) A coordinated opposition with a strong
counter-narrative can cut through,' agreed Gostyńska-Jakubowska."

> Commentary: Yes, indeed, but what is it?

October 15, 2019
The Financial Times [19]

"PiS will be less dominant in Poland despite big poll win"

Commentary: PiS won, but it's not all bad.

"Jarosław Kaczyński's ruling party faces checks on its power as economic clouds gather...The conservative-nationalist party increased the number of votes it won from 5.7m in 2015 to more than 8m in 2019—a jump of 40%. Yet when the new parliament assembles, PiS will be in a weaker position than four years ago—and the party's next term in office could, paradoxically, be trickier than the last."

Commentary: Wishful thinking again. The defensive position:

"If opposition senators can co-operate, it will at least allow them to delay legislation, making it harder for PiS to ram through controversial bills in the middle of the night and at breakneck speed, as it has in the past. (...) Aleks Szczerbiak, professor of politics at the UK's University of Sussex and Agata Szczesniak, a commentator from OKO.press, an online news portal."

Commentary: The economic headwinds argument:

"The economic weather may also prove less favourable than during PiS's first term. Poland's growth rate has averaged more than 4% since 2015, and been a big factor in the government's ability to fund the welfare schemes that have underpinned its success. But in recent months the German economy has begun to slow, and Polish companies—enmeshed in the German supply chain—are starting to feel the impact."

Commentary: And then acceptance:

"Despite the challenges, however, PiS still has strong cards. It is by far the most popular party. (...) Civic Coalition, has problems of its own: it lacks a charismatic leader; has struggled to renew itself since 2015; and seems unclear whether to try to beat PiS by consolidating its appeal to Poland's liberal voters or winning back moderate conservatives..."

Commentary: Therein lies the rub.

---

19   James Shotter, "Law and Justice Will be Less Dominant in Poland Despite Big Poll Win," *Financial Times,* October 15, 2019.

October 16, 2019
Financial Times [20]

"Editorial: Poland must not slide further into illiberalism. Conservative national-ism has taken a firm hold in central Europe." The editorial board. (...) When Po-land's conservative-nationalist PiS party won elections in 2015, many western liberals saw it as a short-term aberration."

> Commentary: Western liberals is a very broad and, in many ways, contested no-tion. And many of them, us, didn't see it as a short-term aberration. Perhaps sit-ting in the *FT* offices, the kinds of liberals being referred to didn't meet the pop-ulist masses too often, perhaps only to step over them on the way to the office.

"Poland's 1990s embrace of 'shock therapy" reforms had, after all, made it one of the most vibrant ex-eastern bloc economies and an advert for the 'Europe-an project.'"

> Commentary: With or without shock therapy, Poland was likely to catch up. The type of capitalism that did emerge was, for many, then and now, far too close to the Anglo style, when a more German safety net might have worked better.

"The center-right PO, in power for eight years, had been weakened by sleaze scandals and voter ennui, but would surely bounce back."

> Commentary: Strange comment, wishful thinking.

"Civil society remained robust..."

> Commentary: Meaning Polish friends were still quite nice, the ones that spoke English in coffee shops and on social media.

"PiS, meanwhile, had masked its true nature by keeping its abrasive leader, Jarosław Kaczyński, in the wings, allowing more voter-friendly figures to front its campaign..."

> Commentary: Oh, how cunning! And not entirely true. PiS was a known en-tity. And then the usual suspects.

"Certainly, PiS has followed some of the playbook of Viktor Orban's Fidesz in Hun-gary in entrenching itself in power. One of its first acts was to neuter the con-stitutional court. (...) It has reduced public media to little more than a pro-gov-ernment cheerleader. (...) In combining Catholic-infused social conservatism

---

20   "Editorial: Poland must not slide further into illiberalism. Conservative nationalism has taken a firm hold in central Europe", *Financial Times*, October 16, 2019.

with generous family subsidies, it has found a formula that resonates, especially with voters who felt left behind in the wrenching post-communist transition. Its 500-zloty ($128) per month child benefit scheme boosted both incomes and esteem among the less well-off..."

Commentary: The language oozes paternalism.

"Helped by continuing strong growth, it confounded many economists' predictions that it would be unaffordable."

Commentary: The *FT* simply couldn't believe that anything other than market forces works. And then the language of social conservatism:

"The ruling party goes beyond merely embracing conservative family values, and rallies support in part through ugly efforts to stoke fears of 'others': Muslim immigrants in the 2015 campaign, LGBT rights this year. (...) Western capitals fear Warsaw will push on with contentious legal reforms, attempt to rein in privately owned news outlets, and tinker with electoral rules."

Commentary: Do they?

"PiS would do better to build on its popularity while trying to heal the country's divisions. Mr Kaczyński has framed his goal as correcting and completing a revolution that went off-track."

Commentary: Explain please.

"It would be a tragedy if Europe's sixth-largest economy, cradle of the 1989 anti-communist uprisings, were to slide back from democracy into a form of one-party rule..."

Commentary: A child again, not quite grown up. Looking at Westminster and the failures of British democracy, this is somewhat ironic.

Oct 17, 2019
The Economist[21]

"Zlotys for tots win lots of votes: Poland's ruling populists win again. Lavish welfare and a divided opposition keep PiS in power."

Commentary: Headline says it all really. The plebs are being bought off. Even if true, still clutching at straws.

---

21 "Zlotys for Tots Win Lots of Votes: Poland's Ruling Populists Win Again," *The Economist*, October 17, 2019.

Part 3: Post-Mortem

October 21
The Guardian [22]

"Poland's rightwing populist win should be a wake-up call for democrats world-wide"

> Commentary: Mudde is the go-to guy on populism. His analyses are insightful, yet practical: how to combat the populists.

"The victory of the ruling rightwing PiS party calls into question ideas common in the fight against populism. Mudde argues that PiS victory calls into question at least four received ideas common in the fight against rightwing populism. (...) 'Rightwing populism will fail in government' and 'Rightwing populist parties moderate in government'. In the eyes of populists, elitism is not about your official position, or even personal class background, but about your morality.'"

> Commentary: Not sure who thought that in 2015. PiS was well organized, had a coherent plan, bridged the business-people divide, didn't frighten off foreign capital.

"While PiS campaigned on a rather moderate and vague platform in 2015...it implemented a much more radical program in government."

> Commentary: And?

"High(er) turnout hurts rightwing populists: Higher turnout did not bring the expected result, a lower score for the rightwing populists. In fact, not just the radical right PiS did better; so did Konfederacja, a 'confederation' of mostly extreme-right forces under the leadership of the anti-democratic misogynist Janusz Korwin-Mikke. (...) All of this should give liberal democrats pause... Consider what we're seeing: rightwing populists' open attacks on liberal democracy do not deter their supporters, particularly in highly polarized societies."

> Commentary: Template stuff. Little understanding of the discursive elements. The appeal of the masses, the need for structural change, the mass emigrations. The article asks us to consider how we can combat the baddies and save our system of civic governance.

---

22   Cas Mudde, "Poland's rightwing populist win should be a wake-up call for democrats worldwide," *The Guardian*, October 21, 2019.

October 24, 2019
The Guardian[23]

"How liberalism became 'the god that failed' in eastern Europe"

Commentary: How did it all go so wrong? A valiant effort by *The Guardian*.

"After communism fell, the promises of western liberalism were never fully realized—and now we are seeing the backlash (...) The origins of populism are undoubtedly complex. But they partly lie in the humiliations associated with the uphill struggle to become, at best, an inferior copy of a superior model."

Commentary: Hurrah, some context, some attempt to understand the emotional, the collective. But a superior model? Oh, come on, please!

"Discontent with the 'transition to democracy' in the post-communist years was also inflamed by visiting foreign 'evaluators' who had little grasp of local realities. (...) a nativist reaction in the region, a reassertion of 'authentic' national traditions allegedly suffocated by ill-fitting western forms. (...) Imitation of the west as a well-travelled pathway to normality. But reformers underestimated the local impediments to liberalisation and democratisation and overestimated the feasibility of importing fully worked-out western models. (...) The post-national liberalism associated with EU enlargement allowed aspiring populists to claim exclusive ownership of national traditions and national identity. (...) But a subsidiary factor was the un-argued assumption that, after 1989, there were no alternatives to liberal political and economic models. This presumption spawned a contrarian desire to prove that there were, indeed, such alternatives."

Commentary: An excellent article, touching all the key points, but again only really flirting with perhaps the critical issue, the liberal west's systemic disparagement of alternatives after 1989.

October 26, 2019
The Guardian[24]

"Not everything is perfect—as reflected in political flux—but the region is wealthier and healthier than ever before."

23 Ivan Krastev and Stephen Holmes, "How Liberalism Became 'the God that Failed' in Eastern Europe," *The Guardian*, October 24, 2019.

24 Shaun Walker, "'This is the Golden Age': Eastern Europe''s Extraordinary 30-year Revival," *The Guardian*, October 26, 2019.

Commentary: We'll meet again, don't know where, don't know when... Not everything is perfect, no. Cue setting, something positive:

"A new business development on the outskirts of Gdańsk, filled with the offices of multinational companies. (...) The economic demands of Solidarity, which had sprung up at the huge Gdańsk shipyard and was led by Lech Wałęsa, rippled through Poland and then the rest of central and eastern Europe during the 1980s."

Commentary: Solidarity had many and diverse demands. The success thesis:

"A range of metrics demonstrate that the transition from communism to capitalism has been a remarkable success: economic spurts of growth that any region of the world has ever experienced. People live longer, healthier lives. Air quality is better, and individuals are on average twice as wealthy."

Commentary: Stir gently and add your favourite source:

"'This is the golden age for the region,' says Marcin Piatkowski, a Polish economist."

Commentary: And then, the poor will always be with us:

"Such optimism often feels misplaced, given that many people in the region still feel left behind."

Commentary: Really? And cue Balcerowicz, again.

"The 'shock therapy' reforms that speedily pushed Poland and other countries in the region into capitalism have come in for criticism, but Leszek Balcerowicz, the architect of Poland's reforms, still believes they were the best option for the country in the circumstances. 'If you move fast from a bad system to a better one, you release new forces for growth,' he says.

Commentary: And then recognition that capitalism has its downsides too:

"Additionally, while the statistics may show that on average even the poorest parts of society are better off than they were 30 years ago, this is little comfort to those in former industrial areas or rural regions where there is an overwhelming sense of decay; indeed, that decay can feel ever more pressing when compared to the progress experienced in shinier areas."

Commentary: But...

"But in place of the hulking shipyard, a number of smaller companies building yachts have sprung up in Gdańsk and elsewhere on Poland's Baltic coast, and many of them have become successful. (...) Going forward, the key will be moving away from an economic model of western European countries outsourcing production to the east, and towards one that sees ideas and innovation developed inside the region."

October 30, 2019
The Guardian[25]

"Democracy is under attack in post-Wall Europe – but the spirit of 1989 is fighting back"

Commentary: We, the readers, know what to expect from Timothy.

"Thirty years after the fall of the Berlin Wall and Europe's velvet revolutions, a new generation is standing up to the populists..."

Commentary: So, he starts, straight off the bat: bad populists, but there is hope.

"Imagine someone who had witnessed the liberation of western Europe in 1945 returning in 1975, only to find the dictators coming back. That's rather how it feels revisiting central Europe 30 years after the velvet revolutions of 1989."

Commentary: Really? Some people actually lived there all that time, not in some odd abstract way, visiting the good and the kind, the noble, but the rough, the small towns where things don't work so well, where the trains are late or non-existent, where an avocado is an exotic experience.

"At a rally in Gdańsk in June, I heard European council president Donald Tusk call on his fellow Poles to learn from the example of the Solidarity movement of the 1980s in opposing the country's nationalist populist PiS party government. Yet PiS triumphed again this month in a general election."

Commentary: Why these two things are brought together is unexplained.

"The future triumph of anti-liberal authoritarianism is no more inevitable than was the future triumph of liberal democracy."

Commentary: Umm, yeah.

"No wonder commentators are rushing to paint a chiaroscuro picture: from yesterday's glorious light to today's encircling darkness."

Commentary: Commentators like Garton Ash?

"Overstatement is often felt to be essential to get your voice heard in an overcrowded internet marketplace of ideas, and so we read of the coming death of democracy, a new age of the dictators, and so on. This is simplistic and shortsighted. Our mistake after 1989 was not that we celebrated what happened in central Europe as a great triumph for freedom, democracy, Europe and the west. It was all of that. Our mistake was to believe that it was the new normal, the

---

25   Timothy Garton Ash, "Democracy is Under Attack in Post-Wall Europe – but the Spirit of 1989 is Fighting Back", The Guardian, October 30, 2019,

direction history was travelling. Now we are in danger of making the same mistake, only in the other direction. (...) Strictly speaking, 'illiberal democracy' is a contradiction in terms, like fried snowballs. However, the term is useful to describe the condition of a democracy that is being eroded, but has not been completely destroyed."

Commentary: Having accused some of overblowing the end of the world thesis, he immediately calls on a rather hyperbolic term himself.

"Inevitably, the focus of most writing about this 30th anniversary, including my own, has been on the question: 'what has gone wrong?'"

Commentary: For many that is not the question.

"But if the post-Wall generation in central Europe fights for the liberties it has grown up with, and the EU starts standing up for democracy in its own member states, there is every reason to believe that the 40th anniversary, in 2029, will again give us cause for celebration."

Summary

Fusion of news and commentary: The wall, Chinese or otherwise, that separates news from comment and analysis in newspapers is quite thin. Often the stretch of an arm over a desk or dividing wall in an office. Sometimes the divide sits within the same human being, one day news, the next a feature. The commentary and analysis are informed by news written by the same people. Let me see, whom to consult on this piece. Am I available? Commenting on and analysing things (facts) that are established by a series of news reports that use similar discursive devices to frame the conversation is pernicious, of course.

Fact and source selection: Framing debates, controlling narratives, exercising a performative and political function. *Gazeta Wyborcza*, old friends, the liberals and the conservatives at work and play. A certain new elite class, a fusion of intelligentsia and new capital, manifested nowhere better than Agora and *The Guardian*.

The goal: To keep as much of the status quo as possible, but generally make us feel as if we are doing something, and are on the right side. Managing the political defeat of a certain version of Polish capitalism, of local client elites. PiS, in fact, was not very radical in its economic redistribution, its fiscal policies and relations with foreign capital. If the goal of the liberal media was to control the articulation of alternatives, it worked in many ways to circumscribe PiS's radicalism. This was, after all, the same period as Corbyn was being vilified in the UK election build up. There will always be some losers and the left behind if one assumes a shared direction, a shared project and stakeholders with equal benefits and leverage.

Chapter 10

Hiatus—the Election that Wasn't, May 2020

By the time April crawled, exhausted, into May, the Covid-19 lockdown had entered its eighth week. Wise people said things would never be the same again and, indeed, words and phrases once ghettoized in sociology seminars came into everyday use. This was the "new normal," they said. But the old normal seemed pretty much alive and kicking too.

The omens were far from auspicious. Europe's oldest primeval forest, Białowieża,[1] had just been badly burned, killing swathes of rare wildlife, drought beckoned, while the global economy teetered on a cliff edge. Poles remained in lockdown as PiS pushed ahead with May 10's presidential election. The field at this stage upon which the battle for "the PiS project" would be won or lost wasn't the election result, so much as if and when and how an election would go ahead.[2]

A worried PiS tried to rush through several citizens' bills in April. At the top of the pile was a return to a proposal to tighten already restrictive abortion rules.[3] Another proposal was aimed to curb sex education in schools,[4] while another, introduced by Far-Right activists, would have banned restitution of pre-World War Two Jewish property in Poland in cases when no heirs were alive.

---

1   In 2019 European Court of Justice ordered an end to logging in the forest, finding that it posed a clear threat to the United Nations World Heritage site. The ruling was a major defeat for PiS

2   Charlemagne, "How Hungary's Leader, Viktor Orban, Gets Away With It," *The Economist*, April 2, 2020.

3   Proposed as a citizens' initiative, the draft legislation would ban abortion if prenatal tests show serious, irreversible damage to the fetus, one of the few instances in which the procedure is allowed in Poland.

4   The "Stop Pedophilia" bill's backers sent a document to parliament: See Rhuaridh Marr, "Poland Debates Law to Ban Sex Education by Labeling Teachers as Gay Activists and Pedophiles," *Metroweekly*, April 22, 2020.

Morawiecki reiterated the election would go-ahead on either May 10, 17 or 23 by postal ballot and the idea of a change in the constitution was floated, giving Duda a 7-year term. Having already appointed supportive judges to the Constitutional Tribunal as well as the Control Committee of the Supreme Court, anything seemed possible. Lower house Speaker Elżbieta Witek on April 6 asked the Constitutional Tribunal if she could change the date of the election based solely on what she said was already in the constitution, without the latest legislation having to be passed, stuck as it was in the senate. But constitutionalists questioned if this was, well, constitutional. It seemed that management of the crisis was becoming a central part of the election campaign, or rather, the non-campaign. PiS' gradual opening of public spaces, although science-sanctioned, sometimes appeared neatly politically choreographed[5]—even weaponized—if not always successfully. For example, the lockdown seemed to be more enforced for some and less for others, with government ministers at the Smoleńsk disaster 10th anniversary wearing no masks or gloves.

A Stick to Beat the EU: The EU and others warned that holding the election under lockdown conditions would undermine democracy. Freedom House published a report noting that Poland was no longer a "consolidated democracy." But solidarity within the by now UK-less 27-nation bloc was conspicuous by its absence.[6] And as EU unity weakened, Brussels' usual targets were rolled out, the guns targeted at PiS (and Fidesz/Orbán in Hungary).

Meanwhile, the worse the constitutional crisis became, the more PiS banged its anti-EU drum, starting another round of tit-for-tat with Brussels.[7] "I am convinced that the Covid-19 crisis has made many people aware of the weakness of the EU, as well as the key role played by the nation states," Kaczyński said in April.[8] Morawiecki claimed in parliament that Poland "has not received a single cent from the EU [to fight the virus]," while Ziobro, said "the EU had compromised itself" in the crisis.

---

5   On April 27, Duda was seen chatting in a telephone conversation with Pope Francis. A Polish contingent of disinfectants would reach the Vatican in the coming days to be distributed to the needy. And back to the profane, on May 1 Duda said the government would hike unemployment benefits.

6   The European Commission said on April 24 its rules allowed individual EU countries to block coronavirus aid from going to companies based in tax havens. On April 8, Morawiecki said large companies wanting some of his government's $6 billion bailout fund must pay domestic business taxes.

7   "A Postal Vote in Poland Could Entrench Populists," *The Economist*, April 16, 2020.

8   An ECFR opinion poll in April revealed one of the deepest divides between Poles who support Duda and those who backed the opposition was in their attitudes towards Europe. "Poland's Presidential Election: Three Battles for the Future of Europe Piotr Buras," *European Council on Foreign Relations*, May 6, 2020.

Opposition from Within PiS's Bloc: With the actual opposition having decided not to contest the election, opposition within PiS and its parliamentary bloc rose to the occasion. Duda and Mazowiecki, in an unusual win for the centrist/technocratic wing within PiS, forced the expulsion of the head of public television, TVP, Jacek Kurski,[9] an ally of Kaczyński. The TVP guns soon turned on commercial television broadcaster TVN, accusing it of anti-Polonism and "fake news." [10]

Then it was the turn of Gowin, who made his power play, apparently failed and fell on his sword. A mini-act of apparent self-sabotage, but it left a public hole in the United Right's common front. There were 460 MPs in parliament and 231 needed to obtain a majority. The United Right had 235 MPs, of which 200 belonged to PiS, 18 to Agreement and 17 to United Poland. If only five Agreement MPs left the coalition to join the opposition, PiS would lose its majority. PiS enforced party discipline and secured a slim majority to put the postal election motion on the parliamentary agenda, exploiting the absence of some opposition lawmakers. But the dispute hinted at an emerging crack in the PiS-led conservative alliance. PiS then scrambled to buy Gowin's MPs' support by promising legislative gifts. Gowin meanwhile had reportedly been negotiating with opposition parties and there were suggestions he was working on a plan that would elect him as Sejm speaker, making it difficult for PiS to manage parliamentary business effectively, in exchange for helping to install an alternative government supported by opposition parties headed by a new center-right political formation, Koalicja Polska (Poland Coalition, made up of Kukiz'15 and the Polish Peasant Party, PSL).[11]

Opposition Frames its (Non-)Position: Nine former Polish prime ministers and presidents said on April 30 they would boycott the election. In a statement, the ex-leaders called on the 30 million eligible voters to boycott the vote.[12]

---

9   "Poland's TVP Public Television Rift Reveals PiS Party Split," *Deutsche Welle*, March 3, 2020.

10   In intellectual defense of PiS, "one gets the impression that the contact lists of foreign correspondents of newspapers like *Le Monde* for example, have been filled for 25 years with the same phone numbers of journalists from *Gazeta Wyborcza*." Agata Wereszczyńska, "Foreign Media Reports: Poland's Image in the Western Press," *The Warsaw Institute Review*, June 22, 2017.

11   Aleks Szczerbiak, "Will the Polish Government Collapse?" *The Polish Politics Blog: Analysis of the Contemporary Polish Political Scene*, May 4, 2020.

12   The statement was signed by former presidents Lech Wałęsa, Aleksander Kwasniewski and Bronisław Komorowski and some former prime ministers, including Ewa Kopacz, Kazimierz Marcinkiewicz, and Leszek Miller.

PO candidate Małgorzata Kidawa-Błońska called the election a "coup d'etat not only against our democracy but also against the life and health of Poles. This election will not be democratic, and the result is fixed in advance. We cannot take part or encourage Poles to take part in this farce, this election must not go ahead on May 10."[13]

In late April the outgoing head of the Supreme Court, Prof Małgorzata Gersdorf, said PiS was moving the country towards an authoritarian state.[14] Retiring after a six-year term she cited the party's determination to hold the election by postal vote and the sidelining of the state electoral commission.

Duda appointed judge Kamil Zaradkiewicz. The move also raised concern in the EU. The bloc's Values and Transparency Commissioner Vera Jourova told *Rzeczpospolita* that recommendations from the Council of Europe were for countries not to carry out "fundamental changes" to electoral rules in the year leading up to elections.

Tusk said the plan was "nothing like an election." Polish voters should boycott a presidential election out of "basic human decency," he said. "If you don't know how to act, be decent," he said, paraphrasing a quote from the late anti-communist activist, Władysław Bartoszewski.

On April 9 the ECJ ordered Poland to suspend immediately the disciplinary chamber of its Supreme Court, a body that can punish judges, and freeze a new law restricting judicial independence. Then, late on May 6, Deputy Prime Minister Jacek Sasin said the election would be held in June at the earliest. Duda and the Solidarity union, which was close to PiS, agreed a platform including a pledge to provide financial help to those who lost their jobs because of the pandemic.

The Hangover: "Kaczyński's party has made a fool of itself," *Gazeta Wyborcza* pronounced grandly on May 8, with a strong whiff of Schadenfreude.[15] "The mood in PiS circles can be summed up in two words: gigantic hangover. After repeating for weeks on end that the elections would be held on May 10 or another day in May, because this was the only solution that complied with the constitution, now it has been forced to admit that this was false. Jarosław Kaczyński had to back down... We have a government

13 "Poland: Opposition Slams Presidential Election by Post," *Deutsche Welle*, April 25, 2020.
14 Adam Easton, "Polish State Becoming Authoritarian, Top Judge Gersdorf Says," *BBC News*, April 30, 2020.
15 "Giant Hangover in the Government Camp," *Gazeta.pl*, May 8, 2020. Author?

made of plywood—and that's the nicest possible way to describe it. After all, in the last few weeks Poles have become the world's laughingstock." The second phase of the battle for the presidency had begun.

Sikorski weighed in. With the PiS beast wounded, why not, after all? "Kaczyński is trying to turn the country into a Roman Catholic dictatorship," he wrote on May 8. "He [Kaczyński] wants to create a Catholic state of the Polish nation. His vision is that of Salazar, or rather Franco, but adding strong support from the US," Sikorski told *EUobserver* in an interview. "If Hungary has become the European Union's first coronavirus autocracy, Poland looks set to be the second...Europe must not remain silent...This is not the moment for Europe to be silent. International organizations have to face up to their responsibilities."[16]

Opposition MPs then called for the dismissal of Jacek Sasin, the deputy prime minister who had been tasked with organizing the presidential election, and accused the government of risking public health for political gain. "Today we are starting the process of holding accountable those who are responsible for the embarrassment that is the presidential elections," Budka, PO's leader, said. The Left, meanwhile, submitted a notification to the prosecutors' office demanding information on whether there was a legal basis for a postal ballot.

Feeling a little beleaguered on the home front, its divisions exposed to an already irritated public, and few friends in the EU, PiS turned to the US and the Vatican for some kind of reassurance. On May 8 Duda placed a paid article in *The Washington Post*.[17] "The situation we are in today shows how much a nation-state is needed to ensure and maintain security and peace," he wrote. According to Duda, Poland had acted "quickly, aggressively and effectively to limit the spread of the disease" caused by the virus. Duda argued for "building the unity of free world countries."

Beyond the Pale?[18] Only a few days after celebrating Poland's May 3, 1791 constitution, PiS was busy trying to work out how to circumvent the present

---

16   "Kaczyński Turning Poland into 'Franco's Spain,'" *EUobserver*, May 8, 2020.

17   "Balancing National Sovereignty and International Cooperation: Conclusions from the Coronavirus Pandemic," *The Washington Post*, May 8, 2020.

18   The Pale of Settlement was a term applied to the area within the Russian Empire which was restricted to Jewish settlement. The region was established as part of imperial Russia after the introduction of a large number of Jews as a result of territorial acquisitions following the three partitions of Poland (1772, 1793, and 1795).

one. In a move that would have had dead communists smiling from their graves in admiration for its Orwellian double think, Kaczyński issued a statement late on May 6 saying the May 10 vote would be annulled once the Supreme Court had certified that the election hadn't actually happened, a feat it could only achieve after an election that wasn't going to be held, had been held.

Such a cancellation was the result of an agreement between two party leaders—Kaczyński and Gowin. "Simply put, in a democratic country, the government decided—consciously—not to organize the election of the head of state," a senior EU official in Warsaw said.[19] At the same time, while it was impossible to organize an election because of the pandemic, there was no apparent reason to declare a state of natural disaster, as provided for in the constitution.

Many observers raised their eyebrows at the confidence with which the Kaczyński-Gowin agreement anticipated a Supreme Court decision, but Kaczyński was likely betting on the fact that PiS felt it had already achieved control of the body. Schrödinger's election, *Politico* called it.[20] Trying to make the crisis out to be a positive and normal part of the democratic process, in an interview with *Gazeta Polska*, Kaczyński said it was no secret the coalition was divided. The three-party coalition had "quite a radical wing and a very moderate one, too. Friction between them is nothing new, I think," Kaczyński said.

But what was new was Morawiecki reportedly handing in his resignation in protest against rushing the election. At the May 9 Kaczyński-Gowin meeting Kaczyński declined it. Some commentators suggested that members of a conservative faction within PiS—including Ziobro—had triggered the talks simply in order to blow up the deal with Gowin as a means of forcing a government collapse, enabling Ziobro to get rid of a rival in Morawiecki.

Anyway, a few days after agreeing with Gowin, Kaczyński was already considering reneging on the deal. Influenced by Duda's electoral team and other allies, Kaczyński reportedly wanted to see if he could push for a vote on May 23.

Meanwhile, two candidates, Szymon Hołownia and PSL leader, Władysław Kosiniak-Kamysz, were gaining in opinion polls. In a poll by

---

19 Piotr Buras, head of the Warsaw office of the European Council on Foreign Relations think tank, told *Reporting Democracy* on May.13.
20 Jan Cienski and Zosia Wanat, "Poland's Schrödinger's Election," *Politico*, May 5, 2020.

IBRiS, Duda had 45% with the second most popular candidate, Hołownia had 19.5%. "It turns out that reality is not as flexible as Jarosław Kaczyński's mind," Hołownia said in a press conference on May 11.

"Hybrid" Election? As many Poles awoke to the first snow in May for several years on May 12, Gowin's relationship with his Accord colleagues in parliament appeared to have become a bit, umm, frosty. Although his fate had probably been determined the week before after he publicly challenged the might of Chairman Kaczyński, few had expected his political assassination to come so quickly and from within his own party, even if the knives may have been quietly sharpened at PiS HQ on Warsaw's Nowogrodzka street.

PiS, meanwhile was facing another, perhaps bigger, threat in the shape of Hołownia, after an IBRiS survey had given him 19.2%, second place behind Duda on 45%. As friends in his world, that of Warsaw media, were keen to reiterate, Hołownia's success lay largely in how he had played social media. "No-one can beat him on the internet," Anna Mierzyńska, an internet analyst, told *Onet*. "He emanates energy and freshness. His erudition and eloquence are conducive to listening to him," Bartosz Czupryk, specialist in image and political marketing, positively oozed.[21]

PiS Acts Before it's Too Late: Meanwhile, as if to highlight its increasingly blatant illiberal credentials and also perhaps because of rising fears that Duda was no longer a shoo in for re-election if the poll were to go to a second round, the government said it was drafting legislation obliging NGOs to declare any foreign sources of financing. Environment Minister Michał Woś told Catholic broadcaster *TV Trwam* that the ministry had set up a working group tasked with "making NGOs' finances more transparent."[22] "Poles have a right to know whether they are indeed organizations that work in the interests of Poles... Those that have nothing to hide have no reasons to be afraid," Ryszard Czarnecki, a PiS MEP, said.

EU Toothless and Tangled: Meanwhile, after judges in the German city of Karlsruhe in early May questioned the European Central Bank's authority to buy bonds to be used for quantitative easing, complicating the ECB's efforts to keep the eurozone alive, the EU's legal framework was thrown into

---

21   Magda Wrzos, "Hołownia zdobył mistrzostwo internetu. Z tym medalem goni Dudę," *Onet.pl*, May 12.

22   "Polish Government Considers Law Forcing NGOs to Declare Foreign Funding," *Reuters*, May 11, 2020.

chaos. The court in Karlsruhe had effectively overruled the ECJ in Luxembourg, which had previously given the ECB a green light.

Euroskeptics of course smirked. What, after all, had been holding back the Polish and Hungarian descent into illiberalism but the ECJ? So it was hardly surprising when Morawiecki wrote an enthusiastic letter to a German newspaper, praising the Karlsruhe verdict as "one of the most important judgments in the history of the EU" because "it was a reminder that it's member states which decide what the EU's institutions may do, not the other way around."

Wounded PiS Counters: The opposition does not recognize democracy, it blocked the elections and the government has done everything to meet constitutional deadlines, Kaczyński said on May 12 in an interview with *Gazeta Polska.*[23]

The decision as to whether Kidawa-Błońska would continue to be a candidate in the presidential election "would be made in Brussels or another place where Donald Tusk is now most often," Kaczyński claimed. "If he does not want to, and probably will not, who else can they put up? They do not have, at least in my opinion, a substitute who can change their position in a short campaign. For Tusk himself this perspective is probably not very tempting, because it has a high or even very high risk of failure. (...) In the most radical of all cases so far, it turned out that our opposition does not recognize democratic rules. It does not respect the rule of law. They did not shy away from blocking the elections for a very simple reason: they would suffer a serious defeat in them. They used the coronavirus epidemic," he said.

Kidawa-Błońska reportedly declined to withdraw from the election, even though the party leadership had put the suggestion to her. Schetyna, aiming to return as PO chief, was said to be looking for ways to keep Kidawa-Błońska in the candidacy. Schetyna had pulled her into the party rank's a few months earlier, after all. When, before the parliamentary elections in fall 2019, it turned out that Schetyna was polling very low, he appointed Kidawa-Błońska as the PO candidate for prime minister. Then, although he had promised her he would run for president, he supported Poznań President Jacek Jaśkowiak in the primaries. The new head of PO, Boris Budka, then made a pact with

---

23 "Kaczyński: uratowaliśmy możliwość przeprowadzenia wyborów zgodnie z prawem," *Onet*, May 13, 2020.

Kidawa-Błońska and promised her PO's candidacy in exchange for support in the clash with Schetyna during the PO leadership election in early 2020.

So, Farewell, then, Kidawa-Błońska: In fairness, she had never really wanted to be there, so when Kidawa-Błońska resigned it was probably with relief. Trzaskowski, and Sikorski—both Oxford alumni—were waiting in the wings. Tusk had reportedly done equally well, although Trzaskowski would fare better in a possible clash with Duda if it were to go to a second round, which was now clearly PO's hope, assuming it could unite the other opposition candidates behind its own.

Tusk had announced in late 2019 he would not run. For months, the possibility of his comeback to Polish politics had been one of the most widely discussed topics in Poland, but he said the country needed "a candidate who has not been burdened with the baggage of difficult, unpopular decisions. I have been burdened with such baggage since I was the prime minister." His popularity rating was also low, lower even than Jarosław Kaczyński's.[24]

Meanwhile, the cognitive linkage between PO and the EU was reinforced when Andreas Vosskuhle, president of the German Federal Constitutional Court, told *Die Zeit* in an interview that he no longer considered the Constitutional Court in Poland a partner. "If you want to gain absolute power in the country, then you must quickly subordinate yourself to an independent constitutional court," Vosskuhle said. "This is no longer a court that should be taken seriously, it is a dummy," he said, adding that it takes at least a generation to build an institution such as the Federal Constitutional Court, which enjoys trust. "But it would probably only take a few months to destroy them," he added.

Julia Przyłębska, president of the Constitutional Tribunal, of course didn't take kindly to the words. "The scandalous statement of the president of the German Constitutional Court is not befitting of honest public debate. I am embarrassed that a person performing such an important function speaks in such a way," she said. The Polish Embassy in Berlin, headed by Andrzej Przyłębski, husband of Julia Przyłębska, announced it would demand a correction to be included in *Die Welt*.

The Cult of Jarosław: "From our point of view, these are more or less equivalent candidates. Neither one nor the other of these gentlemen are suitable

---

24 The Amber Gold scandal, which came to light in 2012, was one of the biggest business scandals in Poland since the fall of communism in 1989.

for the position of president," Kaczyński told Polish Radio on May 15, when asked to assess Trzaskowski and Sikorski. "These gentlemen are different, but from the point of view of all Poles, it does not matter. God forbid that these people would influence the whole country. I will not describe the effects, because I do not want to be rude here."

The Supreme Court—tasked, among other things, with assessing the validity of elections—faced a battle about its future, electing a new First President after Małgorzata Gersdorf ended her mandate the previous month. But some judges accused Kamil Zaradkiewicz, the interim court president appointed by Duda, of abusing the system in a bid to force through a PiS-friendly candidate.

On May 15, Trzaskowski was elected KO candidate in the presidential election.

Kaczyński and EU Size Up: Kaczyński, when asked about the statement of Vosskuhle, said "unfortunately Germany is changing very slowly" and "until certain German attitudes towards Poland change, there will never be good relations. This is the attitude of old Prussian nationalism. I say Prussian, so as not to say something worse."

Meanwhile, Juan Fernando Lopez Aguilar, head of the justice committee in the European Parliament, said on May 15 he wanted to tighten article 7 on the rule of law in a report to be adopted as the position of the European Parliament.

TVP Gets the Ball Rolling: Public television, TVP's main news program presented the president of Warsaw as a "human defect," a reference to the failure of the Czajka sewage treatment plant in Warsaw under Trzaskowski. "Man-defect fights for the palace," appeared on the TVP info bar. "There was chaos in Warsaw, will there be chaos in Poland?" followed a moment later. Further moments later, an invited pundit, *Sieci* journalist Michał Karnowski, told TVP that Trzaskowski "had told us about the fact that the world is changing, that a new wave is starting. I hope it will not be a sewage wave." To stress the effect, TVP displayed a screen cluster assembled from statements by Trzaskowski, in which the capital's president speaks about the failure of Czajka. "TVP's timetable for the next two months: Czajka, the depravation of minors, re-privatization of Jewish property and homos" Rafał Madajczak wrote in *Gazeta.pl*.

"Your Pain is Better Than Mine": In the early part of the period that followed the constitutional crisis frenzy of early May and before the election, traditional proxy forms of discursive joisting filled the void, functioning in symbolic high definition to reproduce the culture war. First off, Polish public radio was accused of censoring an anti-government song that topped the charts. Veteran musician Kazik Staszewski's song *"Twój ból jest lepszy niż mój"* (*"Your pain is better than mine"*) was announced as the number one single on Polish Radio Trójka's music chart. The song, a collaboration with Wójtek Jabłoński, complains about the tenth anniversary of the Smoleńsk disaster on April 10, 2020, when several ruling party politicians were criticized for not observing restrictions on public gatherings while attending the memorial. The host of the Trójka chart show resigned.

Your Film is Better Than Mine: Four days later, public television, TVP aired a film by Sylwester Latkowski suggesting that several well-known celebrities had attended sex parties. The film named no names but added to an atmosphere of suspicion. Its role in the battle to distract from the fallout of the earlier film was clear.

Meanwhile, Duda appointed Justyna Kotowska from the Institute of Psychiatry and the Ombudsman for Children appointed Dr. Hab. Błażej Kmieciak as members of the state commission for clarifying cases of juvenile sexual abuse, just in case anyone had forgotten the body actually existed. These were the first signs of activity in the commission for almost eight months, since its establishment, but they showed that PiS a) cared, b) was doing something about the problem, and c) didn't need morality lessons from PO or anyone else.

Gloves Off: The soap operaization of Polish politics, actually politics everywhere, continued into June. "If Duda were to lose, would Kaczyński resort to using the court to annul the result?" the Leftist commentator Sierakowski asked on June 5.[25] Duda had already selected Małgorzata Manowska, a former PiS deputy minister, to serve as First President of the Supreme Court, the institution that would certify the election. By June 4 polls indicated the Trzaskowski effect might actually be working and a Plan B might in fact be needed.

As to distract from this whiff of foul play, Kaczyński upped the discursive ante, calling opposition MPs "rude scum" after PO chairman, Budka, was accused of talking over a speech in parliament by MP Barbara Nowacka. On the same day, PiS won a vote of confidence in parliament, a vote called by ...

---

25 Slawomir Sierakowski, "The Polish Opposition's Last Chance," *BalkanInsight*, June 5, 2020.

PiS. PiS spokeswoman, Anita Czerwińska, weighed in: "PO wants to be an arbiter of elegance, while it was PO who introduced brutality, aggression and coarseness into the public debate many years ago."[26]

Meanwhile, it was widely reported that Kosiniak-Kamysz might be joined by Hołownia in a new political grouping (potentially together with Gowin's party) to lead the opposition. PO's future was on the line and Trzaskowski started to act, unveiling a plan to eliminate the public news channel (TVP Info) and ban editorializing on all major public channels, so that they could never again be used for government propaganda. Underwhelmed was perhaps the appropriate response.

Kaczyński Locks Down on Familiar Rhetoric: "The victory of the PO (KO) candidate would mean a huge political, social and moral crisis," Kaczyński wrote in a letter to PiS members on June 9. "This huge undertaking is still ongoing and requires continuation for many years." It was such an obvious reiteration of values and reaffirmation of enemies that it didn't seem to warrant much analysis. But it was also apparently a defensive posture, falling back on tried and tested discourse. It was as if the first phase of the "revolution" still needed safeguarding, namely that the mythological framework had stalled at the first of Bouchard's hurdles, that of casting doubt on existing narratives, whether mythological or not. Some on the "other side"—of course!—sensed weakness. Some saw it as a sign that Kaczyński was in fact contemplating new parliamentary elections, in part driven by recent polls that gave PiS a 26% lead over PO.

Anyway, for the time being, Kaczyński was content to plough some existing furrows: the opposition was corrupt, anti-democratic, anti-family, anti-Polish, and had sold Poland out to foreigners. "I am addressing you at a special moment. Poland—like other countries—is struggling with a serious epidemic and economic crisis. A social crisis has also appeared in some countries," he started.

> The opposition is still defending the old system, defending the privileges of the elites, who seek to subordinate Polish affairs to foreign influences and maintain the remains of former dependencies from the time of the Polish People's Republic (communist Poland).

---

26 *Gazeta.pl*, June 5, 2020.

He delved back into the swamp, way back to 2002 in fact, and the Rywin scandal and what he called "massive manipulation."

Previously used social engineering techniques were sharpened and the lie reached such proportions that one can safely say that the media built a kind of counter-reality, a virtual world, having virtually no relation to facts. This was possible only thanks to the existence of a media monopoly of forces defending social evil.

The old rule that a lie repeated many times permeates the public consciousness and in this sense becomes the truth, is still present in the opposition's actions, even when basic human decency and national loyalty would dictate abandoning these unworthy methods of action.

The equation is of civil rights and economic rights in the following sentence is instructive: "Under the rule of PO, basic civil rights were violated, for example the sale of valuable enterprises and open plunder of ordinary citizens." The lack of clarity in the economic dimension of civil society discourses in Poland referred to elsewhere in this work was again evident here.

Tanks on Democracy's Turf:

Nevertheless, a definite advantage in this sphere still belongs to the supporters of the old system. A significant part of the courts behave like political institutions, so they are the exact opposite of what they should be. (...) The opposition does not conceal the fact that it intends to violate the constitution, as well as the law. PiS, unlike PO and other opposition parties, has never questioned democracy. However, democracy must include a sphere of agreement, including consent to abide by the law, honoring election results and basic loyalty to the nation and the state. Whoever rejects these principles becomes an anti-democratic, anti-state, anti-constitutional and, in fact, external force.

Further in the letter, the PiS leader noted that the opposition had suffered "numerous defeats" over the previous five years and had failed to regain power. "Nevertheless, it still has great potential and is able to harm not only PiS, but above all Poland."

The cognitive fusion of party and state is a commonly observed aspect of PiS discourse, but it was so apparently effortless here that one might be forgiven for wondering if the great leader himself was not believing his own propaganda.

The same applies to the constantly spread of statements about the alleged inefficiency of the PiS government in the fight against the epidemic or the inability to counteract the deepening economic crisis. (...) After the change of the PO candidate for president, a fraudulent attempt was made to convince the public that a representative of the extreme left, whose views had already found a clear expression in the way Warsaw was governed (during which he became known as an ardent supporter of LGBT ideology). He presents himself as a Catholic, a continuator of Solidarity and even a person referring to the tradition of President Lech Kaczyński.

Nationalizing Gender Discourse: Duda a week later called the promotion of LGBT rights an "ideology more destructive than communism." On June 14, he asked international media to "stop distributing fake news" after extensive coverage of a campaign speech in which he compared what he called LGBT "ideology" to Soviet-era communist indoctrination. "Yet again, as part of dirty political fight, my words are put out of context. I truly believe in diversity and equality," Duda tweeted in English, tagging media organizations including *Reuters, The Associated Press* and *The Financial Times*. But Duda a few days later said such teachings were a form of "neo-Bolshevism" in a campaign speech in Brzeg, saying his parents' generation had not fought communist ideology for decades only for Poland to face a "new ideology (of LGBT rights) that is even more destructive... Truth has become a scared little creature," Duda said.

UK Coverage: In the UK, the trickle of news coverage that wasn't Covid-19 fixated continued to be split between the pro-Brexit and pro-Johnson *Telegraph/Times* and the anti-Brexit and anti-Johnson *Guardian*, with *The Economist* and *The FT* anti-Brexit and largely pro-Johnson, to simplify. "Poland-as-news" thus played into this mix of messages, at once a figurehead for those carrying an anti-EU banner and a harbinger of the end of liberalism by those of another persuasion.[27]

---

27 Piotr Buras, "First Hungary, Now Poland: It's Time for Europeans to Speak Out Against COVID-19 Power Grabs," *Euronews*, April 15, 2020.

May 5, 2020 [28]
The Guardian

The Guardian view on Poland's presidential election: call it off.

Commentary: *The Guardian* had long since picked its side and had chosen to take the fight to populists in Warsaw, but also in London and Washington. An editorial in *The Guardian* on May 5 called on PiS to postpone the election in Poland. It is not known how this was received at PiS headquarters, if at all, but the editorial was widely reported in the Polish press. This was followed by a piece in the paper by Garton Ash:

"Liberal internationalists have to own up: we left too many people behind... In Britain, it's the Poles themselves who are the target of white working-class anger... Populists channel these widespread grievances into paranoid paths. But the grievances nonetheless have a foundation in reality and it behooves us to recognize that the causes do lie, at least in part, in free-market, globalized liberal capitalism as it has developed since its historical triumph in 1989. Yes, this is the world we liberal internationalists built—even if we didn't all have our own hands in the bankers' till."[29]

Commentary: It behooves us also, perhaps, to wonder a little about things closer to home. This was just a handful of weeks after all after Keir Starmer had replaced Jeremy Corbyn, an advocate of many of the antidotes to populism now advocated by Garton Ash, as leader of the UK's Labour party.[30]

Also, in the first round of British reporting on the election that wasn't, *The Guardian*, *The New Statesman* and *The Financial Times* got the ball rolling. Nothing particularly unexpected or new, straight news reporting, but subtle use of language to designate and in fact recreate semantic hierarchy. A casual and implicit framing of the election as one on which PiS would do whatever it took to win, in the same spirit it had adopted since 2015. We were reassured that "serious" people, defenders of human rights and opposition MPs,

---

28 "*The Guardian* View on Poland's Presidential Election: Call it Off. Editorial." *The Guardian*, May 5, 2020.

29 Timothy Garton Ash, "A Better World Can Emerge After Coronavirus: Or a Much Worse One," *The Guardian*, May 6, 2020.

30 Alex Zevin, *Liberalism at Large: The World According to the Economist*, (London: Verso, 2019), 392; Timothy Garton Ash, "The Battle for EU Membership is Lost, but a European England is Still Possible," *The Guardian*, December 14, 2019; Owen Jones, "Corbyn and Sanders May Have Gone, but They Have Radically Altered Our Politics," *The Guardian*, April 16, 2020.

were also watching. This of course places us, readers, in a position of moral superiority, with a front row seat in the theater where PiS's anti-democratic show is top of the bill.

The New Statesman piece[31] reads as if it had to be rewritten by editors in London who knew little about Poland and had to start from scratch. But weighing through complicated news about a faraway country about which they knew little was just too much. The text seems designed to keep the standard narrative pot boiling.

The Guardian piece[32] is perfunctory and slightly sarcastic. Who speaks? Who doesn't? A Leftist MP and opposition journalist running for presidency. The Leftist MP articulates the sense of the absurd that the piece implies but doesn't flesh out. Keeps the bad guys in their bad space, allows the good guys to speak.

Another Guardian piece[33] reports on one film and not the other. In relation to Poland, the UK broadsheets focused during the phony war period between the non-election and the election on political-cultural skirmishes largely on cultural issues, mirroring the discursive framework established in Poland itself. The Financial Times,[34] on May 22, for example, reported "Warsaw faces the music as Polish pop song ignites censorship row," while The Spectator on May 29 also engaged in a spot of the liberal arts.[35]

Unclear what the symbolic aspects the author refers to are, but he seemed very confident in his dismissal of the "symbolic," an area he associated with "the Left" and "progressives."

---

31 Annabelle Chapman, "Why Poland's 'Ghost Election' Sends a Warning About its Democracy," The New Statesman, May 12, 2020.
32 Shaun Walker, "Poland Holds Ghost Election with 0% Turnout," The Guardian, May 11, 2020.
33 The Guardian, May 17, 2020.
34 James Shotter, "Poland Postpones Presidential Vote after Bid to Defy Pandemic," Financial Times, May 6, 2020.
35 Ben Sixsmith, "Poland is Having its Own 'Dominic Cummings Moment,'" The Spectator, May 29, 2020. Other articles included: James Shotter, "Covid-19 puts Polish Logistics and Transport Groups to the Test," The Financial Times, May 29, 2020.

Chapter 11

Diary of British Media Coverage of Poland's July 2020 Presidential Election

Part 1: Britain's Media Picks its Polish Horse

June 12, 2020
The Guardian[1]

"Gay rights and homophobia are likely to be major issues in Poland's delayed presidential election after the frontrunner pledged to 'defend children from LGBT ideology.' (...) polls showed his lead narrowing. (...) liberal mayor of Warsaw, Rafał Trzaskowski. (...) PiS has been accused of democratic backsliding. (...) It has often hit out at gay rights and what it calls 'LGBT ideology', in rhetoric that is popular with parts of its base and the Catholic church." (...) "Government and church leaders have on various occasions compared "LGBT ideology" to communism, Nazism and the plague. (...) Marek Jędraszewski, the archbishop of Kraków, denounced foreign ideologies that he said 'undermine the institution of marriage and the family.'"

Commentary: PiS's 'conservative base' here is a loaded fantasy beloved of amateur psephologists and that new breed of sociologist-journalist. Trzaskowski is a 'liberal,' we are told, which is awkward, but let's move on. Throw in a reference to the Catholic Church and the deal is sealed. Marek Jędraszewski, the archbishop of Kraków, will do. We, good Guardianistas, read the code and know how and where the pieces fit together. Then drag

1   Shaun Walker, "Polish President Issues Campaign Pledge to Fight 'LGBT Ideology,'" *The Guardian*, June 12, 2020.

the "other side" in and the spectacle of democratic rivalry, with issues, debate, an open discursive space within which participants understand and accept standard rules, is made. It pleases us to think in these terms but adds very little other than British normative expectations onto a foreign terrain.

June 17, 2020 [2]
The Guardian

"Donald Trump will receive Poland's nationalist president in the White House, giving Andrzej Duda a probable electoral boost just four days before a presidential vote (...) In reality, the White House visit will be a coveted photo-opportunity and campaign boost for Duda. (...) PiS has been accused of eroding democratic norms in recent years (...) Duda has frequently used homophobic rhetoric during the campaign, pledging to "defend children from LGBT ideology" and comparing the LGBT rights agenda to communist dictatorship. (...) liberal challenger Rafał Trzaskowski... has been attacked by media loyal to Duda as an "extremist" for his backing of LGBT and other minority rights."

Commentary: So, it was to be liberals versus nationalists. Still not obvious what a Polish liberal or a Polish nationalist was. The article then implies cynical use of the trip to the US: an "Electoral boost." It suggests a relationship of inferiority, casually accepted, as if we can assume that is the case and perhaps even the reasons why. "In reality" tells us this is about bad faith. In fact, it is so false, we can discard the reporter's veneer of objectivity and just tell the reader that the reality is different. It is so obviously different, this is not a value judgment or opinion, but a fact.

June 19, 2020[3]
The Guardian

"Duda tweeted in English to accuse a number of media outlets, including The Guardian, of spreading 'fake news' about his views on LGBT issues. He did not clarify which reports he believed were false or taken out of context. (...) Rafał

2   Shaun Walker, "Trump Gives Poland's President Duda Pre-Election Boost with White House Invite," *The Guardian*, June 17, 2020.
3   Shaun Walker, "Polish President Scales Down Homophobic Rhetoric as Election Nears," *The Guardian*, June 19, 2020.

Trzaskowski, the liberal mayor of Warsaw.... is a slick campaigner who speaks multiple languages, but is struggling to shake off a reputation as a condescending member of the metropolitan elite and broaden his appeal in the provinces. (...) 'Of course he's talented, and he's a fully European intellectual, but that's not necessarily a recommendation in the elections,' said Adam Michnik, the veteran editor of liberal newspaper Gazeta Wyborcza, which has supported Trzaskowski's candidacy. (...) However, large swaths of Poland remain deeply conservative, and Trzaskowski has tried hard to avoid firm declarations of support for LGBT rights during the campaign."

Commentary: LGBT+ rights are morally on the "right" side, one that "we" represent and PiS wants to roll back. No need to explore or dig deeper, just find your outrageous quotes and a real person to articulate the pain and the discursive formula is ready to bake. The economy is doing badly, so focus on LGBT+. Trzaskowski is urbane, "very European," and a member of the "metropolitan elite." Reads as if the author is simply reiterating the division between these imaginary Polska As and Polska Bs. The meta narrative is now so absurd, that both sides deploy a language that parodies the others' simplification of its own narrative. Michnik's quote is an example of this. He is clearly proud of Trzaskowski, but is telling us, foreigners, that it's still 'Injun Country' out there. The reference to PiS's failure to say precisely where and when the foreign media had maligned PiS tells us a lot about the author's mindset. A touch of the colonial bully. He wants to engage this foreign leader on his own terrain with the challenge of an empirical comparative content analysis of non-Polish language media?

June 20, 2020 [4]
The Economist

"Gay 'ideology' is worse than communism, says Poland's president. (...) Facing a tough election, Andrzej Duda needs enemies. (...) ruling populist Law and Justice (PiS). (...) Liberal, pro-European Mr. Trzaskowski (...) the beginning of the end of PiS rule."

Commentary: A fairly neutral description of the events of the previous three months reframes the existing paradigm: PiS (populist/nationalist) versus

---

4   Playing the family card, *The Economist*, 20 June, 2020

PO (pro-EU/socially liberal). The notion that only populists need their enemies is again given a run off the bench. But without the demons of PiS, one is left wondering what the other side offers other than more of an old model that quite blatantly didn't work terribly well for all. How PO appeals to the floaters, those sympathetic to PiS' "anti-progressive" line on gay marriage, but who are fed up with democratic backsliding, judicial conflict, etc., is not explained. Also, there is no recognition that PiS is also pro-EU, allowing the reader to presuppose that it is a certain version of the EU that is better than others.

June 21, 2020 [5]

The Financial Times

"...the liberal mayor of Warsaw is the main challenger to Duda. (...) This gave his Civic Platform party a chance to replace its struggling candidate Malgorzata Kidawa-Blonska, whose support had withered into single digits."

> Commentary: the same Kidawa-Błońska who the *FT* hailed as the soft-spoken antidote to PiS?

Ben Stanley, associate professor at SWPS University in Warsaw: 'The stakes are high. Since 2015, the conservative-nationalist PiS has been able to rule largely unfettered, buttressed by Mr. Duda's support for its often controversial agenda. An opposition president, armed with the office's veto powers, would be a check on the ruling party—and Mr. Trzaskowski has made this one of his main selling points. Duda is not independent and in this day and age, we need a strong president who is going to control the monopoly of the government,' he said in an interview with The Financial Times.

> Commentary: "We"?

"PiS promised people a strong state ... but we are now seeing that it didn't materialise. (...) Duda has the public media squarely behind him (...) he's got that [government] machinery behind him."

> Commentary: The lack of a strong state, one assumes, is a reference to the mishandling of the presidential election and perhaps alas more widely of the Coronavirus lockdown.

---

5   James Shotter, "Warsaw's liberal mayor mounts election challenge to Andrzej Duda" *The Financial Times,* 21 June, 2020

"Trzaskowski's rise in the polls built on re-energising Civic Platform voters, many had drifted to other candidates after Ms. Kidawa-Blonska called on them to boycott the May election. (...) We don't want Poland the way it is today," said Olga, who had travelled 20km with her mother to watch Mr Trzaskowski speak. 'I'm on the left side of Polish politics. Duda is not my president.' If Mr. Trzaskowski is to oust Mr. Duda, though, he will also have to win over moderate conservatives.

Commentary: Moderates? Did we ask her about abortion, gay rights, or immigrants?

Aleks Szczerbiak, professor of politics at the UK's University of Sussex: 'He won't win just by mobilising the large towns and metropolitan areas. He's also got to be able to win support in small town provincial Poland. (...) A lot of the things that give him credibility with the big city urban electorate—the fact he comes across as very urbane, educated, speaking many languages, being very liberal on social and cultural issues—are potentially the things that are very problematic for him,' Prof Szczerbiak added. (...) State media has also sought to sow doubt over his support for the '500 plus' child benefit programme that has been one of PiS's most popular policies among less well-off voters. He has affirmed his support for 500 plus, and contrasted his plans for investments 'around the corner' from ordinary voters with PiS's promises of mega-projects, such as a new airport hub near Warsaw.

Commentary: Did people believe him on 500+?

In last year's parliamentary and European elections, focusing on 'culture war' topics proved to be a vote winner for PiS. But, so far, the strategy does not appear to have slowed. Trzaskowski is the polyglot son of a jazz musician.

Commentary: Is PiS, and only PiS, is focused on the "Culture Wars"?

June 21, 2020[6]
The Sunday Times

Addressing a crowd of 200 supporters in a cobbled square near a church in the medieval city of Torun, Robert Biedron, a candidate in next Sunday's Polish presidential election, held up a Bible in his right hand. He revealed a copy of the country's constitution in his other hand, declaring: "For me this is the guide."

---

6   Dariusz Kalan, "Poland's youth backs gay atheist Robert Biedroń for president in land of the 'LGBT-free zone,'" *The Sunday Times*, 21 June, 2020.

Atheist and openly gay, Biedroń is anathema to the ruling right-wing Law and Justice Party.

Commentary: It was not clear if Biedroń was a left-winger in any sense other than support for the liberal causes he had become associated with.

June 25, 2020 [7]
The Guardian

"Poland's public broadcaster has entered the paranoid realm of the far right." ... "Come with me on a tour through the magical world of the evening News programme on Polish state television (TVP). (...) We start on Sunday 14 June. The first item marks the 80th anniversary of the first deportation of Poles to Auschwitz in 1940. But in the entire news item, lasting more than four minutes, the words 'Jewish victims' do not appear once." ... "Soon the programme turns to what can only be described as pure election propaganda for Trump's pal Duda. (...) After berating Poland's independent media, the News turns to differences between Duda and Trzaskowski. Now the Jews do get an explicit mention, as the programme characterises the two candidates' allegedly different responses to Jewish restitution claims, or, as the announcer puts it "giving money back to the Jews for the second world war. (...) Then comes an attack on Trzaskowski for his 'way of thinking, thinking not in line with Polish interests'. This is evidenced by the fact that he participated in a meeting of the Bilderberg group in the Swiss resort of Montreux: ... "Cut to another supposedly expert interviewee, who says: 'The Germans export to us candidates for the highest positions, such as [Donald] Tusk, and now such a German candidate is Trzaskowski.' (...) The next day News tells us that President Duda's 'family charter' envisages "the defence of children against LGBT ideology". ... "Returning to the Jewish restitution theme, the announcer makes this truly despicable claim: 'Experts have no doubt [that] the stream of money that currently flows from the state budget into the pockets of Polish families will dry up if Trzaskowski, after his possible victory in the presidential election, will seek to satisfy Jewish demands.' (...) Polish state television makes Fox News look like the Canadian Broadcasting Corporation. (...) I have been writing about Poland for more than 40 years and have constantly struggled against a

---

7   Timothy Garton Ash, "For a bitter taste of Polish populism, just watch the evening news," *The Guardian*, 25 June 2020.

widespread western stereotype of this fascinating, complicated country as stiff-necked, narrow-minded, reactionary, nationalist and antisemitic (...) Now here is state television comprehensively reinforcing that stereotype.(...) What can be done about this? First, Polish voters can vote out Duda. Second, we need to defend media pluralism. Media scholars distinguish between internal and external pluralism. (...) public television was always inclined to sway under pressure from governing parties, although incomparably less crudely than today. (...) the historic Gazeta Wyborcza, weeklies such as the Polish Newsweek, online platforms such as onet.pl, and the independent journalism site oko.press, TVN, which is owned by the US-based Discovery channel. (...) Fakty is not BBC-style impartial: it clearly favours a more liberal, pro-European Poland and is strongly anti-PiS. But unlike the so-called News, it is still definitely professional, high quality, reality-based journalism. (Think something between CNN and MSNBC.)

Commentary: The "we" used here is ambiguous. We, the people? We, *The Guardian* readers? We is most certainly not the fools who will fall for PiS propaganda. Perhaps some of this "they" could be "we" if they weren't so dumb. Garton Ash tells us he has been writing about Poland for 40 years and when in Warsaw no doubt always meets up with the same ex-underground intellectuals and/or their children now bemoaning the barbarians in power, without realizing—perhaps—that they, like all revolutionaries, eventually become the target of the counter-revolutionaries at the next table. *Gazeta Wyborcza*, TVN, and *onet.pl* are "we," i.e., on the right side. The other side is simply creating mendacious news, for example dabbling in ancient racialized tropes that view Otherness through the prism of a dichotomy of "Polish" and "Jewish." Garton Ash goes on to defend Poland from itself, or its worst self. They may be peasants, but they are my peasants. The piece betrays an absence of understanding of the forces that were underpinning PiS's success. Yes, what happened at TVP was awful, but perhaps public discourse and news work differently in Poland, not just because of a history of communism, but because a deeper layer of Polish culture works in ways not fully commensurate with the BBC and its relationship with British society and the British establishment. Internationalist liberal sentimentality wafts throughout the piece, with its sneering about "supposed" experts. It was very easy for someone in Garton Ash's position to be critical of PiS, less so of those whom he supports. Imagine a Polish account of the BBC for Polish readers from a renowned Polish academic based on talking exclusively with friends from *The Guardian* and on sporadic visits watching BBC News for a week. It was hard to imagine Garton Ash had the depth of detailed historical knowledge of TVP to debate the role of TVP in Polish public life. For him, again, it had a touch of the Ancient Greeks about it, not really living people.

June 25, 2020[8]
The Times

"Of all the gifts President Trump could bestow upon a visiting statesman, the most precious is a shot at political survival. (...) Last night the first foreign dignitary to walk into the White House since the US went into lockdown was President Duda of Poland, a man in need of all the good news he can get. (...) After five years in power, Mr. Duda is facing his sternest test yet on Sunday, with an ebullient liberal rival threatening to eject him from office. His previously commanding lead in the polls has crumbled over recent weeks and the ultimate outcome of the vote is now too close to call."

Commentary: The colonial theme. Duda pays his tribute to The Emperor in return for reflected glory at home, support from the US's 10-million-strong Polonia community and possibly a few more US troops on Polish soil.

June 26, 2020[9]
The Guardian

"A disgracefully homophobic campaign may have backfired on President Andrzej Duda. (...) the disgraceful drumbeat of homophobia in Mr Duda's bid for re-election has been unrelenting and shameful. (...) an MP from PiS and member of the president's campaign team told viewers: 'Let's stop listening to these idiocies about human rights. These people are not equal with normal people.' (...) With wearying predictability, Poland's populist right tends to ramp up its culture wars when election time comes around. (...) The rhetoric is cynical and manipulative, intended to mobilise a deeply conservative, mostly rural base. (...) But the licence

8   Oliver Moody, Maria Wilczek, "Donald Trump's meeting with Andrzej Duda may determine the future of Poland," *The Times*, 25 June 2020.

9   "The Guardian view on Poland's election: pride versus prejudice. Editorial," *The Guardian*, 26 June 2020.

given in recent years to extreme prejudice has steadily changed the reality of LGBT lives on the ground. (...) The 48-year-old Mr Duda, a devout Catholic, has promised to ban LGBT education in schools and refused to allow same-sex marriage." ... "As election day nears, however, there are heartening signs that the old polarising playbook may be misfiring. (...) Warsaw's liberal mayor, Rafal Trzaskowski, has spooked the president's team. (...) Despite relentless attacks from state media. (...) but could prove a turning point."

Commentary: Regardless of the ostensible value and validity of its argument, *The Guardian* seemed again to be positioning itself as the moral arbiter of another country's government. The editorial reads like a kind of post-colonial admonishment. If only "they" shared our values things could go back to normal. But what PiS has done is "disgraceful," "shameful," and there is a "wearying predictability," to this, given the "deeply conservative rural base." Throw in the obligatory idiotic quote from someone in PiS. But there is hope, still. This election may be a turning point, and the LGBT+ community, like the vanguard (working) class of old, could be the fulcrum of resistance and a harbinger of a better future. It is not clear how damaging the editorial was on the ground in Poland two days before the election, but the fact of seeking to shame an elected foreign government is awkward to say the least, and also likely counter-productive.

June 26, 2020[10]
The Guardian

"Trzaskowski could easily pass as a Polish Emmanuel Macron: he is good-looking, young, well-educated, speaks foreign languages, ostentatiously comes from the intelligentsia, but is still a devoted family man. He offers a polite vision of European-ness and Western-style free-market politics, which some Poles miss and aspire to. Others, of course, influenced by PiS's relentless anti-EU propaganda, hate such an outlook. (...) Poland is caught between the prospect of Viktor Orbán-style anti-democratic governance or neoliberal neglect of workers' rights, regardless of whose candidate wins. One thing is certain: as long as PiS rule

---

10 Agata Pyzik, *Poland casts its vote as a nation divided. But can the election deliver true change? The Guardian*, 26 June 2020. *The Guardian*. Followed by *The Guardian*, June 29, Poland should get less from Covid-19 fund due to rights record, claim EU member states; *The Financial Times*, June 29, Poland's run-off election to force candidates to reach beyond their bases

persists, there's no chance of the party's long-running lockdown on freedoms being lifted anytime soon.

Commentary: PiS doesn't care about these things, although we have no context as to who was making the accusations. But, wait, we have a new Macron. He is into Western-style free-market politics, whatever that is. He is European, as opposed to PiS, which is, well, what?

Part 2: Round Two in the Presidential Election

July 5, 2020 [11]
The Observer

"LGBT rights are among issues at stake in Poland and beyond. (...) Duda has courted further controversy by making homophobic rhetoric a cornerstone of his re-election campaign. (...) Trzaskowski has promised to be a more tolerant and open face of Poland in Europe. (...) Barack Obama called Trzaskowski, and they discussed 'the importance of Polish democracy', according to Trzaskowski. (...) Traditional voting...older voters and residents of small towns and villages heavily favouring Duda. (...) can win in big cities. Winning the whole country will be much harder, but would send a signal that Poland is not travelling further down the path of illiberalism towards Viktor Orbán's Hungary. (...) PiS has offered a cocktail of nationalism, historical grievances, rightwing social and cultural policies, and generous direct welfare payments, most notably substantial monthly child support payments. It has proved a winning combination at the ballot box. (...) There are two schools of thought about support for PiS, one is that it's about money and the other is that people are affected by the rightwing, Catholic propaganda. (...) PiS is much more skilful in appealing to deep emotions than liberal politicians have, and liberals need to learn from that." (...) "political divide is more complicated, and simply putting PiS support down to class issues masks a failure among progressive politicians to inspire people." (...) 'This distinction is too comfortable, because it's always 'us' looking at 'them', and it's something between pity and contempt,' said Karolina Wigura.

---

11 Shaun Walker, 'Knife-edge Polish presidential race could slow the march of populism,' *The Observer*, July 5, 2020

Commentary: Talking again with the same supporters of PO. Karolina Wigura is an insightful human being, but solidly "inside the bubble," as she herself would probably acknowledge. There is nothing wrong with knowing your audience, but it is still relentlessly one-sided. Hoping for a way to unlock the secret that keeps populists in power. But a very similar rehash of old analyses, half wishful thinking, an outline of the old divisions. Opponents who know they are smarter than the populist masses, but still need to persuade these masses to vote for a project that has lost its shine. Nothing on what Trzaskowski offered other than stymying PiS.

July 9, 2020 [12]
The Financial Times

"intense struggle between conservative nationalism and liberal centrism. (...) the faultlines of Polish society run deep and the two camps often spurn compromise. (...) Their disputes extend beyond economics to questions of identity, culture and private morality. ... The election's outcome will be of critical importance to Polish democracy and the nation's place on the global stage (...) It will fall to the next president either to advance or to resist controversial government policies which, in the past five years, have tarnished Poland's impressive record since it shook off communism in 1989. (...) assault on the independence of Poland's judiciary. transformation of the state media into a machine spewing out pro-government propaganda. (...) PiS remains the legitimately elected government, popular on account of its high-spending social and welfare policies. (...) For Poland, political moderation is more than a good in its own right. It is an insurance policy for its security in the world."

Commentary: The absence of any deeper reflection on what stymied liberal opposition seems to be a precondition of any media written post-mortem after the election of populists.

---

12 Opinion,'Poland faces a choice over its place in the world,' *The Financial Times*. July 9 2020

July 9, 2020 [13]
The Guardian

"A referendum on the 'Third Republic': a pluralistic democracy, or a majoritarian democracy with no effective constraints on the ruling party. (...) fissures of
class, culture and geography. (...) Duda and Trzaskowski are the faces of the two
Polands (...) Duda represents a Poland that is provincial, conservative and Polo-
nocentric. (...) For the cosmopolitan tradition in Polish culture, the social hierarchy is built on contempt for those considered to be less cultured, a deeply rooted attitude that originates in the contempt felt by the gentry for the peasantry,'
said Maciej Gdula, a sociologist at the University of Warsaw. (...) For the rightwing
tradition the social hierarchy is based on ethnicity, manifesting itself as hostility towards minorities, whether it be Jews, Muslim migrants, or members of the
LGBT community (...) At the centre of the cultural divide is the contentious role
played by the Catholic church in Poland's public life."

> Commentary: An unusually perceptive reflection on the class dynamics and
> snobbery of the enlightened middle class. But no real analysis of social
> structure, power relations, or anything to tell us where these things arose
> and how they are maintained. The liberal ideal stands alone on its own.

July 13, 2020 [14]
The Guardian

"A bitter campaign laced with homophobic language and accusations that Trzaskowski would sell out Polish families to 'Jewish demands'. (...) 'complete state
capture...dismantle already damaged system of checks and balances in a similar way that has already happened in Hungary. (...) Tapping into old antisemitic tropes, Duda's campaign and the pro-government state media also repeatedly cast Trzaskowski as working on behalf of a 'powerful foreign lobby' linked to
George Soros and the Bilderberg group. (...) critics say the commission and member states have failed to do enough to prevent a more recent slide in the rule of
law, despite initiating a sanctions process known as Article 7 against both Poland and Hungary that could in theory lead to the suspension of their voting rights

---

13   Christian Davies, 'Future of 'Third Republic' defines run-off vote in Poland,' July 9 2020, *The Guardian*
14   Jon Henley, 'Andrzej Duda's re-election set to intensify Poland-EU tensions,' July 13 2020, *The Guardian*.

in the European council. (...) Poland, one of the EU nations least affected by the coronavirus crisis, was set to become one of the biggest recipients of the bloc's pandemic recovery fund despite its government's attacks on the judiciary and LGBT community. (...) 'Poland is making a mockery of our values and gets rewarded for it,' one senior EU diplomat said. That is unacceptable."

Commentary: Just as the EU decides on its next budget round, PiS is making a mockery of "our values."

July 13, 2020 [15]
The Guardian

Editorial: "Polish liberals must find a way to reconnect with non-urban voters. (...) It is worth rewinding a few days to an interview with Jaroslaw Kaczyński (...) Kaczyński warned that Mr Duda's liberal opponent, Rafał Trzaskowski, lacked a 'Polish soul'. The evidence, he said, was Mr Trzaskowski's unpatriotic willingness to even consider Jewish restitution claims in relation to the second world war. He went on to hint at a need to 'repolonise' sections of the media partly under foreign ownership. And, emphasising a running theme of Mr Duda's successful campaign for re-election, Mr Kaczyński predicted an opposition victory would see Poland capitulate to an 'LGBT offensive', corrupting the minds of the young. (...) It is not hard then to sympathise with the 48.8% of voters who backed Mr Trzaskowski, in the hope of making Poland a more open and tolerant country than Mr Duda and PiS will allow it to be. (...) bitter defeat also carries a stark lesson for opposition parties. (...) in the parts of the country sometimes referred to as 'Poland B', which have seen less of the benefits of globalisation, PiS's redistributive programmes are popular and inspire fierce loyalty. (...) to navigate a route back to power, Poland's opposition must find a way to win back the trust of communities that have come to associate greater economic security with the cultural conservatism and bigotry of PiS. It is a task greatly complicated by the continuing influence and sway of conservative elements in the Catholic church. But for Poland's heartbroken liberals, it must become the priority between now and the next electoral opportunity to turn back the illiberal tide."

Commentary: Again, who are these liberals? A reference to Polska B, but nothing more.

---

15   The Guardian view on Poland's election: a good day for intolerance,' July 13, 2020,

July 15, 2020[16]
The Guardian

"Anaemic grey clouds hung over much of Warsaw as the city's liberals and pro-gressives came to terms with the fact that it will almost certainly be another three years, during parliamentary elections in 2023, before they get a chance to challenge (...) 'This was not a normal, fair election held in a liberal democracy,' said Agnieszka Graff, a public intellectual and professor of cultural studies at the University of Warsaw. (...) But as they lick their wounds – with many nursing hang-overs, talking of emigration, or both – Polish liberals and defenders of the rule of law are caught between their anger and frustration at what they regard as a playing field tilted by state authorities in the incumbent's favour, and a discom-bobulating mixture of dread and cautious optimism engendered by a close result that only a month or two scarcely seemed imaginable. (...) The extreme partisan-ship and toxic rhetoric has shocked Polish moderates and garnered internation-al attention and criticism. (...) 'The elections were neither fair nor constitution-al, but there's nothing that can be done about that now,' said Marcin Matczak, a law professor at the university of Warsaw. (...) "Some worry that Rafał Trzas-kowski's strong showing will mask what many regard as the abject failures of Po-land's leading opposition parties to hold Law and Justice effectively to account. (...) 'PiS's successful long march through the institutions have been hampered by ideological disagreements and factional disputes.' (...) 'We have been delud-ing ourselves – we simply assumed that Poland was a western country, but we didn't actually do what was necessary to make it a western country,' said Graff. 'We still have an authoritarian school system, and moral values are dominated by the Catholic Church, which is also authoritarian. So why are we surprised when our politics is authoritarian too?'"

Commentary: **You've been framed**

The language used to describe what PiS does tends to use word like "bribes," "bungs," and the people who vote for it as "the left behind," "losers." PiS won because it offered more money. The ordinary people quoted always have to come from somewhere, as if this mini-backstory justifies their voice being heard; they are talking not just for themselves but for a group defined

---

16   Christian Davies, 'It feels like it's game over': Polish liberals despair after Duda's win," July 15, 2020, *The Guardian*.

by the reporter. They make a brief appearance and then disappear before an expert interprets their words. We are given their context ("she came to the rally on a bus..."), a framing device that is rarely used for business or other analysts. The frame already tells us that our reporter has entered actual foreign terrain and actually talked with actual people. But the framing of the place and the speaker seems designed to conjure up certain notions. Sometimes an angry, shouty, drunk may appear in a piece for extra color. PO will usually be semantically associated with the side the experts describe: "rule of law," "democratic integrity," etc. Verbs used to describe how PiS people speak are also different. They tend to "scoff," while others may "argue." We get a few Church figures thrown into the mix, but they are generally quotes from its more rabid parts. LGBTQ+ people are invariable cast as "brave" and fighting "a lone battle." Very little, if nothing, on trade unions or Solidarity; little or no analysis of class or social structure, a definite focus on demographics (age mainly, PiS voters are older, and gender: men like PiS more) and region (Polska B is backward, etc). A more nuanced understanding of how the crude dichotomization of PO-PiS into the two basic and unchanging forces in Polish society came about and was sustained was lacking.

July 17, 2020 [17]
The Economist

"In the opposition, eyes are on Mr Trzaskowski, who won over 10m votes. Some politicians in Civic Platform suggest that he could lead a new movement that could unite the fragmented opposition, which includes moderate conservatives, liberals, agrarians and the centre-left. In an interview with a privately owned television broadcaster on July 14th, he announced plans to 'rebuild political parties' and use the "civic energy" of the election to build a modern, European Poland. He said he also intended to stay on as mayor of Warsaw. After years of a conspicuous lack of leadership and vision within the opposition, Mr Trzaskowski is offering his liberal compatriots a dash of that elusive quality: hope."

Commentary: **A fragile flower**

The "moderate conservatives, liberals, agrarians and center-left" represent competing interests and ideas. It is a coalition held together mainly by its

---

17 July 15, 2020, *The Economist*.

opposition to PiS. Hope is not in shortage among the 51% who voted for Duda, one assumes.

July 15, 2020 [18]
The New Statesman

"Already, some in PO are speculating that Trzaskowski could lead a broad movement. Here are eight suggestions to start with:
1. Have a programme
Whatever one thinks of the current ruling party, PiS has a consistent ideology and programme (...) the opposition has tended to be vague, reactive or has cobbled together a programme just before an election (...) it needs to figure out what it truly stands for. Falling back on simply being 'against PiS' is not enough (...) it needs a simple set of policies that can last for several years, not just one election. For example, this might include making a commitment to introduce civil partnerships, rather than dodging or wavering on the subject."
2. Beware of one-hit wonders
There have been several "one-hit wonders" in Polish politics over the past decade...recent examples include the centre-left 'Spring' party or the liberal 'Modern'. To avoid this fate, Trzaskowski's movement needs to appeal to a wider sentiment and avoid cult-of-personality territory."
3. Build on the cities. 4. ...but venture outside them
That said, Poland is not just Warsaw, Wrocław, Gdańsk and other major cities, and the opposition cannot limit itself to relatively comfortable, urban voters.
5. Have the "old guard" step back
The opposition should cultivate young leaders – ones socialised in today's Europe
6. Let women shine
The opposition should move talented women politicians into the foreground and give them the opportunity to lead (...)stand up to the social conservatism of PiS and its traditional ally, the Roman Catholic Church in Poland.
7. Anchor Poland in Europe
PiS has long accused the opposition of being unpatriotic. Trzaskowski does not 'have a Polish heart and soul', said PiS's chairman Jarosław Kaczyński during the

---

18   Annabelle Chapman, "Eight Ways Poland's Liberal Opposition can Build on the Presidential Election," *The New Statesman*, July 15, 2020.

campaign. This is a false choice. The opposition should instead focus on a strong Poland in a strong Europe.

8. Think long term

Politics is a long game and winning elections is only part of it. Deep political change involves stepping out of one's comfort zone, engaging with new social groups, and gradually transforming the language of politics into one of respect and tolerance."

> Commentary: The lack of critical self-awareness continues in this article published three days after Duda's win. *"Politics is a long game,"* we are told, thankfully. The piece doesn't bother to question its—or our—moral superiority from the start. "We" are clean, untainted, better. "We" support gay people, immigrants, minorities. When the author calls for the opposition to "Have a programme" the heart sinks. Does she have any program in mind, or just one that is "consistent," like the PiS one? "It needs to figure out what it truly stands for." Perhaps the "truly" only works here if one assumes the opposition had before this only worked out what it stood for half-heartedly, that there was an inauthenticity about its reason for existing as a political entity. Not, perhaps, that its emptiness was precisely what it stood for. "It needs a simple set of policies that can last for several years, not just one election. For example, this might include making a commitment to introduce civil partnerships, rather than dodging or wavering on the subject," the article notes. This is so lacking in conceptual acumen as to be slightly disturbing. And in a notionally Left-of-center weekly current affairs magazine, it smacks of failure to see beyond the world "we" inhabit. "The opposition should instead focus on a strong Poland in a strong Europe." Sounded very much like a PO soundbite.

Summary

The fusion of news and comment was apparently more or less complete by the presidential elections of 2020. The lack of reflection on the rise of populism, belittling a la Applebaum of any Leftist analysis as simplistic, was becoming a dangerous omission among ostensibly the cleverest (most talented?) among us.

The alliance of liberal media in the UK and Poland was sealed. We will go down with you, the UK liberal intelligentsia promised, just like we did in 1980/81. Liberal institutions were doing fine and LGBTQ would be the new vanguard of a liberal Poland. There would be no question of following PiS down the rabbit hole of a bigger state, of redistribution, of talking with and about the masses.

Perhaps the weakest element of *The New Statesman* and other similar articles[19] was the failure to grasp PiS's success in structural and socio-economic terms. The focus was on how to regenerate the opposition and again, in largely symbolic and vague ways. Nothing on the economic foundations of social class, nothing of notions of elite self-perpetuation and intra elite rivalries.

Part 3: Unfinished Business

The whispers grow louder. The king is sick, he is weak. Brutus lurks in the wings, weapon in hand. But the actors haven't been informed that this is a Mel Brooks' production of *Julius Caesar* and the dagger merely a plastic replica of the real thing. Public television, TVP—in the best traditions of authoritarian censorship—meanwhile relays news from anti-government demonstrations in Belarus, resolutely ignoring this 2020 retro version of the early 1990's *War at the Top* on its doorstep. Even the ghost of Debord whispers, 'this has gone too far.' As the images of police batons striking heads in Minsk flash on the screen, Ziobro's political life is already ebbing away from him, the spectacle relegated to a meta secondary news cycle event.[20] His Warsaw press conference a personal Ides of March, fittingly delayed during the year of Covid-19 until September 21. It has the feel of a show trial, where the accused admits to the crimes he is accused of and begs forgiveness, though he knows the gallows await, whatever he says. "I believe the United Right (PZ) coalition is good... I am convinced that this project has a big future ahead of it and can do a lot of good for Poland," Ziobro pleads.

Succession Can Wait: Hammy theatrics aside, the question that (re-)arose in September was a crucial one, that of post-Kaczyński succession. All revolutions succumb to fatigue sooner or later and either fizzle out or must be renewed afresh. But when to strike and who will be the first to do so?

---

19   Sean Walker, Standing up for the 'real' Poland: how Duda exploited rural-urban divide to win re-election, July 18, 2020, *The Guardian*.
20   Douglas Kellner, Media Spectacle and the Crisis of Democracy: Terrorism, War, and Election Battles, (London and New York: Routledge: 2005).

The outcome of the ideological and personal struggles between PiS's holy trinity of Kaczyński, Ziobro and Morawiecki was always going to define the next phase of the party's "project." With no election due for three years, the coalition wanted to use the period to expand its aging voter base, but at a time of economic difficulties aggravated by the coronavirus pandemic, it was split over how to do so. The period after the delayed presidential election was characterized by a continuation of the infighting that had marked the period between the planned date of the election and its execution, Ziobro (and Gowin, again) playing a high-stakes game, with echoes of Andrzej Lepper and Roman Giertych, 2005–7, a game that ended in PiS spending the next eight years in opposition. Ziobro was not even talking to his formal superior, (the prime minister), and rarely appearing at government meetings. It was an open secret that the most important ministers often consulted straight at Nowogrodzka Street over the head of the head of government, who himself spent several hours there almost every day. But it was not only a struggle on a tactical and personal plane, it was also a battle over the PiS strategic soul, a choice between a harder-edged nativist project, as Ziobro preferred, a market-driven nationalism-soft version a la Morawiecki, or a strategic balance of the two.

Toil and Trouble: Or that is how the discursive framing instruments, in particular those calibrated for foreign consumption, most obviously the *Financial Times*,[21] constructed the choices available. No doubt Trzaskowski, the new darling of the liberal center, was weighing up which of the two men would best allow him to play the stable-centrist card, the Biden approach, one might say. Would PiS return from the epic to the ordinary ("water in the taps"?) and challenge PO on its own terms or unleash a second revolutionary round?[22]

The *FT*, and others, would of course prefer to feel PiS could be tamed, with Morawiecki open for business, his more vulgar friends not invited to the party. But sustaining such liberal centrist sensibilities requires stables to be booked and invitations issued. Let the uninvited by default define the new center, allow their absence to reframe perceptions of the ideological and political balance with the hope of splitting the beastly populist beast. It might

---

21   Christian Davies, "The Power Struggle at the Heart of Poland's Political Turmoil," *The Financial Times*, September 19, 2020.

22   Tom Blackburn, "A Biden Victory Cannot Bring Normal Back," *The Guardian*, September 19, 2020; See also Fintan O'Toole, *The Politics of Pain: Postwar England and the Rise of Nationalism* (London: Liveright, 2019).

also be good for business, reclaiming a seat at the high table in Warsaw after a 5-year hiatus, an interview and a bit of ideological leverage perhaps exerted in that terribly polite British way. Maybe Lionel might even drop in for an "interview" a la Vladimir Putin.[23] *FT* eyelashes had after all already flickered in Morawiecki's direction several times since he became top dog in Warsaw. Wine and dine the prime minister then and throw Ziobro into a Corbyn-shaped media black hole. And what better way than a new round of moral panic? Ziobro as a mix of Feliks Dzerzhinsky and Joe McCarthy.[24] Journalists of course live for intrigue in the court, the whispers offering redemption from that hollow feeling of insignificance, clinging to a sense of being there when history is made. Coalition government is intrinsically rife with whisperers and hence scooping opportunities. Add into the mix Western editors' potent distaste for PiS, and the chance to dabble in power politics becomes an even headier brew. But it is a selective and political choice, one self-legitimized perhaps by defense of the ideals of liberal-democracy and ends justifying means, but a dangerous game and one predicated on understanding Kaczyński's psychology.

The Financial Times,
September 19: [25]

A New Folk Devil: "hardline justice minister...Mr Ziobro and his allies staked out hardline positions. (...) "Mr. Ziobro positions himself as heir to Jaroslaw Kaczynski...who is understood to be considering a withdrawal from front-line politics." (...) "a ruthless political operator...Seen by his admirers as an uncompromising fighter against crime and corruption, critics claim his political opponents had a habit of getting caught up in his investigations. (...) 'There are people even within the United Right who consider him as someone who would do anything to destroy his enemies,'" said Mr. Szacki. It is not just liberal Poles who are scared of him — many on the right are scared of him too.' (...) In July, Mr. Ziobro announced a plan to withdraw Poland from the

---

23 https://www.youtube.com/watch?v=pcmZFJRikqM.
24 Stanley Cohen, *Folk Devils and Moral Panics: The Creation of the Mods and Rockers* (London: MacGibbon and Kee, 1972); Amanda Rohloff, *Shifting the Focus? Moral Panics as Civilizing and Decivilizing Processes* (London: Routledge, 2011).
25 Christian Davies, "The power struggle at the heart of Poland's political turmoil," *The Financial Times*, September 21, 2020.

Istanbul Convention on the prevention of violence against women, which he has described as a 'feminist invention that is meant to justify gay ideology.'"

Morawiecki, a Man with Whom We Can do Business: "prime minister Mateusz Morawiecki, a relative moderate widely seen as Mr. Kaczynski's preferred successor.." (...) "According to reports in the Polish press, the justice minister has been putting pressure on Mr. Kaczynski to consent to a merger between their parties, and pave the way for Mr. Ziobro and his allies to assume control of Law and Justice after Mr. Kaczynski's departure. But Mr. Kaczynski, keen to secure Mr. Morawiecki's future elevation to the leadership, is resisting. Were Mr. Ziobro to be excluded from the ruling camp, an empowered Mr. Morawiecki could be in a position to seal an alliance with centrist factions, leaving Mr. Ziobro to decide whether to seek a reconciliation or to try to outflank Law and Justice by forging an alliance with the far-right."

Shifting the Ideological Center: As Ziobro threatened to shift the United Right sharply to the Right, the apparent erstwhile center shifted subtly with him, shunting effective opposition from PO to Morawiecki, the technocratic manager, a man who by rights was "one of us," an ex-banker after all, hardly one of the rabble. Trzaskowski, thus recalibrated, then became someone of the liberal-left—measured in LGBT/gender sympathies if little else—even if his statements on progressive taxation, among other things, were far from it. The actual Left became thus the Far Left, fading even further from view, not needed in this ideological Potemkin. In the abstract semiotic calculations of selected newspaper scribes, the ideological matrix seemed desperate—even if unaware of its desperation—to protect a market-driven agenda at all costs, by exclusion, mainly, of ideas that threatened shareholder dividends. Mirroring the Biden approach to the US's upcoming election, PO could be anything that might dislodge the populists. If Trazaskowski failed that test, Morawiecki would be insurance. Whatever it takes, we will clear up the mess the day after the counter-revolution, they said. In lieu of any real political or social momentum, ideas or strategy, the LGBTQ fig leaf approach thus again forced its way center stage. A sigh of resignation in the *FT* editorial office in London. Somehow thus, in a curious counter-logic, Kaczyński—who, we are told in numerous media reports, was a cat lover—is semi-humanized, rehabilitated, and the hopes of those who believed he could be tamed, rekindled. The king lives.

War at the Top, Again: The crisis started in August when Ziobro positioned himself as the most zealous element of the ruling camp, criticizing the "technocratic faction" around Morawiecki. The strains emerged public-ly when Kaczyński spoke of a cabinet reshuffle to reduce ministry numbers in early September. SP, with 19 seats, and Accord, with 18, then refused to back an animal rights bill submitted by Kaczyński and parliament passed the bill with support from PO, with 356 votes in favor, 75 against and 18 absten-tions. The bill, popular among young Poles in urban areas, alienated farmers in PiS's rural electoral base.

Morawiecki had been resisting efforts by the ultras in the ruling coalition to ratchet up a government crackdown on LGBT and women's rights, wary of further undermining Poland's ties with the EU. Ziobro, meanwhile, had demanded Morawiecki veto the European Council budget over threatened rule of law conditionality. Ziobro then went full Ziobro, calling for an out-right ban on gay marriage and urging Poland to leave the Council of Europe's Istanbul Convention on combating violence against women. Only a few days earlier he had accused the EU of waging an "attack on democracy" after the European Parliament passed a resolution criticizing lax adherence to the rule of law and discrimination against women, LGBT people and minorities in Poland. He said the EU was trying to impose its agenda and values on Poland and disrespecting the majority views in the largely Catholic nation. Poland and Hungary "are a constant target of leftist attacks," he said. Morawiecki, meanwhile, on a visit to Lithuania, said his government had "no major issues" with Brussels, but that there is a certain "lack of understanding" by the EU of the need to mend Poland's justice system. Our kind of chap.

The conflict had entered a critical phase in September. Until then, Zio-bro had been Kaczyński's armed wing to take over the courts, and the pres-ident had more plans in the area, aiming to throw out most of the judges on the Supreme Court, and no-one in PiS could do it as ruthlessly as Ziobro. The situation was aggravated by the fact that the zealots voted against the draft of the second important law for Kaczyński—on the ban on breeding fur an-imals and on a limitation of ritual slaughter. "Poland's standards regarding animals should be no worse, or even better, than those in western countries," said Kaczyński, the cat-lover.

Threats swirled around Warsaw's salons. Gowin's people, it was whispered, and above all the Ziobrists—headed by Ziobro's wife and brother—could be re-moved from state-owned companies. Kaczyński had reportedly ordered Jacek Sasin, deputy prime minister (from June 2019) and the minister for state assets, to check which companies "belonged" to Ziobro three weeks before the coalition affair came to public attention on September 19. The list of companies in which Ziobro's people held prominent positions was long. A prominent position in the Link4 insurance company was held by his wife, while his brother worked for the bank Pekao. Ziobro was also reportedly favored by people on the boards of Orlen, Tauron, Elektrociepłownia Będzin and PGNiG. In addition, he had also managed to place "dedicated associates" on several supervisory boards, at Kraków Airport, Grupa Azoty and Polski Holding Obronny.

Ziobro tried to deflect attention as best he could, but the game seemed up. First off, Smolensk. A Polish court issued a detention warrant application for the three Russian flight controllers on duty on April 10, 2010, the first step to issuing an international arrest warrant. The prosecutors alleged the controllers "had anticipated that a catastrophe might occur" before giving a conditional clearance for landing to the pilots. Next up, bank owner Leszek Czarnecki was accused on September 21 by prosecutors of cheating clients of Idea Bank. Ziobro, finding time in an unusually busy schedule, repeated the antimonopoly office's statement from 2019 that Idea Bank had misled clients when selling them bonds issued by debt collector GetBack. Roman Giertych, once head of the LPR and by 2020 Czarnecki's lawyer, said the accusations were "grotesque and related to media speculation that he might be dismissed as a result of tensions in the ruling coalition."

But Kaczyński now had Morawiecki in his pocket after the premier had failed to forge a new center-right formation with PSL, his threat to Kaczyński thus blunted. His offer had been a joining of the peasant party to the coalition with PiS in provincial assemblies. However, the talks ended in failure, with PSL leader, Władysław Kosiniak-Kamysz, against and no other coalition possibilities in the Sejm stood out: no question of cooperation with PO or the Left, and the Confederation had no interest in joining the PiS cabinet. The Confederates indeed presented themselves as spokesmen for aggrieved farmers. PiS could go it alone, but a minority government would mean political vegetation, problematic if your goal—like Kaczyński's—was to fundamentally rebuild the state. Meanwhile, opinion polls showed PiS falling short of a majority in a snap election and its two smaller coalition partners failing to meet the threshold to win seats.

Kaczyński's Conditions for Ziobro: Enter—and exit—Bogdan Święczkowski, the national prosecutor politically close to Ziobro. Kaczyński demanded

Święczkowski (also an ally of Father Tadeusz Rydzyk) be sacked, a painful blow to Ziobro, who had known Święczkowski from his student days at the Jagiellonian University in Kraków. During the first PiS-led government in 2005–7, Święczkowski had been head of the Internal Security Agency, and Ziobro minister of justice.

Kaczyński also demanded from SP that it withdraw its veto on the act on the ban on breeding fur animals and support it in the Sejm after it returned from the Senate, where significant amendments would "probably" be tabled. Ziobroists would also have to support the bill giving impunity for officials in the event of breaking the law in connection with a pandemic, again after "significant" legislative changes. Kaczyński then demanded the separation of the prosecutor's office from the Ministry of Justice and, perhaps crucially, that SP abandon its postulates regarding LGBT+.

Monkey or Organ Grinder? Ziobro himself clearly did not want a conflict with Kaczyński, but with Morawiecki, whom he saw as a foreign body on the Right. But in the Sejm, finding a new majority would be a miracle and early elections a huge risk. Hence the entry of Kaczyński to the government. The then current head of government was after all an active participant in the conflict, instead of an arbiter. Some important PiS politicians were reluctant to support Morawiecki, although they would not openly oppose him because of his backing by the president.

Chapter 12

Synthesis—Finding a Voice Between the Sublime and the Ridiculous

Poland comes fairly low down on the British editorial list of priorities. Something big has to happen to reach the news. "I'm afraid Belarus has just replaced Poland in the 'scary Eastern Europe' category, and we apparently do not belong in any other," Konstanty Gebert told me in August 2020. However, given this set of politico-commercial constraints, the Poland story that did emerge after PiS came to power was oddly consistent across the broadsheet news coverage of Poland. This narrative structure and lexical tool kit was deployed perhaps most clearly during the two national elections of 2019 and 2020 and the European election of 2019. British media, for one reason or another, created a textual framework to explain to a British, and also a wider audience, a complex historical process operating on multiple, and often highly fluid and opaque levels, simultaneously.

To simplify, one can divide the period chronologically. The language used in the first stage, leading up to the October 13, 2019, election, was one of "handouts," "an anxious business community," "losers/winners" and concerns for the LGBT+ community. A core frame, both of the center-right and center-left, established what appears to be a narrative that "cultural" issues were PiS's weak point as they exposed the party to claims it was backward, primitive, "Eastern European" in the sense used in the communist-era 1970s and 1980s, implying poor, culturally backward and perhaps in an ambiguous position of "enemy."

The language also split Poles into the "haves" ("the winners") and the "have nots" ("the losers"). Those parts of Polska A, in bigger cities, educated people, younger, were closer to "us." The rest, perhaps like the poor folk of parts of northern England, south Wales and so on, could basically be bought, the poor as merely instruments, lacking agency, who will take something if offered, though it is rarely clear that they really deserve it. The implication underlying the many broadsheet texts of this first stage is that the post-1989 capitalism that Poland had imported essentially worked and there was no need to rethink, reboot or even accept problems existed.

So, battle lines were drawn very quickly in 2015, both inside Poland and internationally. But this dialogical format was one that had been brewing for years: PO, the neoliberal Warsaw proxy versus a resurgent Polish nationalism in the form of PiS. The liberal discourse that *The Financial Times* and others were expressing (or simply leaving unquestioned) was—alongside a toothless left and aging secular-humanistic intelligentsia—coming under attack, seemingly opening the door for alternatives. In this context, the re-emergence of PiS as an electoral force could not be unanticipated. In this case, the narrative arc, if that is what we can call it, went from warnings about a tragedy waiting to happen to the tragedy itself, to its aftermath, resembling the stages of grief, from wishful thinking, denial, to some kind of acceptance. It is interesting, but beyond the scope of this study, to examine this discourse as a function to some extent of the debates that were raging in the UK during this period of Brexit. Certainly, a similar process seems to have occurred, from early warnings of a tragedy being fomented by populists, to sour acceptance of a status quo that was largely anathema to liberal civic discourse, be it of the center-Left or the center-Right. The question seemed to be: why did a society as international, educated, pluralistic, and affluent as Poland's buy into the populist agenda?

In social class terms, PiS was perhaps an expression of a growing middle class, one that hadn't inherited capital—social, political or financial—after 1989. Their politics was perhaps largely informed by concerns that the intelligentsia might eschew. People perhaps who did not know any gays or Jews, who hadn't studied abroad, and didn't speak perfect English. PiS's rise was thus in thus respect a story about the passing of one of the Solidarity wings of the 1989 negotiated transition, that of the liberal intelligentsia, and the rise of the materialistic, individualistic and transactional middle management.

Looking Ahead

1. We Are Past Nowhere: The first stage of the post-communist transition since 1989 was perhaps an interlude, not the destination at all, as many had thought, or hoped. Or perhaps the destination was indeterminacy. Disorder and stasis are real enough after all. Referring back to Bouchard's "sociology of myth," the first stages of his three-stage myth-making process seemed to have been largely achieved by 2019. Disruption of existing narratives, although heavily contested at each turn, was a fact. The narrative had clearly disrupted the existing status quo, with protagonists facing a rising number of intensifying conflicts and mini-climaxes, but as of 2020, we had seen no clear or decisive turning point, ritualization and sacralization proving somewhat harder to attain. But given that the next stages of ritualization and sacralization are incompatible with a liberal democracy and that Kaczyński will move aside, eventually, leaving PiS facing existential choices, the future was far from certain at the end of 2020.

2. PiS Read the Wind Better Than Others: Defined against a geopolitical background of insecurity and threats, perhaps PiS was just faster than its rivals in understanding the electorate. Perhaps Poland was simply reverting to type. Wasn't this New Normal a lot like the Old Normal? Values tended to be less informed by secular and multicultural influences than in western Europe.

3. Some Threats are Real: These phenomena also took place against the backdrop of a rapidly changing external environment. Increased insecurity in Central and Eastern Europe created by the unrest in Ukraine and Russia's increasing regional belligerence; the weakening of the EU after Britain's exit; the war in Syria and the inflow of refugees into Europe—alongside a rise in antipathy in Europe towards them and in the CEE region towards the EU for demanding intake quotas; the hardening of nationalist-infused regimes from Ankara to Budapest and beyond; and Trump-driven nativism in the US giving a sense that things would not be "normal" again, that is, if by normal, one means the social, economic, and political compacts that grew out of the collapse of communism in 1989, whether we call these processes globalization, neoliberalism, or something else.

4. Myth is Real: As the consensus political discourse after 1989 was largely unable to understand the need for a left alternative at all,[1] after 2015 it sought factual—empirical—holes in the PiS narrative, without understanding it as an act of faith, a story that is either accepted in its entirety or not at all. So,

---

1   Jo Harper, "Hoping, Doping and Coping," DW.com, March 7, 2017: Interview with German political scientist Wolfgang Streeck, a professor at the Max Planck Institute for the Study of Societies in Cologne

when PiS tells its story, one that has very little overlap with the "globalist" one, it posits a binary choice of interpretative frameworks. The notion of other truths is discarded. The liberal Western—Anglo-American—media, rooted in the empirical tradition, when confronting the apparent intransigence of inductive continental thinking did not cope very well. It was an attack on a way of life, a whole self-sustaining system of thought and action. Both stories are in some senses then about betrayal, the "Globalists" of the guiding hand and coffers of Brussels, PiS's of the sellout of Polish industry and historical identity.

5. Liberalism is "Problematic": sorry Gideon! Liberalism is a nebulous term, and democracy takes many forms. The liberalism out of which the nineteenth-century *Economist* and *Financial Times* sprouted, also came under the spotlight, not for reporting untruths, but for failing to understand the power of belief in politics and also its own role in defining and defending a certain truth as if it were somehow neutral, objective, and perhaps even scientific. The standard benchmarks—mostly embedded in the mythology of the "Westminster Model," and the "Washington Consensus"—had to be explained in a way that had not appeared necessary in 1989 in Eastern Europe or perhaps since 1945 elsewhere, in particular in their Western European and North American heartlands. The predominant counter-hegemonic discourse—of sectional interest, division and conflict, and elites and the rest fostered with decreasing success in the West by Marxist thinkers—had been rebuilding in more inchoate ways since the 2007–8 financial crisis, and found expression in the absence of a politically coordinated Left.

It is interesting at this point to return, briefly, to Kołodziejczak and Wrześniewska-Pietrzak.[2] Overlaps can be seen in the rhetorical mechanisms of narrative creation among populists and their opponents:

(i) Topos of power. "A silent majority where the roles 'good' and 'bad' are rigidly assigned." Liberalism provides a rich discursive canon of terms that divide in moral terms. "Populist" is the perhaps just the latest term to describe a working class that no longer has the same industrial function and power of

---

2   *"Kognitywizm jako sposób interdyscyplinarnego (politolingwistycznego) badania populizmu na tle polskich analiz dyskursu populistycznego,"* Małgorzata Kołodziejczak i Marta Wrześniewska-Pietrzak (*Badania nad dyskursem populistycznym: wybrane podejścia,* by Agnieszka Stępińska and Artur Lipiński, Uniwersytet im. Adama Mickiewicza w Poznaniu, Wydawnictwo Naukowe Wydziału Nauk Politycznych i Dziennikarstwa Poznań 2020.

the past. The workers could wave national flags and fight the police in 1989 but not in 2019.

(ii) Topos of oppression. "Arouses fear of a political opponent, mobilizes the people against the oppressor. Performative speech acts in this narrative flatter 'the people.'" The people are actually only those people worth reaching, the opinion formers and their followers. All legitimation relies on flattering the people in one form or another.

(iii) Topos of complaint. "Laments the fate of the people exploited by evil power, exposing its unjustifiable wrongs, traumas and feelings of being underestimated." Gazeta, KOD and others complained about PiS rather a lot.

(iv) Topos of change. "Rejection of what is now. Closely related to feeling of instability, a reaction to crisis. The savior will tame the oppressor. A sense of justice and morality of the so-called ordinary man." Again, a struggle over this ordinary man, changing him for the better, to be more like us.

6. Hybrid Democracy is Still Democracy: Perhaps PiS represented the first step towards what the transition paradigm terms a form of hybrid democracy. Not every political liberalization necessarily leads to Western-style democracy, after all, as the Arab Spring illustrated. In many cases we witnessed the emergence of so-called "hybrid regimes"—semi-authoritarianisms or electoral authoritarianisms that also include competitive authoritarianisms, new authoritarianisms, or neo-authoritarianisms.

7. Journalism Too Important to be Left to Journalists: This book was originally intended to be about how foreign journalists write what they write about Poland, a kind of meta-analysis, seeing journalists not as objective recorders of fact, but as interpretative conduits for ideas and experience, fitting often slippery facts into competing narratives. But as most journalists either don't understand their role or understand it very well and have chosen to bypass the more difficult moral terrain they tread, this became problematic. The disinclination of most Western media to countenance rethinking—in Poland also—is well illustrated in a *Financial Times* editorial from May 2016:

> As an all-purpose insult, "neoliberalism" has lost any meaning it might once have had. Whether it is a supposed sin of commission, such as privatization; one of omission, such as allowing a bankrupt company to close; or just an outcome with some losers, neoliberalism has become the catch-all criticism of unthinking radicals who lack the skills of empirical

argument. It gives succor to oppressive regimes around the world which also position themselves as crusaders against neoliberalism, subjugating their populations with inefficient economic policy and extreme inequality using the full power of the state. [3]

The fragment provides an insight into the newspaper's ideological predilections. "Some losers" is a term that pops up often in discussion in the Western media of Poland's so-called Polska B, as it does in explaining Brexit, the rise of Trump and Le Pen. It is a line that reveals much. As mainstream economics has tended to minimize labor as just one factor of production among others, these "losers" may be those whose factory was closed down and whose electricity bills rose after their public owned utility was privatized. As true in Detroit and Bolton as it would be in Skarbimierz. [4]

"It has become fashionable to blame all the world's ills on neoliberalism. But such cheap rhetoric often comes across like middle-aged men wearing baseball caps back to front, desperate to look cool, but not really getting it." [5] Thus wrote the British business magazine *The Economist* in 2017. Hard as it might be to imagine anyone at *The Economist* wearing a baseball cap back to front at any age, perhaps this guardian of the liberal, if not also the neoliberal, flame had a point.

8. Class Still Not Disappeared: PiS successfully built a working electoral coalition, but it was based largely on an exclusivist rather an inclusivist social model and was reliant on ad hoc measures that did little to deal with structural economic and demographic problems. It was not based on a vision of civil society that genuinely sought to find lasting solutions for those on the receiving end of globally shifting capital, and a largely unreformed state, even perhaps adding to institutional inertia and bureaucratic blockages. If anything, it was merely replacing one clique with another, except this time with less access to international capital markets, investment and so on.

But the center-Left had no traction in Poland, and the liberal center was far too self-preoccupied and unsure of its social status to find a language that

---

3   *The Financial Times'* editorial from May 30, 2016. Others deserve credit for noting at least some of the contradictions. Adrian Karatnycky in *Politico*, for example, on 12.15.15. And also Charles Crawford in *The Daily Telegraph*.

4   James Meek, "Somerdale to Skarbimierz, James Meek follows Cadbury to Poland," *London Review of Books* 39, no. (date): 8–20.

5   *The Economist*, September 29, 2016.

even touched many people's daily concerns. The latter failed to countenance any shift in thinking towards more collectivist and collaborative solutions as to how to oust PiS and return Poland towards a stronger democratic and legalistic path. The Left seemed to be stuck in permanent limbo between cynical ex-communist apparatchiks and trendy neo-Marxist thinkers. It embraced the Rainbow Formula of minority rights and lost much of the support it may have had among the working class, organized in unions or not. The building of a mass movement would require a vision that took PiS's strategy seriously and understood shifting class dynamics. That may be an unlikely eventuality given the splits within the intellectual classes and between them and the new moneyed middle classes. But some form of social democratic solution seemed in late 2020 to be the most likely to oust PiS.

9. Post-Post-Colonial? The reaction against perceptions of Poland as a post-colonial experiment was a defining feature of PiS's claim to legitimacy. A Poland that rejected external assignation, that defined itself. There were those, of course, who would argue that PiS' assault on the institutions of liberal democracy was quasi-authoritarian and that liberal ideals needed to be reinforced. But simply lumping "populist PiS" in the same bag as the various baddies of the liberal, Western, order missed some key points. A modernism that eschews some aspects of the liberal idiom is possible after all.

10. Testing Initial Hypotheses

a) British press coverage was inclined to favor certain notions of what was news in Poland. Poland, bluntly, was economically "remarkable," but politically "naughty."

Yes, but. Coverage changed, with more nuance after the initial bombardment in 2015 of "nationalist" and "far-right" PiS headlines. This was visible in both reporting and features, with Garton Ash even acknowledging, belatedly, that his version of liberal internationalism was one of the factors creating conditions for the rise of the "populists."

b) The benchmark for "good" behavior tended to be what was accepted in newsrooms in Brussels, London, Berlin, Paris and Washington. Interpretations of what the "West" represented, and notions of what 1989 represented, lay at the heart of the discourse, be they center-left or center-right.

As Britain Brexited, the notion of a simple, unilinear version of Europe left with it. The conflict over federal versus national, north-south, etc., replaced in many ways the neo-colonial language of East-West.

c) This kind of neo-colonial imprint was maintained via a Polish elite, many of whom were educated in the West.

This elite turned out to be weaker and smaller than the initial assumptions expected. It had actually very little traction among Poles of all social classes and the emerging business class was perhaps less interested in the "British Model" other than whiskey, Brogues and the language itself.

d) News and opinion merged in many reports of what was happening in Poland. The "illiberality" tag informed how most news was reported.

This was still a problem. The language used in news was still simplified and in a sense performative, in that it created something where it didn't fully exist or added sharper lines than existed. Picked up by feature writers, the notions of truth and fact became entrenched and harder to correct when a reporter would go back into the field.

e) Alternatives to prevailing economic orthodoxies were discursively marginalized. This was based on a hierarchy of values and perceptions more in connection with Western audiences than Polish realities.

This also changed, as many UK broadsheets started, in particular as Covid-19 went on, to recognize that change was needed, both ameliorative in the short-term and longer-term. The language of "bribes" and "bungs" to the "transition's losers" used in Poland suddenly appeared less in kilter with the core discourses emanating from Fleet Street.

f) British (Western) news coverage underpinned PiS claims to legitimacy—that it was more "national" than the agenda favored in the Western media; that it was standing up to Brussels, Berlin, etc.

This was perhaps exaggerated, although there is clear evidence that PiS used the foreign media much the same way Trump talked of "Fake News," to wave a fist at all those who didn't understand the "deeper project." But the real impact of the international media was probably quite limited domestically within Poland, given that few Poles would have access to it. The question seemed to be, however, if this actually worked for PO or for PiS. Given that few PiS voters probably read foreign news, and their access to it was mediated by the Church pulpit or PiS scaremongering, whatever was written or said by *CNN, Die Welt* and *The Guardian* was largely irrelevant. For the British reader, meanwhile, Poland's continued role as "Eastern European," as poor, backward, and so forth perhaps altered as increased coverage showed a more nuanced picture of the country, one where similar dynamics were at work.

Poland became not so different from us, then, even if the "us" we identified with was either the middle-class pro-LGBT+, anti-PiS protestor in Warsaw or the fruit pickers next door "taking our jobs" in Peterborough.

11. Synthesis? Understanding your opponent, or not seeing them as an opponent in the first place, is always and only about losing power if the game you are playing is a zero-sum one. The "other side" threatens the game itself, both sides agree. A *Guardian* voice is needed, but perhaps a more eclectic one, written not only by privately educated "liberal" journalists for whom 'populists' may just be another word for the great unwashed, those swayed by simplistic messages and dark threats. To humanize "them" one first needs to understand that someone else will always have to clean the shit off the streets. And to do that requires real change.

Index

1989, 4, 8, 12, 3, 7, 15, 21, 25, 29, 30, 31, 37, 38, 39, 46, 48, 52, 53, 56, 60, 61, 65, 69, 71, 72, 74, 75, 77, 78, 79, 80, 81, 82, 92, 99, 104, 117, 118, 127, 131, 132, 139, 141, 143, 155, 161, 173, 188, 189, 190, 191, 193

abortion, 33, 40, 41, 47, 95, 129, 147, 167
anti-Semitism, 23, 39, 92, 93
austerity, 9, 10, 17
AWS (Solidarity Election Campaign), 30

Biedroń, Robert, 167, 168
Blobaum, Robert, 75
boilerplate, 123, 133
Bouchard, Gerard, 158, 189
Bourdieu, Pierre, 7, 14
Brexit, 7, 8, 9, 10, 22, 23, 24, 86, 87, 106, 107, 115, 116, 124, 132, 133, 145, 160, 192
British media, 87, 187

capitalism, 11, 22, 23, 25, 26, 43, 51, 54, 74, 77, 78, 85, 119, 120, 138, 142, 144, 161
Catholic Church, 23, 31, 37, 45, 79, 96, 101, 127, 134, 163, 176, 178
Chowaniec, Urszula, 5, 9, 96, 97
climate change, 8, 12, 106, 110
Cold War, 8, 21, 54, 55, 91
communism, 12, 3, 6, 30, 33, 37, 43, 45, 48, 73, 77, 81, 85, 92, 96, 99, 103, 117, 118, 119, 127, 141, 142, 155, 160, 163, 165, 169, 173, 189
corruption, 33, 34, 119, 124, 182
Critical Discourse Analysis (CDA), 15, 116

Darasz, Jan, 14, 34
Davies, Christian, 14, 87, 135, 176, 181

Davies, Norman, 3, 83, 84, 86, 102
Deutsche Welle, 14, 17, 35, 91, 149, 150
discourse, 7, 8, 15, 18, 19, 24, 25, 29, 30, 31, 32, 33, 39, 40, 49, 51, 53, 54, 55, 56, 57, 58, 61, 62, 69, 75, 116, 136, 145, 158, 160, 169, 188, 189, 190, 193
Do Rzeczy, 99
Duda, Andrzej, 12, 44, 56, 83, 87, 96, 104, 110, 148, 149, 150, 151, 152, 153, 155, 156, 157, 160, 164, 165, 166, 167, 168, 169, 170, 171, 172, 174, 175, 176, 178, 179, 180

economy, 12, 5, 14, 21, 40, 46, 65, 66, 68, 69, 73, 74, 100, 107, 116, 117, 118, 120, 125, 126, 135, 137, 139, 147, 165
elections, 7, 12, 8, 12, 32, 33, 39, 40, 82, 94, 98, 103, 110, 119, 126, 132, 138, 150, 151, 154, 156, 158, 165, 167, 176, 179, 186, 187
elites, 11, 15, 18, 31, 39, 40, 42, 58, 99, 105, 132, 144, 158, 190
European Commission, 34, 106, 116, 148
European Parliament, 94, 95, 156, 184
European Union, 22, 133, 151

Fairclough, Norman, 15, 32
film, 95, 96, 157, 162
Forbes, 10, 91
France, 16, 74, 106, 108, 110

Garton Ash, Timothy, 3, 4, 6, 25, 60, 65, 84, 86, 143, 161, 168, 169, 193
Gazeta Wyborcza, 14, 3, 36, 47, 97, 98, 99, 118, 126, 144, 149, 150, 165, 169
GDP, 4, 100, 108, 109
Germany, 4, 12, 94, 98, 100, 107, 108, 109, 156

Gross, Jan, 61, 93, 101

habitus, 7, 14, 48, 83
Holocaust, 92, 94, 99, 102, 103, 105

illiberalism, 7, 25, 43, 85, 116, 138, 154, 172

immigration, 10, 17, 22
intellectuals, 15, 49, 56, 58, 67, 69, 72, 73, 74, 75, 99, 169
Janion, Maria, 53, 56
Jews, 31, 40, 57, 61, 79, 91, 92, 93, 94, 101, 151, 168, 174, 188
Kaczorowski, Ryszard, 82
Kaczyński, Jarosław, 32, 35, 36, 37, 38, 39, 43, 51, 53, 92, 93, 94, 96, 98, 99, 100, 101, 105, 148, 149, 150, 151, 152, 153, 154, 155, 156, 157, 158, 180, 181, 182, 183, 184, 185, 186, 189
Kaczyński, Lech, 61, 102, 160
KO (Civic Coalition), 44, 116, 156, 158
KOD (Committee for the Defense of Democracy), 47, 75, 130, 191
KOR (Workers' Defense Committee), 34

left-behind, 131
legitimation, 38, 191
LGBT, 41, 48, 91, 94, 95, 96, 116, 123, 124, 126, 127, 128, 129, 132, 134, 136, 139, 160, 163, 164, 165, 168, 171, 172, 174, 175, 183, 184, 186, 187, 195
Lukács, György, 15

Marxism, 11, 12, 13, 19, 56, 57, 68, 73, 96
Michnik, Adam, 68, 69, 74, 75, 98, 99, 165
Mudde, Cas, 16, 17, 22, 136, 140
Muslims, 31, 91, 93, 94
myth, 8, 23, 31, 189

nationalist, 9, 14, 30, 32, 33, 34, 36, 40, 43, 47, 52, 53, 66, 75, 76, 86, 94, 115, 125, 126, 134, 135, 137, 138, 143, 164, 165, 166, 169, 189, 193
Nazis, 57, 101
neoliberalism, 25, 37, 100, 189, 191, 192
Newsweek, 38, 98, 169

ONR (National Radical Camp), 92

Opposition, 16, 41, 69, 73, 91, 99, 121, 122, 135, 149, 150, 151, 157, 178
Ost, David, 43, 46, 47, 66, 73, 74

PiS (Law and Justice), 5, 14, 4, 7, 11, 12, 13, 22, 24, 29, 30, 31, 32, 33, 34, 35, 36, 37, 38, 39, 40, 41, 42, 43, 44, 45, 46, 48, 52, 53, 61, 62, 66, 68, 71, 72, 75, 83, 84, 85, 86, 88, 91, 92, 93, 94, 95, 97, 98, 99, 100, 101, 102, 103, 104, 105, 106, 107, 110, 116, 117, 118, 120, 121, 122, 123, 124, 125, 126, 127, 129, 130, 131, 132, 133, 134, 135, 136, 137, 138, 139, 140, 143, 144, 145, 147, 148, 149, 150, 151, 152, 153, 154, 156, 157, 158, 159, 160, 161, 162, 163, 164, 165, 166, 167, 169, 170, 171, 172, 173, 175, 176, 177, 178, 179, 180, 181, 182, 184, 185, 186, 187, 188, 189, 190, 191, 192, 193, 194, 195
PO (Civic Platform), 11, 24, 29, 30, 31, 32, 34, 36, 39, 40, 41, 42, 43, 44, 45, 46, 47, 48, 51, 61, 66, 71, 100, 106, 116, 122, 123, 124, 127, 135, 138, 150, 151, 154, 155, 157, 158, 159, 160, 166, 173, 177, 178, 179, 181, 183, 184, 185, 188, 194
Polish Peasant Party (PSL), 41, 42, 45, 149, 152, 185
Polish People's Republic (PRL), 37, 45, 48
Polish Socialist Party (PPS), 66
Polish United Workers' Party (PZPR), 33, 37, 48, 66, 69, 78, 92, 119
Politico, 14, 12, 42, 61, 91, 152, 192
Polityka, 14, 49, 60, 73, 82, 96, 97, 98, 122
populism, 9, 10, 16, 17, 18, 30, 33, 71, 79, 119, 124, 136, 140, 141, 168, 172, 179
Porter-Szűcs, Brian, 14, 30, 37, 46
post-colonial, 51, 99, 118, 193
press freedom, 133

Radio Maryja, 36, 39, 93, 95
Razem, 44, 45, 119, 129
refugees, 93, 132, 189
rule of law, 8, 15, 21, 22, 41, 42, 67, 75, 108, 133, 134, 154, 156, 174, 176, 177, 184
Russia, 34, 54, 55, 56, 58, 61, 106, 108, 109, 110, 151, 189

shocktherapy, 138, 142

SLD (Democratic Left Alliance), 30, 32, 33, 37, 42, 44, 45, 46, 66, 119

Smoleńsk, 39, 61, 97, 102, 104, 148, 157

Social Democratic Party of the Polish Republic (SdRP), 33, 66

Solidarity, 6, 24, 29, 30, 31, 32, 35, 36, 46, 66, 75, 78, 79, 92, 96, 101, 119, 133, 142, 143, 150, 160, 177, 188

Soros, George, 6, 99, 174

Soviet Union, 8, 48, 54, 85, 102, 109

spectacle, 7, 15, 48, 164, 180

taxes, 4, 40, 42, 85, 148

The Economist, 11, 5, 8, 10, 25, 84, 85, 87, 115, 139, 147, 148, 160, 165, 177, 192

The Financial Times, 14, 4, 12, 61, 76, 83, 85, 87, 107, 115, 119, 131, 137, 160, 161, 162, 166, 171, 173, 181, 182, 188, 192

The Guardian, 5, 3, 7, 8, 10, 11, 12, 13, 14, 16, 17, 22, 25, 56, 60, 84, 87, 88, 115, 118, 126, 128, 129, 130, 135, 140, 141, 143, 144, 161,

162, 163, 164, 168, 169, 170, 171, 174, 175, 176, 180, 181, 194

The Telegraph, 51, 85, 87, 117, 118, 133

Trump, Donald, 13, 7, 8, 9, 10, 15, 16, 24, 47, 88, 109, 110, 164, 168, 170, 189, 192, 194

Tusk, Donald, 21, 34, 41, 102, 106, 122, 124, 143, 150, 154, 155, 168

TVP (Polish Television), 12, 84, 87, 98, 105, 130, 149, 156, 157, 158, 168, 169, 170, 180

UD (Democratic Union), 33, 35

unemployment, 77, 148

UP (Labor Union), 66

UW (Freedom Union), 29, 32, 33, 75

Van Dijk, Teun, 15

Wiosna, 44, 119, 123

women's rights, 41, 53, 129, 184

World War II, 57, 61, 65, 94, 101, 102, 109, 147